# Ill Effects

How do the media really affect people? Can cinema, television and video be blamed for problems in society? Are young people as vulnerable to the influences of 'video nasties' and horror movies as is often claimed?

*Ill Effects* is a radical re-examination of the whole 'media effects' debate. It questions not only whether the media are capable of directly influencing people but also whether the idea of 'effects' is the most useful way of conceptualising the relationship between the media and audiences.

*Ill Effects* looks at the reasons why the media are routinely blamed for horrific events such as the murders of James Bulger and Suzanne Capper and the Hungerford massacre, as well as for perceived trends such as the alleged 'death of the family' and the rise of 'yob culture'. The authors' concern goes beyond individual cases: they discuss the development and current state of play of research into media effects, the remarkable power of 'common sense' notions of media effects and the way in which the effects issue has become embroiled in debates about censorship and freedom of expression. They suggest how audiences *really* respond to media texts, and argue that there is an urgent need for informed and interdisciplinary approaches to the study of the media.

**Contributors** Martin Barker, David Buckingham, Ann Hagell, Patricia Holland, Mark Kermode, Graham Murdock, Tim Newburn, Julian Petley, Willard D. Rowland, Bill Thompson, Ian Vine.

**Editors** Martin Barker is Head of School of Cultural Studies at the University of the West of England. Julian Petley is a Lecturer in Communications and Information Studies at Brunel University.

# Communication and Society
## General Editor: James Curran

**Television Producers**
*Jeremy Tunstall*

**News and Journalism in the UK**
A Textbook, Second Edition
*Brian McNair*

**In Garageland**
Rock, Youth and Modernity
*Johan Fornäs, Ulf Lindberg and Ove Sernhede*

**The Crisis of Public Communication**
*Jay G. Blumler and Michael Gurevitch*

**Glasgow Media Group Reader, Volume 1**
News Content, Language and Visuals
*Edited by John Eldridge*

**Glasgow Media Group Reader, Volume 2**
Industry, Economy, War and Politics
*Edited by Greg Philo*

**The Global Jukebox**
The International Music Industry
*Robert Burnett*

**Inside Prime Time**
*Todd Gitlin*

**Talk on Television**
Audience Participation and Public Debate
*Sonia Livingston and Peter Lunt*

**An Introduction to Political Communication**
*Brian McNair*

**Media Effects and Beyond**
Culture, Socialization and Lifestyles
*Edited by Karl Erik Rosengren*

**We Keep America on Top of the World**
Television Journalism and the Public Sphere
*Daniel C. Hallin*

# Ill Effects

## The media/violence debate

**Edited by Martin Barker and Julian Petley**

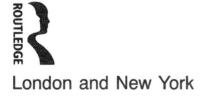

London and New York

First published 1997
by Routledge
11 New Fetter Lane, London EC4P 4EE

Simultaneously published in the USA and Canada
by Routledge
29 West 35th Street, New York, NY 10001

Phototypeset in Times by Intype London Ltd
Printed and bound in Great Britain by
Clays Ltd, St. Ives PLC

*British Library Cataloguing in Publication Data*
A catalogue record for this book is available from the British Library

*Library of Congress Cataloging in Publication Data*
Ill effects: the media/violence debate / edited by Martin Barker and Julian Petley.
    (Communication and society)
    Includes bibliographical reference and index.
    1. Violence in mass media – Great Britain.   2. Mass media – Influence.
3. Mass Media – Social aspects – Great Britain.
    I. Barker, Martin.   II. Petley, Julian.   III. Series:Communication and society
(Routledge (Firm))
    P96.V52G745   1996
303.6'0941 – dc20    96–25087

ISBN 0–415–14672–0 (hbk)
ISBN 0–415–14673–9 (pbk)

# Contents

# Contributors

**Martin Barker** is Head of School of Cultural Studies at the University of the West of England. He is the editor of *The Video Nasties: Freedom and Censorship in the Arts* (Pluto, 1984) and author of *A Haunt of Fears: The Strange History of the British Horror Comics Campaign* (Pluto, 1984) and *Comics: Ideology, Power and the Critics* (Manchester University Press, 1989).

**David Buckingham** is Lecturer in Media Studies at the Institute of Education, London. He has conducted several major research studies of children and television. His publications include *Children Talking Television* (Falmer, 1993), *Reading Audiences: Young People and the Media* (Manchester University Press, 1993) and *Moving Images: Children's Emotional Responses to Television* (Manchester University Press, 1996).

**Ann Hagell** and **Tim Newburn** are researchers at the Institute of Policy Studies, London, and are authors of its report *Young Offenders and the Media* (1994).

**Patricia Holland** is the author of *What Is a Child?* (Virago, 1992) and *The Television Handbook* (Routledge, forthcoming). She has taught communications at Goldsmiths College and has worked as a film editor and television producer.

**Mark Kermode** writes for *Q*, *Sight and Sound* and *Fangoria*, and also reviews films for BBC Radio 1. His doctoral thesis was on modern horror fiction.

**Graham Murdock** is Reader in the Sociology of Culture at Loughborough University and Professor of Communication at the University of Bergen.

**Julian Petley** lectures in Communications and Information Studies at

Brunel University. He has written widely on media coverage of the James Bulger case.

**Willard D. Rowland, Jr**, is Professor of Journalism at the University of Colorado. He is the author of *The Politics of TV Violence* (Sage, 1983).

**Bill Thompson** is Lecturer in Sociology at the University of Reading. He is the author of *Soft-core* and *Sadomasochism* (both Cassell, 1994).

**Ian Vine** is Lecturer in Social Psychology in the Department of Interdisciplinary Human Studies at the University of Bradford. He is the author of *Liberty, Morality and Sexual Censorship: The Politics of Pornography* (Cassell, forthcoming).

# Introduction

## Martin Barker and Julian Petley

*The end of March 1994; my diary hardly records what I was doing, but I know very well what I actually did. I opened my newspaper to read that, apparently, twenty-five of my colleagues – all leading experts in my field – had changed their minds on the vital question of 'media violence and the young'. A new report had been published whose conclusions were so damning that they had no choice but to abandon their traditional 'liberal' stance, and call for further restrictions on 'violent videos'.*

*What happens when something like that hits? I had a combination of reactions. I hadn't seen this report; indeed, I didn't even recognise any of the names associated with it. Who were these people whose report was clearly of such importance that it could command all those headlines? But I'm frequently called by journalists for a 'quick quote' on this issue. How could I comment if/when the phone rang?*

*Another part of me said: here we go again. Without seeing the report, I could almost guess. It would be the kind of farrago of dodgy claims that had emerged in 1984 from the Parliamentary Group Video Enquiry. When eventually I got a copy, five days later, I realised how wrong I was: this one was even worse. It had not a single fact to its name, good or bad. It was a thin tissue of claims whose only virtue was that they were what every politician and newspaper wanted to hear.*

*I spent the next three weeks on the phone, talking to people* actually *working in the field, putting together a response from twenty-three leading media researchers. Except that one has to try, I might as well not have bothered: we were* not *what they wanted.*

Martin Barker

*On the last day of March 1994 I was walking through Harrow around lunchtime. I had just appeared at Harrow Crown Court as a witness for the prosecution in the case of two young men accused of beating up a London Regional Transport official several months earlier. I had been a witness to the assault, so thoughts about violent behaviour were very much on my mind that day.*

*Walking towards Harrow-on-the-Hill station my eye was suddenly caught by the headline of an early edition of the* Evening Standard: *'U-turn over video nasties.' I was amazed. Who'd performed this 'U-turn'? I wasn't aware of any of my colleagues even researching this particular topic, let alone doing 'U-turns' on it. Had I somehow missed out on some important new piece of academic research on the media? If so, who was responsible for it, and what did it say?*

*I bought the paper and, standing in the street, eagerly scanned the front page. What I read both calmed and worried me at the same time. Calmed me because I realised that those who'd performed the alleged 'U-turn' were not media academics but were in fact a group of psychologists, psychiatrists and paediatricians, none of whom had any particular expertise in the media. And, reading behind the headline, it soon became clear that they had, in fact, no new evidence to offer for their position. Nor had any 'U-turn' been executed, since several of these alleged media 'experts' had spoken out in similar terms before.*

*However, I was also filled with an awful sense of foreboding. It was only a few months since the press had tried to pin the blame for the murder of James Bulger on the video* Child's Play III; *and, although this ploy had been exposed as ridiculous nonsense, the papers were, as ever, in scape-goating mode, always on the look-out for sensational items with which to stoke the mood of generalised public disquiet over matters of Law and Order, and always with the pat authoritarian solution ready to hand. Had there been anyone around that I knew, I would have bet them a large sum of money that this story would dominate the next day's papers – and not simply the tabloids either.*

*The next day, with a sinking feeling, I bought all the papers. I would have won my bet hands down. I thought, looking back on ten years of battles with the 'video nasty' myth, 'here we go again . . .'.*

Julian Petley

This book has come out of the reactions of a number of us to the Newson Report. As individuals, many of us have responded before to the kinds of press and political panic about 'dangerous media'. But in November 1994 fifty researchers, policy-makers and industry representatives met for a weekend conference. Organised by the editors of this volume, it was entitled 'Challenging the Effects Tradition'. It's fair to say that one major reason for the conference was the blank silence we met when we issued that counter-statement to the Newson Report. Excepting the *Times Higher Education Supplement* (who reprinted the entire statement) and Richard Boston in the *Guardian* (who commented in fact on the silence), not one newspaper took any note. Yet the Alton–Newson bandwagon was still rolling.

We made strong attempts to reach representatives of the Labour and

Liberal Democrat parties – to no avail. Not one MP would meet us, even to discuss the issues. Yet the fields of media studies, film studies, communication studies and cultural studies were in a healthier, more advanced state than ever before. For once, we felt, there was a chance that media researchers could speak back, and try to change the dominant agenda about 'media effects'. But, first, we had to talk to each other, to see how far there was agreement on the issues and on effective ways of engaging with the public debates. If we didn't, we felt, then apart from anything else the credibility of our whole research tradition was at risk.

To date, the initiatives have been small. This book is the biggest. It is an attempt to try to put into the public sphere the evidence and arguments that are so obvious to us, but which elsewhere tend to hit the stone wall of incomprehension. To put it baldly, there are many who won't be won over or even understand what the contributors in this book make clear. This book is not addressed to those whose minds are so firmly closed on the issue of 'media violence' that, when they speak, slogans drop from their mouths. This book is addressed to those who are worried, who sense that something is very wrong with those arguments but find it hard to say why and how. We want to provide ammunition to the unconfident.

In it, then, we have tried to bring together essays on each of the key aspects of the debate. Rather than use this introduction to tell our readers in advance what each author has done, we've chosen to indicate a number of main points of controversy from which the book has grown.

## ACCESS TO THE MEDIA

We really should have known. When Elizabeth Newson issued her report, the press, radio and television were lining up to cover it. When we tried to state the opposite case, no one wanted to hear. We were the irritant in the jar of Vaseline, not saying what was wanted. Newson not only said the 'right things', she also had a sponsor. David Alton, MP, a committed Roman Catholic, was the perfect broker for her media coverage. But what he got out of it was a cloak of respectability for views which he was promulgating for much more complicated reasons.

There is a real problem with the state of our press in Britain today. A complex of changes has steadily undermined its capacity and willingness to ask difficult questions. Seventeen years of Conservative government, coupled with an opposition which more and more people find hard to distinguish from the other side, have drastically narrowed the intellectual agenda. Shifts in ownership and struggles for readership have reduced staff, and placed ever more emphasis on 'entertainment' and 'human interest' stories. The idea of the press as a critical forum, asking awkward questions of those in power (other than about their private lives), seems increasingly bizarre. Even in exceptional cases, such as the Arms-to-Iraq scandal, investigative work is done largely by television. But television is not going to risk its own position by seeming to question the motives or logic of the moral campaigners.

For these reasons, there are real difficulties in getting any kind of public space for alternative views about 'media influence'.

## THE MOTIVES OF CENSORSHIP CAMPAIGNERS

Those who argue for and practise censorship are no doubt genuine in their belief that certain images are 'harmful' to those who watch them and should therefore be banned. But this view is usually part of a much wider ideological package which its proponents would have us accept, or would like to impose upon us. For example, it is clear that behind the myriad finicking diktats of the pre-war British Board of Film Censors lay a quite conscious determination to protect the *status quo* and the Establishment (Trevelyan, 1973; Phelps, 1975; Pronay and Spring, 1982; Mathews, 1994). Similarly, the famous campaign against 'horror' comics in the 1950s was not ultimately about the comics at all but a matter of defending a particular conception of 'Englishness' and of childhood (Barker, 1984a). Likewise, as Tracey and Morrison (1979) have pointed out, behind Mrs Whitehouse's endless attacks on sex, violence and bad language on television there lies a perfectly coherent viewpoint which is opposed to secular attitudes in general, and to all forms of modernism, of which 'permissiveness' is but a symptom. Thus it was not in the least surprising to find her involved in the original 'video nasties' campaign along with a constellation of similar interests which eventually formed itself into the infamous Parliamentary Group Video Enquiry (see especially Brown in Barker, 1984b). And finally, of course, one discovers that behind much of the lobbying for the Alton Bill, including the Newson document, there lurked the Movement for Christian Democracy, a group with a quite specific moral agenda which, in its own words, used the Bill as a means of 'coming of age politically' (Petley, 1993). To point this out is not to subscribe to a conspiracy theory of history, nor is it an attempt to belittle opposing views by revealing what lies behind them, thus avoiding serious discussion of those views. It is, rather, to suggest that arguments about 'effects' (and therefore, usually, censorship) do not exist in an ideological vacuum and generally tend to spring from deeply felt beliefs about how society should – and shouldn't – be organised and regulated. They are not simple 'proofs of harm', in some para-medical sense.

## DANGEROUS CLASSES

One clue to the operation of these ideological discourses is to be found in the campaigners' claims about who is at risk. Upon whom are the media supposed to have their 'effects'? Not the 'educated' and 'cultured' middle classes, who either don't watch such rubbish, or else are fully able to deal with it if they do so. No, those who are most 'affected' are the young, and especially the working-class young. Here 'effects' theory meets up with what Pearson (1983) has called the 'history of respectable fears' and Cohen (1972) 'folk devils'. In the nineteenth century the music hall and 'penny dreadfuls' were blamed for inciting the lower orders to hooliganism, and almost from its inception the cinema was accused of encouraging 'copy-cat' crime. In the 1930s Hollywood was blamed for the growth of 'motor bandits', and in the 1950s the behaviour of the Teddy Boys was laid at the door of *The Blackboard Jungle* and *Rock around the Clock*. The language of generational fear and class dislike peppers a good deal of 'effects' literature, and most certainly informs the 'video nasty' affair – see in particular the *Video Violence and Children* report of the above-mentioned Parliamentary Group Video Enquiry. In more recent times, and in particular in the wake of the murder of James Bulger, the latest to join the list of 'hooligans' are members of the so-called 'underclass', victims of the 'dependency culture' and of a mythical 'permissiveness' which has led to the break-up of families, who sit around all day psyching themselves up on violent videos and then go out to commit horrific crimes as a direct result.

## THINKING ABOUT CHILDREN

Campaigns about the media have an inevitable accompaniment: the incantation of phrases about the 'need to protect children'. This is the flip-side of the worries about 'dangerous classes', of course, since they are often spoken of as 'childlike'. Only rarely does this come right to the surface; when it does, it is revealing. So, in a classic essay on delinquency in 1868, magistrate Matthew Hill voiced his view that the problem with the delinquent was that he grew up too fast; 'he must therefore be turned again into a child' (on this see Barker, 1989, p. 33).

Usually, though, just to repeat the phrases about children is enough – who but a fool or a villain would not want to protect them? It somehow is never enough to reply that real, live children are complex beings who survive many worse things than a scary story or two. The reason for this is that this whole discourse is not about real, live children but about a *conception of childhood* (Coveney, 1967; Cunningham, 1995; Holland, 1992; James and Prout, 1990).

There is now a large body of work looking into the role that ideas of childhood have played in the Western world since industrialisation (Cunningham, 1995; Holland, 1992; Hoyles, 1979; James and Prout, 1990; Steedman, 1990). 'Child' equals 'natural innocence' in a world where that has become a rare commodity. 'Childhood' equals hope for the future where that, too, has become hard to hold on to. We invest much in our hopes for our own children, but our culture invests even more in a demand that 'childhood' should be an ideal arena. As two researchers, who were hardly uncritical of children's media, put it:

> [A]dults create for themselves a childhood embodying their own angelic aspirations, which offer consolation, hope and a guarantee of a 'better', but unchanging future. This 'new reality', this autonomous realm of magic, is artfully isolated from the reality of the everyday. Adult values are projected onto the child, as if childhood was a special domain where these values could be protected uncritically. . . . Thus, *the imagination of the child is conceived as the past and future utopia of the adult.*
> (Dorfman and Mattelart, 1972, pp. 30–1)

The problem here is not simply how misleading this conception of 'child-hood' is. It is so empty as to be manipulable; it can be turned to political uses, charged with the emotions that we do really feel for our children. This was evident recently in the way in which groups ranging from fundamentalists to 'professional carers' managed to start a furore over 'ritual sex abuse' of children – on the back of which many innocent families were deeply harmed.

There are lessons to be learnt from such as this. We need to ask questions about real children as an antidote to these kinds of scare. What harm is done to children who are *over-protected*? How do actual children use the media as part of their growing up (see Hodge and Tripp, 1986, for instance)?

## OTHER MEANINGS OF 'EFFECTS'

In the *Guardian* (10 March 1996) there appeared a report about a direct and highly measurable effect of the media. Apparently, ever since the BBC's 1995 adaptation of Jane Austen's *Pride and Prejudice*, Lyme Hall in Cheshire (where some of the key scenes were filmed) has become the top tourist attraction in Britain. There is no question but that this is a 'media effect', one which should delight media critics since it is so easily measurable.

But of course this is not what the critics mean by 'effects'. In truth, they have a remarkably impoverished notion of them. The only ones that generally interest them are those in which, supposedly, all mediating steps between seeing and acting are removed. That clearly won't work in this case. We might fill in the intervening steps like this: watching *Pride and*

*Prejudice* was itself an enjoyable, romantic experience for many viewers, part of which was seeing the pristine grandeur of Lyme Hall. Almost certainly, then, groups of people will have planned an outing, or a visit.

In other words, here is a determinate media effect whose whole logic is that it is interwoven with people's everyday lives. It involves pleasures and emotions, thinking and planning, and belonging to social groups with specific preferences and resources. That is a *real* media effect, unlike the mythical ones with which this book is concerned. We say this here, to counter the dull inevitable refrain that we are denying all effects of the media. This is simply a nonsense.

## TECHNOPHOBIA/THE 'NEWNESS' OF OBJECTS OF CONCERN

As far back as the sixteenth century it was argued that popular songs were dangerous because they too often presented criminals as heroes. In 1751 Henry Fielding's 'Enquiry into the cause of the late increase in robbers' identified 'too frequent and expensive Diversions among the lower kinds of People' as one cause which 'hath almost totally changed the Manners, Customs and Habits of the People, more especially of the lowest sort' (quoted in Pearson, 1983, pp. 186–7). We have already noted the fears engendered amongst the middle classes by the perceived effects of the music halls, the 'penny dreadfuls' and the cinema upon the 'lower orders'. In fact, in a society so thoroughly shot through with class division and class dislike, every new means of communication, every new medium, has been greeted in much the same fearful fashion, be it radio, television, video or, most recently, new developments in information technology. Far from being welcomed as a valuable educational tool, such technology has been regarded with suspicion and even downright hostility by too many parents and teachers, who seem incapable of seeing it as anything more than a haven for 'computer porn' and paedophile propaganda.

## THE *TRAHISON DES CLERCS*

In a complete perversion of the original meaning of this term (the treason of the intellectuals), contemporary media academics are accused (usually by the pundits of the press, tabloid and broadsheet alike) of refusing to fall in behind populist, common-sense, crudely behaviourist and hypo-dermic notions of 'effects' and of peddling over-intellectualised, irresponsibly libertarian ideas derived from 'fancy foreign theories'. As a result, serious work on the media by media specialists is either ignored, travestied or trashed – all in the name of 'common sense', of course. Few subjects illustrate so clearly the vast gap which now exists between Fleet Street punditry and serious academic thinking as the papers' fatuous, ill-informed, and crudely caricaturial representations of what they think of as 'media studies' – and in particular media academics' attempts to come to grip with the question of media 'effects'. (On the media and 'common sense' see in particular Murdock, in Haslam and Bryman, 1994.)

It is in fact a recurrent problem that when an allegedly dangerous film, such as *Natural Born Killers*, hits the headlines most people who might wonder about the claims simply haven't seen it. So the descriptions and claims by politicians, press and pundits are all that most of us have to go on. And, of course, their languages are well established: it is simply and soley sex, violence and bad language, and these are only 'gratuitous', 'excessive' and 'harmful'. These vocabularies are hard to respond to. Even if you have seen the material in question, how exactly do you prove that it isn't 'gratuitous'? But often their accounts go further, even to the point of inverting the actual plot of a film.

This is no new problem. For more than 150 years, moral campaigners have been making wild claims about the effects of media which they don't like. When in the 1830s Thomas Bowdler claimed that the plays of Shakespeare would corrupt young girls' minds, he was doing something no different from Conservative MPs today claiming that *Casualty* could encourage inner-city violence. Anyone, it seems, is entitled to make extravagant claims. All they have to do is to say that they are 'protecting society' or 'concerned for the young'. These are all the credentials you need to pontificate about the media, and about how their audiences use, understand and respond to them. We don't agree. In several chapters in this book, our authors challenge the right of the campaigners to have 'instant wisdom' on what the 'messages' or 'effects' of the media are.

## THE GROWTH OF MEDIA STUDIES

Academic work whose methods and conclusions support populist, 'common-sense' assumptions and gel with newspapers' own ideological positions is far more likely to receive coverage than that which doesn't. The latter is likely either to be ignored or travestied. (For an example of the former strategy, compare and contrast press treatment of the Newson and Barker documents.) In support of 'facts' to back up their pre-set ideological positions, papers are quite extraordinarily selective in what they choose to cite, often concentrating on quite minor aspects of research reports and ignoring the major ones (see Petley's section on the Gulben-kian report in Chapter 9 of this book). Journalists will also pick up on remarkably abstruse and obscure pieces of work to back up their views (*vide* Melanie Phillips), though they are usually careful to present these as tablets of stone rather than as contributions to on-going, peer-reviewed debates. What will for certain be missing from their accounts is any sense of the overall direction and thinking of the field to which they are contributions.

The field of media studies (and its cognate areas, cultural studies, communication studies, film studies and the like) has mushroomed in the last twenty years. Now there are few British universities that do not have courses, and teachers and researchers for whom this is their prime focus. The same is true in many other countries – with America, the base of the 'effects' approach to the media, being one of the last to see this development.

The rise of this set of disciplines is of immense significance. They have occasioned the development of a battery of ways of investigating the media that can address them at all levels: how they are produced and circulated; the forms they take as 'texts', and how they embody meanings and invitations to their audiences; how audiences learn to make sense of them, to choose or reject them, to evaluate and to use them. Any discussion of 'media effects' that ignores the contributions from this field is now quite simply beyond the pale.

One of the early realisations within media studies was the importance of 'genres'. Audiences for any kind of medium do not come innocent to particular materials. Whether they are coming to romances, westerns, horror, the news, situation comedies, comics or cartoons, audiences begin by learning the *kinds* of thing to expect. They learn the 'rules of the genre' and, in doing so, learn if they are the kinds of material they will enjoy and want to invest in. As you would expect, much research and debate is still proceeding on the precise meanings of 'genres', how exactly they work and by what processes audiences learn what to expect from them. But the significance of this concept is huge. At the very least, the idea that audiences can make sense of a film or a television programme only if they have learnt the 'rules of the genre' seriously undercuts two aspects of the 'effects tradition': if media materials obey certain rules, then it makes no sense at all to detach little bits from the programme and count them to see what 'effect' they may have, because their meaning and possible effects are not detachable from the rule-governed form in which they occur – just as it wouldn't make sense to ask how much Monopoly money is worth outside the game. And if audiences have to learn those rules, have to be able to make sense of the media they encounter, then the more they have learned the rules, the less likely they are to be 'vulnerable' to those media. Rather like learning to do crossword puzzles, learning the principles by which the media work makes their reception more routine. Therefore it also makes no sense to talk of 'cumulative effects', of audiences being 'bombarded' by the media or becoming 'addicted' to them.

Media studies has grown, and its researches clearly have much to contribute to these important public debates. What has been the response to this opportunity for new insights and understandings? Zilch, and worse. In the last few years, the field has been either systematically ignored or abused by politicians. Typical headlines in a collusive press have dismissed it as a suspect non-subject, without once looking at the work that has actually been produced. Too much is at stake to let this pass unchallenged.

## CONCLUSION

This book, then, is a challenge. We are throwing down the gauntlet to those of our colleagues who have kept quiet while, first, claims are circulated which their whole research tradition shows to be absurd and, second, their expertise is smeared by those who do not want to listen to the real arguments. We are challenging those who have been worried by the growth of the new censoriousness, but have felt overwhelmed by the apparent power of the critics' arguments. We are challenging our own students to realise the potential power of their discipline, to speak in public arenas and to try to make a difference. We are challenging, finally, those policy-makers whose minds have not been too closed off from rational debate by the mantras of the 'effects lobby' to discuss these issues with us.

This, then, is not a standard academic book. It is a polemic drawing on a body of academic research. We hope it is both accessible to those who are not well versed in our field and a contribution to clarifying positions within that field. We have not sought unanimity among our authors – the one point in common which we have assumed is a deep unease at the way issues of 'media effects' are used for purposes of control and censorship.

In the chapters that follow, readers will find a number of very different kinds of essay and argument, arranged alphabetically by author since we do not want to privilege any particular angle. Our goal has been to bring together pre-eminent people to present the bones, at least, of the case for changing the agenda on 'media effects'. These questions structured our conference in November 1994, and they structure this book as well. What exactly is meant by 'screen violence', and how is it supposed to be so powerful? Who exactly is it that the campaigners fear – the nameless ones whom they think are influenced by 'dangerous media'? Often these fears are expressed as being about the 'protection of children'. What is this idea of 'childhood', and how does it operate in our culture? And what do we know about how *actual* children respond to various kinds of 'violence' in the media? And, alongside that, what do the *fans* of the condemned media think of and do with the things they love?

There is an unexamined model in 'effects' research about how we might be influenced by the media: what is it, and what are the problems with it? And what interests – political, financial, bureaucratic – lie behind the seventy-year tradition of such research? And, finally, what is it about this body of ideas about 'effects' that it so strongly resists challenges to its validity? These are all questions asked in a field in which, usually, answers are given ahead of the questions being asked. We invite our readers to dare with us to ask the difficult questions, and to see where they lead.

## REFERENCES

Barker, Martin (1984a), *A Haunt of Fears: The Strange History of the British Horror Comics Campaign*, London: Pluto Press.

Barker, Martin (1984b), *The Video Nasties: Freedom and Censorship in the Arts*, London: Pluto Press.

Barker, Martin (1989), *Comics: Ideology, Power and the Critics*, Manchester: Manchester University Press.

Barlow, Geoffrey and Hill, Alison (1985), *Video Violence and Children*, London: Hodder & Stoughton.

Cohen, Stanley (1972), *Folk Devils and Moral Panics: The Creation of the Mods and Rockers*, London: MacGibbon & Kee.

Coveney, Peter (1967), *The Image of Childhood: The Study of a Theme in English Literature*, Harmondsworth: Peregrine.

Cunningham, Hugh (1995), *Children and Childhood in Western Society since 1500*, London: Longman.

Dorfman, Ariel and Mattelart, Armand (1972), *How to Read Donald Duck: Imperialist Ideology in the Disney Comic*, New York: International General.

Haslam, Cheryl and Bryman, Alan (1994), *Social Scientists Meet the Media*, London: Routledge.

Hodge, Bob and Tripp, David (1986), *Children and Television*, Cambridge: Polity.

Holland, Patricia (1992), *What Is a Child? Popular Images of Childhood*, London: Virago.

Hoyles, Martin (ed.) (1979), *Changing Childhood*, London: Writers and Readers.

James, Allison and Prout, Alan (1990), *Constructing and Reconstructing Childhood: Contemporary Issues in the Sociological Study of Childhood*, Brighton: Falmer.

Mathews, Tom Dewe (1994), *Censored: What They Didn't Allow You to See, and Why: The Story of Film Censorship in Britain*, London: Chatto & Windus.

Pearson, Geoffrey (1983), *Hooligan: A History of Respectable Fears*, London: Macmillan.

Petley, Julian (1993), 'In defence of "video nasties" ', *British Journalism Review*, 5:3.

Phelps, Guy (1975), *Film Censorship*, London: Victor Gollancz.

Pronay, Nicholas and Spring, D. W. (1982), *Propaganda, Politics and Film 1918–45*, London: Macmillan.

Steedman, Carolyn (1990), *Childhood, Class and Culture in Britain: Margaret McMillan 1860–1931*, London: Virago.

Tracey, Michael and Morrison, David (1979), *Whitehouse*, London: Macmillan.

Trevelyan, John (1973), *What the Censor Saw*, London: Michael Joseph.

# Chapter 1

# The Newson Report

## A case study in 'common sense'

*Martin Barker*

In June 1994, the *Christian Democrat* celebrated a famous victory. It had forced the Home Secretary, Michael Howard, to amend his Criminal Justice Bill to make the British Board of Film Classification much more stringent about what was allowed on to video. Howard hadn't adopted their amendment – one which had been drafted at a meeting of the Movement for Christian Democracy in March – outright. But its main thrust, without question, was accepted.

How had they done this? By a combination of arguing and lobbying. They had talked of the need to protect children. They had spoken of gratuitously violent films and videos, and how bad they are for the young. And they had played on memories of recent cases where young people, even children, had so obviously gone to the bad. And they got their argument into every newspaper in the land, and on to many radio and television programmes. The effect, as their Parliamentary sponsor David Alton himself put it, was that they had 'changed the terms of reference' in which 'films of this kind' would henceforth be discussed.

That was no small achievement. And it owed much to one thing: a report by Professor Elizabeth Newson published in April 1994, just two weeks before the 'Alton Amendment' reached the floor of the House of Commons – a report which, as this essay aims to demonstrate, was wildly misleading (Newson, 1994). But the most important thing to note is not just its appalling quality of evidence and argument, but that, *because of the nature of what it was arguing, those weaknesses went wholly unnoticed.* What we have, in the Newson Report, is a classic case of 'common sense writ large'. By this I mean that its claims have the same status as medieval witchcraft accusations. When a 'witch' was denounced, a whole array of evidences and proofs could be adduced; but these could only ever convince because those hearing them were already completely persuaded that these were the only likely explanations. You can only believe someone to be a witch if you believe there are 'witch-events'. The facts adduced only look like evidence and arguments if you are already within that frame of reference. So the Newson Report.

In this chapter, I aim to demonstrate just how bad the Newson Report was. But my broader aim is to push to the centre of our attention the question: why don't we spot this more easily? And I focus on the Newson Report because it is so symptomatic. There, condensed within a few pages, are all the marks of a contemporary witch-craze. Few will now remember the details of what Newson wrote. And yet look how the same framework of ideas was so easily reactivated in more recent attacks: on magazines for young girls (for 'encouraging young girls to experiment sexually'); on *The X-Files* (for 'encouraging young people to play with the supernatural'); on any photography of naked children (for 'pandering to child pornographers'); on 'porn on the Internet' (for giving access to a 'vast array of corrupting materials'); and so on and on. Newson's report allows us to see in miniature all these processes.

## HOW DOES 'COMMON SENSE' OPERATE?

The aftermath of the murder of James Bulger in Liverpool gave a huge fillip to the prosecution case against TV, film and video. At the trial, the judge speculated on what might have prompted the killing. He wondered if there wasn't a connection with violent videos. He didn't mention any particular films, but the press had been primed, and one film, *Child's Play III*, became their target. However, it soon became clear that, despite police efforts, there was not a scrap of evidence that the boys had watched the film. Did this failure produce retractions of the claim? Did any of the newspapers, or Alton, or the other campaigners, admit they had been wrong? Not one. So urgent is the wish to find such a link, it seems, that when an exemplar like this falls apart the response is simply to carry on.

In fact, several things happen. Some retreat to the position 'Well, they certainly had/could have had access to films of this sort; after all, we all know children will find ways . . .', or: 'Of course, there is an evil climate that surrounds children from films like this, whether they actually see them or not.' (This apparently weaker position is in fact rhetorically stronger. For what would count as a test of it?) Others escape by arguing 'Well, maybe not that time – but here's another . . .', and cite another new case, in its turn difficult to check.

These strategies were all at play in the Granada TV programme, *TV Violence – Will It Change Your Life?* on 1 May 1994, intended as television's riposte to the threatening resonances of the Bulger case. Granada had arranged for one of the Merseyside police investigators to be present, to 'give the facts'. And he did so, briefly acknowledging that they had found no link. But he continued: no, they hadn't seen that film, but they *had* grown up in a 'violent video culture'. And, to see the harm that could do, look at the case of Suzanne Capper in Manchester, a young woman brutally murdered in a drugs case. Inevitably a warm round of applause greeted this rebuttal. The trouble is, the claimed link in the Capper case was just as bogus, but no one was there to show it. The story most people remember is the story as the press told it – as the Liverpool policeman retold it, having heard it from the press.

Most of us have no chance to check claims in cases like this. We are therefore dependent on how the facts are presented to us by the media. In fact, if we want an example of media effects, this is probably the clearest we can get! And it is very tempting to welcome and accept quick-fix explanations that seem to 'make sense'. They speak in a vocabulary that we recognise. So, even when refuted, such cases don't go away. They linger like ghosts, always half-alive to 'explain' the next 'inexplicable'. Long after the link in the Bulger and Capper cases had been thoroughly disproved, journalists and others were happily repeating them as if they were established truths.

This isn't something new, though it currently has a new vigour. In the 1950s, for example, when there was a scare about the possible effects of horror comics on the young, a story hit the press which seemed to prove the point perfectly. A young Borstal absconder, Alan Poole, was killed in a police shoot-out. The press story was that when the police broke into his hideout they found him surrounded by hundreds of crime and horror comics.

Or did they? Some months later the Home Secretary had to make a statement to Parliament:

> Take the case of Alan Poole the Borstal absconder who shot a policeman and was himself then killed resisting arrest. In that case it was reported in the press that he had a library of 50 of these comics. Indeed a social worker said that he had a collection of over 300. . . . [I]n spite of all the publicity, we found that this particular lad had one 'Western' comic in his possession, and that not a very alarming one.
>
> (cited in Barker, 1984a, p. 30)

Yet, despite this official refutation, the case of Alan Poole was cited as proof for a long time after. It suggests that these claims are not part of a rational debate.

But we need to take this further: these arguments have a very particular nature and structure. There are many horrible events 'out there', but only certain very specific kinds of explanation are mobilised to account for them. In the Bulger case, it seemed to 'make sense' to explain their behaviour by saying they had been 'corrupted' by watching videos – and never mind that they hadn't actually watched them at all. They could have, might have; it could all make sense if they had.

Then, what about this?

FATHER STABBED BABY TO DEATH 'AS SACRIFICE TO WARD OFF EVIL': A father who thought he was Joseph, his wife was Mary and they and their children were on the way to the Garden of Eden killed his 17-month-old daughter as a sacrifice, an Old Bailey court was told yesterday. . . . Before the attack in June, he had . . . watched the film *King of Kings*, about the life of Christ.

(*Guardian*, 21 December 1994)

Not one newspaper which recounted this sad story thought it worth suggesting that *King of Kings* is a potential cause of murder. Why not? Actually there is probably *more* evidence to sustain such a link, because of the tendency for certain very disturbed violent offenders to adopt a 'killer-missionary' role; they explain their violence as a command from God. The reason why such a link wouldn't be proposed is because it doesn't seem 'obvious' – and that is the problem we must explore.

## NEWSON'S ASSUMPTIONS

David Alton may have used the good offices of the Movement for Christian Democracy to prepare and promote his case, but he also apparently had science on his side, in the form of Elizabeth Newson's Report, co-signed by twenty-four other child professionals. I want to put that 'science' to the test. One of the problems has been the disparity between its size and scope, and its impact. Here is a short report, making no claim to present new evidence. It mainly tells of a supposed change of heart by twenty-five people. Its tone is certainly thoughtful and concerned. It makes no obviously wild claims. Follow, then, its narrative, to see where steps are taken that might give us cause to question.

Newson begins with the Bulger case. She is careful not to assert that the two boys really did see *Child's Play III* or other equivalent films. Rather, the boys are depicted as exemplars of a new cruelty in children. Something exceptional must explain this new viciousness. And here Newson acts as spokesperson for a group who have been growing increasingly worried: the child professionals. It is their view that there are now new kinds of film, and that these films have disturbing 'messages'. To confirm this, we are referred to two films as examples, and to a large body of research evidence which (we are assured) now concludes that these messages are doing harm. The conclusion is inevitable: professionals must forgo their traditional liberalism. The problems are just too overwhelming.

We need to get behind this narrative. For it is built on a series of claims, all of which have to be true for her argument to hold up. There are eight such claims:

1 the murder of James Bulger was so special as to require special explanation;
2 such an explanation has to be some singular change. The most singular recent change is the easy availability of sadistic images within films;
3 these films offer a distinctive message which can be traced and correlated with the attitudes and/or behaviour of James's killers. *Child's Play III* might well be an example of such a film;
4 there is also now a new kind of film, in which 'the viewer is made to identify with the *perpetrator* of the act, not the victim';
5 these four propositions are linked to a general claim: 'The principle that what is experienced vicariously will have *some* effect on *some* people is an established one, and is the reason why industry finds it worth while to spend millions of pounds on advertising';
6 this new kind of film is the start of a worsening curve, as film-makers, video games writers and the like exploit the growing potential of their technologies. Therefore their effects are almost certain to get worse;
7 a great deal of research has already been done, with consistent conclusions: 'media violence' is linked via 'heavy viewing' to 'aggressive behaviour';
8 there is now a vast world literature on this topic, which consistently supports this link.

Eight claims, then, so common to debates on these issues they could be endlessly reproduced. Unfortunately not one of them can be justified. Not one of these claims can be supported by either evidence or logic, as I aim to demonstrate. Yet each one looked disturbingly obvious and persuasive. So persuasive in fact that only a fool or a villain would ignore that obviousness. I will tackle them through four key themes around which they are organised: How do we tell what the 'message' of a film is? How can we understand 'media influence'? Is there, as claimed, an overwhelming body of evidence for 'harm'? And just what is 'media violence'?

## HOW CAN WE TELL WHAT THE 'MESSAGE' OF A FILM IS?

There have been claims about 'new, bad media images' for a very long time. An example:

> Granted, my dear sir, that your young Jack, or my twelve year old Robert, have minds too pure either to seek after or to crave after literature of the sort in question, but not infrequently it is found without seeking. It is a contagious disease, just as cholera and typhus and the plague are contagious, and, as everybody is aware, it needs not personal contact with a body stricken to convey either of these frightful maladies to the hale and hearty. A tainted scrap of rag has been known to

spread plague and death through an entire village, just as a stray leaf of *Panther Bill* or *Tyburn Tree* may sow the seeds of immorality amongst as many boys as a town may produce.

(see Barker, 1989, p. 102)

Thus a nineteenth-century campaigner against 'penny dreadfuls'. Or again:

Before these children's greedy eyes with heartless indiscrimination horrors unimaginable are . . . presented night after night. . . . Terrific massacres, horrible catastrophes, motor-car smashes, public hangings, lynchings. . . . All who care for the moral well-being and education of the child will set their faces like flint against this new form of excitement.

Thus *The Times*, eighty years ago (see Pearson, in Barker, 1984b, p. 88). Or again:

I find that many parents and teachers are blissfully ignorant of the contents of comics and they would be wise when the opportunity occurs to examine them in detail. They will not be impressed by the printing, colouring, drawing or literary contents, and they will soon see that the comics can be broadly divided into two classes, harmful and harmless.

Thus one of the 1950s campaigners (see Barker, 1984a, p. 81).

If we look carefully at these three quotations we can discern the core of critics' claims. There are 'bad materials' out there, and we only have to look to know that they are bad. One contact can be enough (if in the nineteenth century the favourite metaphor for this was disease, today it is drug addiction), so the dangers when we are 'bombarded' with 'floods' of these things are incalculable. So how do we tell 'bad' materials from 'good'? Let us take Newson's examples head-on.

*Child's Play III* is not a very good film. But the point is: what *kind* of film is it, and what could reasonably be claimed about it? Not many people will have seen it, and therefore it is interesting to ask readers to fill out a mental image of what it must be like. After all, the film was widely claimed to be the possible trigger for the murder of James Bulger. What sort of a film is it in your imagination?

The most remarkable thing about this film is that a great majority of the film is devoted to a desperate attempt to save a small child from being killed. It is a horror film, no question. In part it is scary, sometimes a bit bloody. But judge for yourselves whether it fits your mental image. Here is a synopsis:

The story is the third in a series in which teenager Andy Barclay is forced to do battle with a 'Good Guy' doll which has been possessed by the mind of a former murderer. The title sequence shows a doll forming out of plastic contaminated with the blood of the murderer: evil is returning. The opening scene shows the chairman of the doll-making company resolving to resume production of the doll. He is a cynical man – 'Let's face it,' he sneers at one of his executives, 'what are children, after all, but consumer trainees?' For that he will get his comeuppance. That night, he takes home the first doll off the production line, and it comes alive and kills him gleefully. 'Don't fuck with the Chuck,' it rudely pronounces.

The remainder of the film takes place around a military academy for the young, where Andy Barclay has been sent to help him 'grow up'. From the start, he is viewed as a troublemaker, and is victimised, especially by a sadistic Sergeant who cuts all their hair, and by the young Lieutenant Shelton. On his first parade, he is saved from the worst of the bullying by the intervention of da Silva, a tough-cookie girl who doesn't mind standing up to Shelton. Barclay and da Silva are attracted to each other. Soon Andy sees on television an advertisement for the newly released Good Guy dolls, and knows trouble is brewing. A parcel delivered for him is opened by Tyler, a tiny wide-eyed black boy who only loves to play. In it is Chucky.

We see Chucky attempting to take over Tyler's body. Interrupted, it reverts to its 'lifeless' form, and is thrown out as rubbish. Chucky uses a ruse to escape from the garbage truck, killing the driver in the process. On the parade ground, Andy guesses what has happened.

There follows a series of episodes as Andy discovers that Chucky is targeting little Tyler; he again and again tries to capture Chucky to destroy him, only to find himself misunderstood and humiliated by Shelton, who sees him just as a wimp. Chucky's level of mayhem rises. Finally, the Colonel dies of a heart attack when confronted with a talking doll.

The next day is a War Game, and it will go ahead in honour of the dead Colonel. Tyler is separated from Andy and da Silva. Andy absconds to try to save him. Chucky meantime has substituted live bullets in one team's guns, and lures Shelton to his death. In the final showdown at a nearby fairground, da Silva is wounded and has to leave Andy Barclay to stop Chucky alone. As Chucky once more begins the chant to transfer his soul into Tyler, an injured Andy manages to throw him off the top of a 'ghost mountain'. Chucky falls into the blades of a wind machine, and is destroyed. The film ends with Andy saying goodbye to da Silva as she is taken away by ambulance – and as he is once more taken into care. . . .

Even this short synopsis demonstrates that *Child's Play III* is the *exact opposite* of everything that was said about it; this is in fact one of a thousand films which show a sort of rite of passage of adolescence: a misunderstood, essentially gentle boy gains courage and a girlfriend through the need to confront evil. Misunderstood and maltreated by the adults around him, he does the right thing, no matter what the cost to himself. This is a very *moral* tale.

Of course that is not all there is to say about this film. Any horror film has to *show* evil to make sense of the hero's struggle. And Chucky is a curious form of evil: the idea of an animated doll, a cuddlesome thing that might turn on you, is 'risky'. But, then, a horror film can only work because it deals in notions which are potentially frightening. Interestingly, the film also displays a most cynical view of big business, and its attitude to children – and it would not be the first time that a political strain in a film has led to attacks on it in the name of 'protecting children'.

If Newson and so many others can be so wrong about *Child's Play III*, let us check the other film she obliquely references as especially dangerous because of that issue of 'identification':

A parallel in a recently released film is where we witness in lit silhouette the multiple rape of a woman by a queue of men, and hear her agonised screams, all in the context of an intent to punish her.

What film is this? It proved very hard to track down. Even Professor Newson herself, when I asked her, was not sure of its title – an odd situation for someone quoting it in a published report. Finally, I identified the film as Peter Greenaway's *The Baby of Macon*. Once again, what kind of film was this, and can it carry the reading that Newson makes of it?

*The Baby of Macon* is, like all Greenaway films, a highly stylised art-house product. Every scene is filmed at slow speed, lit and set like classical oil-paintings. The film deals with social power, symbolised in the conflicts between the Church and a young woman whose baby brother has miraculous powers. Who will control his powers? But there is also a play-within-the-film; we see that the story of the Church, the woman and the baby is being acted to an audience; and below stage we see the actors also living out various conflicts. The scene to which Newson refers comes right at the end of the film. Her account of it is seriously misleading. We do not see the woman being raped in lit silhouette in the way she suggests. An enclosed four-poster bed is just about visible. It is hidden from us by the Church representatives who, having won control over the Baby, calmly ignore the woman's screams while discussing their new power over women. Even this meaning is complicated by the fact that at this point the gap between the story and the actors is breaking down. The 'rape' is meant to be simulated, but the male actors have decided to take revenge for being up-staged by the young actress. They will *really* rape her, but no one will notice, because they will assume her screams are simulated. In no sense at all will this narrative, and this scene within it, support a claim of 'getting the viewers to identify with the attackers'. The whole film is about male domination, and the forms through which it is enforced.

It is precisely these ambiguities, and the deliberate breakdown of the narrative, which make this scene so meaningful, and so powerful. The reason for spending so much time on this is because it throws into relief the question: *how can we know what the 'message' of a film is?* There is now a body of research into film and all other kinds of media, into how they work to produce meanings, and how audiences receive and make sense of those meanings. This is a developing field, and a great deal is still being explored and debated. But two things are clear: neither Elizabeth Newson or any of her co-signatories has any expertise in this field. And the possible 'effects' they imputed to these films, and their audiences, contradict everything practitioners in the field do know – but which nobody wanted to hear.

All this inevitably provokes the question: how do people like Newson get away with making unsubstantiated and insupportable claims about films, on the basis of unblemished ignorance of all such matters? Imagine the situation where a bunch of amateurs published claims about the way 'chemicals' affect the body, claiming that sulphur affects our 'humours', and that if we ingest it in particular ways it is guaranteed to make us hum . . . imagine the scorn that would fall on them. The scorn which is regularly visited on those who do have expertise in these matters looks remarkably like that visited on those who questioned the claims of the witch-finders.

What can we say more generally about the kinds of media material that get labelled in this way? In fact there is a growing body of research which suggests that the labelling of media materials as 'bad influences' is not the innocent process it proffers itself as being. Histories of censorship, for instance, show how repeatedly the censors act in self-serving ways to limit or bar materials which might embarrass them. Yet, in attacking them, they always do so by calling them 'harmful'. Examples are legion. In the nineteenth century, critics of the 'penny dreadfuls' reserved their worst hatred for the 1866 publication *Wild Boys of London*. Yet, when examined (something made difficult by the fact that the police were persuaded to break into the printers, and smash the printing plates), it turns out not to be the catalogue of gang warfare and delinquency that the title might seem to suggest. In fact, the story connects closely with a deep-running sore of the time: the problem of orphans and the urban poor.[1] Annette Kuhn has shown how censorship of early films was predicated on the concerns of Empire, and in particular on the imposition of a definition of proper female sexuality (Kuhn, 1988). Between the two world wars, film censorship was used to prevent embarrassment in foreign affairs (Mathews, 1994).

My own work on the 1950s horror comics campaign showed how particular comics were targeted which dealt with strongly political issues, including anti-McCarthyite stories (Barker, 1984a). In the 1970s, the film

*Scum* was barred from television for a long time; in fact it is a powerful critique of the brutality of the Borstal system, and the way it can make its inmates more desperate and violent. And it raised embarrassing questions at a time when the Conservative Party was pressing the introduction of 'short, sharp shock' schemes for young offenders. Again it was banned on grounds of being 'violent'. In fact it seems that the word 'violence' frequently acts as a code-word for objections made to materials on quite other, often political, grounds. We need to bear this in mind when we come to the final part of this chapter. For it raises acutely the question: Is it meaningful to research into such a question at all?

## HOW CAN WE UNDERSTAND 'MEDIA INFLUENCE'?

In Elizabeth Newson's report, there is one classic sentence which has been heard so often, if in different words, it has become like a mantra. 'The principle that what is experienced vicariously will have *some* effect on *some* people is an established one, and is the reason why industry finds it worth while to spend millions of pounds on advertising.' What does this amount to? One very typical problem faced by those who reject the rhetorics of the anti-media campaigners is the challenge: then, are you saying that television has no influence at all? If that was the case, then advertisers wouldn't be willing to spend all that money, would they? Isn't that sufficient proof that TV must have *some* effect? Given that, what is the problem with admitting that TV violence might cause people to go out and commit real-life violence?

This is, I suspect, the most commonly repeated move by anti-violence campaigners. It was certainly there in 1984 at the height of the campaign against video nasties. The evangelical Christian Action, Research and Education (the equivalent then of David Alton's Movement for Christian Democracy) urged:

> Organisations spend around £1.6bn in advertising each year. They must believe that by seeing an advertisement on TV, on a poster etc, the consumer will be persuaded to purchase a product, make a donation or change their behaviour. The Government itself has used advertising to portray messages about safe sex, drinking and driving, and firework safety in an attempt to change the behaviour of the public. All the political parties make broadcasts before elections to persuade voters to cast their vote in a particular direction. There must be instances when each of us can recall seeing a product that had been recently advertised, and deciding just to 'try it out'. It would be trite to stretch the argument and say that after seeing one episode of violence, an individual is going to commit a crime. But the point is illustrated: what we see *does* affect our behaviour.
>
> (CARE, 1994, p. 29)

This argument is evidently felt to be a clincher. Yet even a cursory examination shows it to be palpable nonsense. The simple error the campaigners make is to assume that, if TV, or film, or whatever, has *some* influence, it must have the kinds of influence they want to ascribe to it. It would be a very stupid person who denied that television had any influence at all – but only if 'influence' includes all the following and many more (add your own examples to our list):

1 interesting us in things we didn't previously know about;
2 making us stay up too late;
3 giving us a sense of our place in the world, through its ability to take us to events as they are happening;
4 making us smile, laugh, be sad, cry, feel nostalgic, patriotic, disturbed, uneasy, want to join in, bored, disenchanted, and disaffected with our own lives;
5 making us think about things, shaking our assumptions, making us complacent, talking to us in languages we feel comfortable or uncomfortable with;
6 and so on.

All these are effects, no question. They are a very small part of any list of possible effects. So, why so firmly dismiss the analogy with advertising, and challenge the idea that television violence might cause violence? There are a number of strands to this argument which must be disentangled in turn.

Consider the following (real) cases:

1 A man takes a gun and shoots his entire family after watching the news. Arrested and tried, he explains his actions on the basis that the world news was so bad there seemed no point anyone going on living.
2 A paedophile is convicted of molesting a young boy. In his house, the police reported, he has a collection of newspaper cuttings about court cases involving paedophiles.
3 An elderly woman commits suicide after watching *Schindler's List*. In a note, she expresses an overwhelming sense of guilt at being a survivor of the Nazi camps.

What is the difference between cases like these and putative cases of television causing violence? In the first case, any explanation would have to refer to the man's mental state (he must have been already depressed, perhaps there were already signs of disturbance or family breakdown, etc.). So it could not be put down simply to the 'effects of the news'; the man's reaction was non-normal, unpredictable, and therefore could not provide us with grounds for judging the suitability or rightness of the news. It was he who was aberrant, not the news.

The second case poses an interesting problem. We are well used to hearing of claims that sexual attackers possessed pornographic materials – with the implication that this provides a causal factor. But we know that the press materials this man collected will have been condemnatory of paedophilia. Yet somehow the man 'used' them. What judgement could be based on this – that we should ban even the word 'paedophilia', lest it stimulate the desires?

In the third case, a women is 'induced' to suicide by a film. Not by the violence of the film (of which there is some, and very disturbing it is, too), but by a sense of deep shame when she relates the film to her own and other Jewish people's lives. Yet curiously my suspicion is that, however sad her death, the judgement would be that this only proves the *worth* and *quality* of the film.

This is not what the anti-media campaigners mean. In each of these cases, they will argue that while TV or press or films were factors they can't be blamed as causes. But when they make claims about TV or films causing violence they change the way the explanation works.

There is something very strange about the way they argue this, as I have argued before (see Barker, 1984b). Their claim is that the materials they judge to be 'harmful' can only influence us by trying to make us be the same as them. So horrible things will make us horrible – not horrified. Terrifying things will make us terrifying – not terrified. To see something aggressive makes us feel aggressive – not aggressed against. And the nastier it is, the nastier it is likely to make us. This idea is so odd, it is hard to know where to begin, in challenging it. Let me start, then, by saying that if it were true, then their own whole analogy with advertising breaks down, and collapses even more completely if we add in that notion of 'vicarious viewing'. This is why.

Mass advertising began in the 1880s, with the arrival of brand names. Research to make that advertising more effective developed in the 1920s. Since then, the overwhelming tendency of advertisers has been towards more and more targeted advertising, precisely because they know that advertising that depends on 'vicarious contact' – that is, on our happening to see an advertisement which isn't really aimed at us, which we haven't selected for any reason – is singularly ineffective.

Advertisers have also learnt another principle, and that concerns the difficulties of negative advertising. From the 1950s at least, advertisers have understood that products associated with negative images are unlikely to be acceptable. The most notorious example of this is the cigarette campaign with the slogan 'You're never alone with a Strand'. The assumption that you might be alone but for the cigarette did no good for its sales, and it bombed. The kinds of film which the campaigners attack are, on this principle, the *least likely to be influential*, since they depend on the construction of feelings of negativity: fear, anxiety, shock, horror, and so on. Advertisers work from the premise that vicarious contact with their materials is the least likely to be effective, and that if it has any 'effect' at all it is likely to be the opposite of what they are seeking. The only advertising materials which use negative images are *educational* materials, which are *intended to make us think critically* – anti-drink/driving campaigns, for instance. So everything we know about the way advertisements work conflicts with the notion that filmic violence is likely to promote audience copying.

## IS THERE A CONSISTENT AND OVERWHELMING BODY OF EVIDENCE IN FAVOUR OF THE PROPOSITION THAT 'MEDIA VIOLENCE CAUSES VIOLENCE'?

It is now common to hear that 'more than 70% of published studies support this conclusion'. A current publisher's catalogue asserts without qualification that

> the consensus among the psychologists, media theorists, sociologists and educators presented is that there is a direct, causal link between the excessive viewing of violence, or the playing of video games, to becoming stimulated to acting violently or to becoming desensitised to violence.

It is certainly true that endless experiments have been conducted. Since the 1930s, in particular in America, vast sums of money have been obtained to test this relationship. But curiously, and with hardly an exception, researchers in this field have hardly ever set up what are called 'critical experiments'.

In any branch of science, not all experiments are of equal worth – and not just because some are better designed or conducted than others. An experiment is useful to the extent that it can add to our knowledge, not just by confirming what we think we know, but by clarifying aspects which are not yet clear. As knowledge accumulates, it becomes necessary to develop theories and models that can make sense of what we think we know. Without theories, information is dry and uninformative. But theories always and of necessity go wider and involve more than the evidence on which they claim to be based. Theories involve generalisations, they assert patterns and causal links, they even perhaps allow predictions. So, a critical test is one which focuses on some particular feature of a theory or model, and asks: are we sure that it really works like that? Designing experiments that really do this is especially hard – because very often theories point towards hidden, non-obvious processes.

Take, then, a simple example. Many claims about media influence talk about viewers 'identifying' with a film character. This is a *theoretical* claim. It amounts to arguing that a viewer may become persuaded by a film *because* (causal linkage) they have identified with a character. There is nothing wrong with claims of this kind. Any theory has to make them. And the theory of media/violence connections frequently depends on it, because it offers an explanation as to how and why people are linked to elements in a film.[2] But note: 'identification' is not something you can *see* happening. An observer can't look at someone, and say: 'Look, s/he is identifying!' Still less can an observer look at four people, and see one as more prone to identification than the others.

So what can researchers do in this situation? They have to develop *models* of what might be going on in 'identification', and then design *tests* to see if things happen according to the predictions of the model. For example, they will have to have measures for who is an 'identifier' (making as sure as possible that there is something there to be measured, of course). Suppose they do this, how will they know if they have done it well? The trouble is, since no one can *see* an identifier – it is not an observable act – there are only limited ways to be sure they have really located the process. Researchers can use *consistency* – using several tests that ought, if they are right, to come up with the same results. They can use *repeatability* – doing the same test several times, while varying supposedly irrelevant conditions. They can test for *critical links* – that is, taking two measures, and seeing if the predicted link is as expected between them. What good science does, then, is to carry out experiments that can help guard against 'experimental artefacts', that is, results that only mean something because of the way the experiment was set up.

In the field of media effects work researchers are extraordinarily careless about such basic requirements of theory as these. In another work, for example, I re-examined the basic research which has been seen as providing the justification for the concept of 'identification'. It had two problems. First, the research was virtually non-existent – concepts such as 'identification' have been so much taken for granted that it has not been felt necessary to test them directly at all. Instead, research has been carried out that *assumes* its presence. Second, the research was grossly self-contradictory – but no one had bothered to check. On only two occasions had research been conducted to see whether the claimed process of 'identification' could be discovered at all – and on both occasions the answer was negative (see Barker, 1989, Chapter 6).[3]

This carelessness about critical tests then links with the other unexplored problem, which we might call the 'problem of accumulated results'. Essentially, it has been assumed that if two studies of media-effects both come up positive, then they can be added together – eventually to generate that '70% of all studies'. Guy Cumberbatch addresses this issue (Cumberbatch & Howitt, 1989). What he shows is that published studies contradict each other on a whole range of dimensions: on which groups are most 'vulnerable'; on the kinds of stimulus that might trigger responses; on whether films make us prone to copy directly, or just generally raise aggressive levels; and on the contexts most conducive to effects. To take just two of his examples: he shows that William Belson's much-cited work in fact conflicts with many others:

> Belson ... finds no evidence that high exposure to television reduces boys' respect for authority, or that it desensitises them, makes them less considerate for others, produces sleep disturbance or (in an earlier study ...) is associated with stealing. Belson's findings contradict many previous studies.

> (p. 48)

Cumberbatch also draws attention to the awkward fact that research has shown that 'aggression can be raised by *humorous* films as much as by aggressive ones' (p. 38). In other words, the studies simply don't support each other. Indeed, to the extent that some of them might be right, then others have to be counted as wrong. It is once again only a grim determination not to ask difficult questions that allows claims like this to go unchallenged.

This tendency can be illustrated in another way. Earlier, I used three quotations drawn from a wide historical period. It is commonplace to researchers that such objections to 'dangerous media' go back a very long way. In the nineteenth century, when such objections first reached full flood, the charges were brought against 'penny dreadfuls' (in Britain) and dime novels (in America). By the turn of the century, music hall (Britain) and vaudeville (America) were the objects of dismay. Then cinema. Then radio. Then comic books. Then television, video, video games, computers, and most recently the Internet. The litany of threats is remarkable for the way each new medium was cited as marking a virtual collapse of civilisation.

But not only did no one think to check or research these claims, or wonder at their extravagance when they could pass so regularly into history; but in fact the claims are mutually contradictory. When 'penny dreadfuls' were attacked, a major part of their danger was the fact that they were found 'on the streets' – they were the street literature of their time. That being so, you might have thought that the security of cinema would make it less dangerous. Not so – here, it was the 'moral dangers of darkness' which appalled critics. But, then, television, which is mostly viewed with the light on, must be less dangerous. Not so – now a new danger emerged, the 'invasion of the home' (though of course that would imply the relative safety of cinema, wouldn't it?).

But cinema and film did, so it was said, have the shared risk that they scroll past you uncontrollably. But, then, in that case, video should have been seen as an improvement because viewers can stop and start it. Ah, not so – now the dangers were that viewers would obsessively rerun their 'favourite bad bits'. But, in that case, film and TV must have been safer than we first thought. Not so, because . . . and so the game goes on. These claims cannot all be true. If one medium is damned, the others must be excused. But the most important point is that all these are made as *ad hoc* assertions, with no attempt to prove or disprove them. Simply, no one has bothered to ask, because it is all so obvious – the witches are out there, aren't they?

## WHAT EXACTLY IS 'MEDIA VIOLENCE'?

Everything I have been arguing comes together at this point. The expression 'media violence' has to be one of the most commonly repeated, and one of the most ill-informed, of all time. It is supposed to encompass everything from cartoons (ten-ton blocks dropped on Tom's head by Jerry, Wily Coyote plummeting down yet another mile-deep canyon); children's action adventure films (the dinosaurs of *Jurassic Park* alongside playground scuffles in *Grange Hill* and last-reel shootouts in westerns); news footage from Rwanda and Bosnia; documentary footage showing the police attacking Rodney King in Los Angeles; horror films from Hammer to cult gore movies; the range from Clint Eastwood as the voiceless hard man of *Dirty Harry* to Arnie as the violent humorist of almost any of his films, etc, etc.

And therein lies the point: no single ground has ever been given for us to suppose that such a list has any single property in common other than that certain critics don't like them. It is a useless conflation of wholly different things. Yet somehow that conflation endlessly continues. And whenever the phrase 'media violence' is used it conjures up one image above all else: an image of motiveless mayhem, to which words such as 'gratuitous' easily attach themselves. A trip to America intervened in the drafting of this chapter. While I was there, President Clinton put his signature to a Bill requiring TV manufacturers to fit 'V-Chips' in TVs; and with immaculate timing a 'new report' on TV violence simultaneously came out. Among its findings was the assertion that over 73 per cent of violence in programmes went unpunished. That sounds worrying. It is the kind of datum that seems to require a concerned response – until we note, as an acid commentary in an American magazine did, that this figure related to punishment of the perpetrator *in that scene*. It went on:

But to do the opposite, a violent program would have to create a scene in which, let's say, a man is shot, a cop sees it happen, and the criminal is arrested on the spot. US television chooses to do things the old fashioned way. There's something called a *plot*.

(*Electronic Media*, 1996)

This is not a point of detail. The moment 'plot' is allowed in, the whole category 'media violence' dissolves into meaninglessness. And that is precisely what needs to be asserted. *There simply is no category 'media violence' which can be researched; that is why over seventy years of research into this supposed topic have produced nothing worthy of note.* 'Media violence' is the witchcraft of our society. This is such an important point, yet its significance seems constantly to get lost. Imagine that medical researchers were to propose a classification of drugs according to whether they taste nice or nasty. Not only that, but they add that they are going to research – and be funded for more than seventy years for the purpose – into the claim that nasty-tasting drugs do you harm, whereas nice-tasting drugs do you good. What would we say? Quite apart from folksy responses, the scientific response would have to be that there is no reason to suppose that 'nasty-tasting drugs' can be a research object at all. Not everyone finds the same drugs unpleasant. Taste may be a wholly incidental aspect of a chemical's behaviour. Finding them unpleasant may equally be a function of being told that you have to 'take your medicine'. And so on. In other words, *it wouldn't be worth doing the research at all, because there is nothing there worth researching.*

Hard though it may be to accept that an entire research tradition is based on thin air, this is my case. I challenge the research tradition to show a single reason why we should treat cartoons, news, horror, documentaries, police series, westerns, violent pornography and action adventure as having anything in common. Let it be noted: for any one of these that is withdrawn from the list, that '70 per cent of all studies' must be instantly reduced, because some of the studies have (usually without telling us) used just such a mix of genres as their research-objects. And every single 'count' of 'acts of violence' will have to be redone, to eliminate those no longer included.

Pending a reply to my challenge, I end this chapter by proposing a different research agenda.

1   Many opinion polls show wide public concern for limiting 'violence' on television and film. Yet the same people, when asked, have much greater trouble naming the films and programmes which they think have too much. My proposal is that we need to research *how different segments of the public develop their category 'media violence', and what they mean by it.*

2   In a study of children's responses to violence, a Dutch researcher found that children simply do not think of cartoons as violent at all – though they agree generally with adults' concerns and estimates about violence (see Morrison, 1993 for details; see also Buckingham, 1996). While media researchers tend to *count* 'incidents of violence', it seems that the children follow the *story-lines*, and are always aware of the *kind* of film or programme they are watching. My proposal is that we need to

study *how children develop a 'sense of story', and how does this relate to their liking for the kinds of material that the critics worry about?*

3  The languages employed to describe how much people use the media are loaded: from 'heavy viewing' to 'excessive'. These judgemental terms distort research. There has recently been a body of research on 'fans', including fans of supposedly problematic materials such as horror (see Kermode in Chapter 4 of this book; also Penley, 1992; Bacon-Smith, 1992; Sconce, 1996; and Sanjek, 1990). My proposal is that we need to study *how viewers who choose to commit themselves to a medium, genre or series differ in their understandings of them from those whose relationship with them is more casual.*

4  We need to deepen our investigation of the moral campaigners, and their relationship to the research community, in a number of ways. The first is the problem of language. One of the disturbing aspects of the anti-media campaigners' way of arguing is their tendency to hyperbole and emotional talk. This infects the researchers who start to talk of people being 'bombarded' with images of violence, of an 'incessant menu' of 'particularly damaging' and 'gratuitous' materials. Even when no damaging consequences are being implied, this kind of language is still used. So reports of the girl who had a fascination (no doubt long since ended) with *Silence of the Lambs* always talked of her as 'addicted' to the film – whereas a man who went to see *The Flintstones* forty times was called a 'fan'. Quite different images of the people and their reasons for seeing the film are conjured up by the two expressions. *We need to research the invasion of 'effects research' by these languages.*

5  Then there is the talisman against which to test everything: the protection of children. This is the cornerstone of common sense thinking on this topic. Replying to a letter from me, Elizabeth Newson said this:

> I have throughout been careful to stick to my last, which is the protection of children, despite the fact that many correspondents have made the point that adults too might be vulnerable to such images, however presented or wrapped up.... I hope that any arguments you wish to present will acknowledge that my case is about children, not adults.

Why does Professor Newson think this makes the argument stronger? Because 'children' in our culture are seen as specially in need of care and protection. Now that really is a hard one to get past – but we have to try. We have to get past it because the argument is making quite illegitimate use of our feelings for our individual children to make a case for something quite different, called 'childhood'. *We need to research the way the lives of actual children have been affected by the predominant image of themselves as incompetent.*

6  What can we positively say about the media preferences of those who become involved in delinquency and crime? As yet, not much. But

the little we do know contradicts all the claims of the campaigners. The ignored study by the Policy Studies Institute (Hagell and Newburn 1994) may have been limited, but it provided at least a genuine starting point. It was ignored because its findings didn't 'fit'. For they found that the only slightly significant differences between delinquent and non-delinquent boys were in the former's liking for *The Bill* and for the *Sun*! Actually, it wouldn't be difficult to offer an explanation of these preferences: *The Bill* as a police procedural, helping them to prepare for what would happen if they get caught; and the *Sun* for its melodramatic view of the world. The trouble is that this *kind* of explanation is not at all what the campaigners want to hear. It treats the delinquents as normal people, using the media in exactly the same complicated ways as everyone else. *We need further research not only into* what *media preferences delinquents have, but also into how they understand and use them.*

7   Finally, there are the anti-media campaigns themselves. From much that is shown in this book, it should be clear that these campaigns are not the innocent things they manage to appear. At best, they are blind and ignorant forms of protectiveness, at worst disguised political campaigns. *We need urgently to research and gather together a historical picture of such campaigns.*

I am not meaning to imply that none of this research has been done – it has, in fragments. But there is now an urgent need to counter-attack; and our part as critical researchers and academics is to pull together what is known, and to press this agenda that will cut away the ground from under them. They hide their nonsense in a fog of their making, but also of our unquestioning.

## NOTES

1 *Wild Boys of London* was published in complete form in 1866, and began republication in 1873, until the police action prevented its completion. At the time of suppression, two parallel stories were running. One concerned a group of boys who had stowed away to the West Indies, where they were captured by pirates. But this was no simple adventure, for the pirates were all escaped slaves roaming the Caribbean looking for slaving ships, in order to free the slaves and kill their captains. The boys debate the morality of such killings, and conclude that they are indeed justified. The second story-line involved the arrival in London of a group of foreigners to pursue their political cause: Fenians. There can be little doubt that the act of suppression was a political act. But what is just as important is that it was passed off as an act of morality, for the 'protection of children'.

2 It is of course not the only one. Another commonly claimed candidate is 'desensitisation'. Lack of space prevents me dealing with all such claims equally, but it must be noted that the two are not compatible with each other. If media influence worked via 'identification', then we would have to concern ourselves with different kinds of film, and different kinds of audience, than if it worked

via 'desensitisation'. They are not simply alternatives we can shift between, or add together.

3 This fact may be uncomfortable to many working within the media studies field itself, where also that assumption has largely gone unquestioned.

## REFERENCES

Bacon-Smith, Camille (1992), *Enterprising Women: Television Fandom and the Creation of Popular Myth*, Philadelphia, Pa: University of Pennsylvania Press.

Barker, Martin (1984a), *A Haunt of Fears: The Strange History of the British Horror Comics Campaign*, London: Pluto Press.

Barker, Martin (1984b), *The Video Nasties: Freedom and Censorship in the Arts*, London: Pluto Press.

Barker, Martin (1989), *Comics: Ideology, Power and the Critics*, Manchester: Manchester University Press.

Buckingham, David (1996), *Moving Image: Children's Emotional Responses to Television*, Manchester: Manchester University Press.

CARE (Christian Action, Research and Education) (1994), *Evidence to the Home Affairs Committee*. London: HMSO, pp. 27–33.

Cumberbatch, Guy and Howitt, Dennis (1989), *A Measure of Uncertainty: the Effects of the Media*, London: John Libbey.

*Electronic Media* (1996), 'Getting moving on violence', 12 February, p. 12.

Hagell, A. and Newburn, T. (1994), *Young Offenders and the Media: Viewing Habits and Preferences*, London: Policy Studies Institute.

Kuhn, Annette (1988), *Cinema, Censorship and Sexuality, 1909–1925*, London: Routledge.

Mathews, Tom Dewe (1994), *Censored: The Story of Film Censorship in Britain*, London: Chatto & Windus.

Morrison, David (1993), 'The idea of violence', in Andrea Millwood-Hargrave (ed.), *Violence in Factual Television*, London: John Libbey, pp. 124–8.

Newson, Elizabeth (1994), *Video Violence and the Protection of Children*, Report of the Home Affairs Committee, London: HMSO, 29 June, pp. 45–9.

Penley, Constance (1992), 'Feminism, psychoanalysis, and the study of popular culture', in L. Grossberg *et al.* (eds), *Cultural Studies*, London: Routledge, pp. 479–500.

Sanjek, David (1990), 'Fans notes: the horror film magazine', *Literature/Film Quarterly*, 18:3, pp. 150–60.

Sconce, Jeffrey (1996), 'Trashing the academy: taste, excess and the emerging politics of cinematic style', *Screen*, 36:4, pp. 371–93.

# Chapter 2

# Electronic child abuse?
## Rethinking the media's effects on children

*David Buckingham*

The figure of the child is at the heart of the majority of debates about media effects. To some extent, this may be inevitable. Since ancient times, the idea of childhood has been invested with far-reaching hopes and anxieties about the future; and, as a highly visible manifestation of modern technology and modern culture, the same is true of the electronic media. The combination of the two is therefore bound to invoke profound concerns about the continuity of the social order and of fundamental human values. It is only natural that we should care about what our children will become.

What remains striking here, however, is that this combination is so often perceived in such negative terms. Children are seen here, not as confident adventurers in an age of new challenges and possibilities, but as passive victims of media manipulation; and the media not as potential agents of enlightenment or of democratic citizenship, but as causes of moral degradation and social decline. Children, it would seem, are unable to help themselves; and it is our responsibility as adults to prevent them from gaining access to that which would harm and corrupt them.

Among the enormous range of material which the media make available to children, it is the category of 'violence' which has, of course, remained the obsessive focus of adult concern. Media violence is seen, not only to encourage children to commit acts of violence, but as itself a form of violence *against* children, committed by adults whose only motivation is that of financial greed. In Elizabeth Newson's terms, media violence represents a form of electronic 'child abuse', which we must have the courage to regulate and resist.[1]

## CHILDREN AS 'OTHERS'

Debates about the negative effects of the media are almost always debates about *other* people. Elite discourses about popular culture have traditionally been suffused with patronising assumptions about the audience, based largely on a contempt for women and other members of the 'lower orders'.[2] Yet it is also children who are often defined as quintessentially 'other', and who have historically been seen to be most at risk from the media. As other contributors to this book will argue, this in turn reflects dominant ideological assumptions about childhood itself.

Children are largely defined here in terms of what they *lack* – that is, in terms of their inability (or unwillingness) to conform to adult norms. While this lack can be perceived in 'positive' terms – as a form of innocence, an absence of guile or artifice, a child-like charm – such formulations are often merely patronising. Relative to adults, children are seen to lack the knowledge, the experience and the intellectual capacities that would entitle them to social power. Vulnerability, ignorance and irrationality are regarded as part of the inherent condition of childhood.

Thus imitative violence, which has remained the central focus of anxiety in such debates, is largely seen as arising from the inability to distinguish between fiction and reality. Children copy what they see on television because they lack the experience and the intellectual capacities that might enable them to see through the illusion of reality which the medium provides. They take what they watch as an accurate reflection of the world, and as a trustworthy guide to behaviour, because they are simply too immature to know any better. And, of course, in expressing our concern about these matters, we implicitly position ourselves as somehow immune from such inadequacies. Using such arguments thus in itself appears to guarantee our rationality and maturity, and thereby distinguishes us from those others whom we take it upon ourselves to protect.

## 'ACTIVE' AUDIENCES

Historically, academic research on children's relationship with television and other media has tended to reproduce many of these assumptions. Particularly when it comes to 'violence', the central aim has been to seek evidence of direct behavioural effects. While media violence could conceivably be seen to produce many different kinds of effect – to generate fear, for example, or to encourage particular beliefs about the nature of crime and authority – the central preoccupation has been with its ability to produce aggressive behaviour, particularly among children. The methodological and theoretical limitations of this research are discussed elsewhere in this book (especially in Chapters 7 and 8); but it is important to note that, in many academic disciplines, research on children and television has largely moved beyond these behaviourist assumptions.

While some advocates of the 'hypodermic' or 'magic bullet' theory are still to be found, effects research itself has increasingly emphasised the role of 'intervening variables' which mediate between television and its audience. Far from seeing the audience as an undifferentiated mass, more recent studies have tended to concentrate on individual differences which lead viewers to respond in different ways to the same messages. Thus, for example, research on the effects of television advertising has increasingly challenged the view that children are simply passive victims of the seductive wiles of the 'hidden persuaders'.[3] Likewise, research on the influence of sex role stereotyping has questioned the idea that sexist portrayals necessarily result in sexist attitudes, and that 'heavy viewers' are therefore more likely to adopt traditional roles.[4] Meanwhile, the notion that television viewing inevitably displaces more 'constructive' activities such as reading books, or that it leads to a decline in print literacy, has been systematically undermined.[5] In each of these areas, the potential influence of television has increasingly been studied in relation to other social forces and influences in children's lives.

Over the past two decades, this tradition has been joined by a range of newer perspectives which have defined children as 'active viewers'. The notion of 'activity' here is partly a rhetorical one, and it is often used in rather imprecise ways. Yet what unites this work is a view of children, not as passive recipients of television messages, but as active interpreters of meaning. The meaning of television, from this perspective, is not delivered *to* the audience, but constructed *by* it.

For example, within the mainstream psychological tradition, there has been a significant – although in some respects rather belated – incorporation of cognitive or 'constructivist' approaches. Rather than simply responding to stimuli, viewers are seen here as consciously processing, interpreting and evaluating information. In making sense of what they watch, viewers use 'schemas' or 'scripts', sets of plans and expectations which they have built up from their previous experience both of television and of the world in general.[6] Making judgements about the relationship between television and reality, for example, is seen to depend both on children's general cognitive development and on their experience of the medium itself: children use formal or generic 'cues' to build up a growing body of knowledge about the processes of television production, which enables them to discriminate between messages they are prepared to trust and those they are not.

Likewise, uses and gratifications research has emphasised the diverse and active ways in which children and young people use the media for different social and psychological purposes.[7] From this perspective, the socialising role of the media is seen to depend upon the users' relationship with other influences, and upon the diverse and variable meanings which they attach to these influences. Thus, for example, television viewing or popular music will have a different significance depending upon the child's orientation towards the school, the family and the peer group. The influence of variables such as age, gender and social class means that different children can effectively occupy different 'media worlds' – an argument which clearly undermines any easy generalisations about 'children' as a homogeneous social group.

Finally, researchers within Cultural Studies have also drawn attention to the complexity of children's readings of the media, and of the social relationships within which they are situated. In common with constructivists, such researchers regard children as 'active' producers of meaning, rather than passive consumers, although they are also concerned with the ideological and formal constraints which are exerted by the text. One important emphasis here is on the social processes through which meaning is constructed, and the ways in which children define and negotiate their social identities through talk about the media.[8] Children's judgements about genre and representation, and their reconstructions of television narrative, for example, are studied as inherently social processes; and the development of knowledge about the media ('media literacy') and of a 'critical' perspective is seen in terms of their social motivations and purposes. These studies have been complemented by more strictly ethnographic work, which has drawn attention to the diverse social contexts of media use, and the power-relationships which are inherent within them.[9]

While there are undoubtedly several pertinent criticisms to be made of each of these approaches, it is important to acknowledge their complexity and diversity. Uses and gratifications research, for example, is often dismissed as merely individualistic – a criticism which simply does not apply to a great deal of work in the field. Likewise, Cultural Studies research on television audiences has increasingly come to be caricatured as a form of mindless populism, and as a denial of politics – a highly inaccurate view which itself seems to reinforce a very limited and parochial definition of 'politics'.

Nevertheless, it is important to be aware of some necessary qualifications here. The notion that children are 'active', 'sophisticated' or even 'critical' readers is, as I have indicated, partly a rhetorical one – a counterbalance to the more dominant view of them as passive and impressionable. Yet, in some ways, the use of such terms could be seen to perpetuate an inverted form of romanticism, in which children are seen not as innocent but as inherently street-wise. At the very least, this rhetoric merely serves to perpetuate the highly polarised nature of the debate, in which the media are seen *either* as enormously powerful *or* as effectively powerless.

Thus, while it is important to emphasise the *diversity* of children's readings and uses of the media, we must also recognise that that diversity is far less than infinite. Likewise, children's 'sophistication' as viewers has definite limits; and it depends to no small extent on the critical perspectives that are made available to them from other sources, such as parents and teachers. And to argue that children are 'active' viewers is not thereby to suggest that they are not influenced by the media, or indeed that 'activity' is necessarily incompatible with negative effects.[10]

Amid these broader developments, however, research on the effects of media violence has remained something of an anomaly. Despite the more complex views of meaning which have been developed by the various research perspectives mentioned above, much of the work on violence has remained stubbornly tied to behaviourist assumptions. To be sure, there has been some recognition of the social and cognitive dimensions of viewers' responses, but these have largely been conceptualised as 'intervening variables' which mediate between the stimulus and the behavioural response.[11]

At the same time, researchers from other traditions have tended to contribute to this situation, either by strategically ignoring the issue of violence, or by suggesting that the debate is based on theoretical premises which are fundamentally incorrect. 'Violence', they argue, does not exist in the sense that the term refers to a given, socially accepted reality; and the notion of 'cause and effect' is an inadequate basis for understanding the complexity and diversity of audiences' relations with the media. To seek for evidence of 'the effects of media violence' is to persist in asking simplistic questions about complicated social issues.

## ACADEMIC RESEARCH AND PUBLIC DEBATE

While these assertions may ultimately be true, they remain essentially negative. And in the heated debates that surround events like the murder of James Bulger they are quickly incorporated into an either/or logic. Are we really saying that the media have *no* effects? Can we prove it? And since we can't, then surely it is better to err on the side of caution. The logic, it would seem, is inescapable – and to challenge it is simply academic obfuscation. In such contexts, the insistence on diversity and complexity which is apparent in the approaches I have outlined above can come to seem not only wishy-washy but also potentially arrogant – as if those who fail to recognise the full extent of this complexity are simply suffering from a lack of rationality or intellectual acuity. Yet again, it would seem that it is only *other* people who are prone to such illogical 'panics'.

This situation is complicated further by the fact that many who seek to challenge assertions about the effects of media violence also wish to hold on to arguments about the power of the media in other areas. Certainly on the left there are widely held beliefs about the influence of the media – in the case of children, in relation to advertising and 'stereotyping' for example – that are based on similar theoretical assumptions (for instance about 'role models') to those espoused by the so-called 'moral majority'. And of course, in some cases, this alliance between the left and the moral right has been quite explicit – most obviously in the case of debates around pornography.[12] In the case of violence, there are many who would dispute the charge that violent television leads to acts of physical aggression, while simultaneously arguing that it encourages an ideology of militarism or traditional forms of masculinity. And there are few on the left who would not advocate some form of state censorship when it comes to issues such as the incitement to racial hatred.

Such tensions and contradictions cannot easily be resolved; but they can quickly lead to a form of paralysis. When compared with the urgency and passion of the pro-censorship lobby, the epistemological meditations of left/liberal academics are bound to seem frustratingly vague, if not downright perverse. We can all agree to challenge the likes of Elizabeth Newson on the grounds of her lack of evidence and her simplistic theoretical assumptions; but it seems to be much harder to articulate a positive alternative, particularly one which will have any kind of purchase on popular debate. To defend media violence on the grounds of 'freedom of expression' or to base one's argument on claims about 'artistic quality' is almost guaranteed to produce incredulity, particularly in the context of a film like *Child's Play III*. And to challenge censorship on the grounds that it is inevitably 'political' – and that the censorship of violent pornography is somehow to be equated with the censorship of news reporting from Northern Ireland – is to take far too much for granted. Of course, this is not to say that there are not important and valid arguments to be made in such terms; although it is to suggest that they are extremely difficult to sustain in the context of public debate. So what might be the grounds for an alternative approach?

## THE DISCOURSE OF 'EFFECTS'

One potential starting point here is to look more closely at the ways in which popular discourses about media 'effects' are actually employed. In my own research into children's and parents' views on such issues, I have frequently encountered such arguments.[13] Both groups will regularly define television as a 'bad influence' – albeit, of course, on those other than themselves. Yet it is important to acknowledge the social functions of such arguments, rather than simply taking them at face value.

For parents, assertions about the negative effects of television appear to confer a considerable degree of social status on those who make them. To lament the harmful effects of television violence and to proclaim the need for strict control represent very effective ways of staking out a position as a 'concerned parent'. Such responses are, of course, more likely to be produced in situations where people are addressed and defined as 'parents', not least in response to the earnest investigations of middle-class academic researchers. As numerous studies have shown, there is a 'social desirability bias' written into such encounters, which leads parents to take up such apparently 'principled' positions and to over-estimate the degree of control which they exert over their children.[14]

What is interesting, however, is that these kinds of generalised assertion about media effects often prove difficult to sustain in the face of the evidence, particularly about their own children. Idealised accounts of parental control frequently begin to crack when one is asked to describe the realities and compromises of family life. Parents will often acknow-ledge that their children imitate what they watch on television, although they will also imply that such behaviour is clearly recognised as a form of 'play', and that it is unlikely to be carried through into real life. Of course, *other people's* children might be led to commit acts of 'copy-cat' violence; but the primary blame for this is seen to lie not with the media, but with what is seen as inadequate parenting.

When talking to children, a similar kind of displacement often occurs. Of course, 10-year-olds will say, television violence can cause violence in real life. But *we* aren't influenced by what we watch: it's only little kids who copy what they see. We might have done this when we were much younger, but we certainly don't do it now. And yet, when you talk to these little kids, the story is the same: 'other people', it would seem, are always elsewhere. There is a kind of infinite regression here, as children in each age group claim to have already attained the age of reason some years previously. Such anecdotes about media effects are often part of a broader 'narrative of the self', in which children construct a positive identity through disavowing the immaturities of their younger selves.

Similarly, both children and parents will regularly cite cases such as the murder of James Bulger or the Hungerford Massacre[15] as evidence of the negative influence of media violence – despite the lack of evidence which characterises such stories. Yet, at the same time, such arguments are often surrounded with a considerable degree of ambivalence, qualifi-cation and inconsistency. In the case of the Bulger killing, for example, most of the people we interviewed challenged the notion that the film *Child's Play III* alone had been to blame; and many of the children in particular mocked such arguments, asserting that they were symptomatic of the hypocrisy and hysteria of the popular press.[16] Unlike most of the press, they insisted on the need to explain such actions in the light of a broader range of social and psychological influences.

Ultimately, however, the concerns of parents and of children were rather different from those of politicians and other social commentators, and indeed from those of most researchers in this field. The central concern among the parents in my research, at least in relation to their *own* children, was not that they would become aggressive as a result of what they had seen, but that they would be emotionally disturbed or upset. Likewise, older children agreed that younger ones should not be exposed to such material, on the grounds that they might find it too hard to handle. In this respect, a 'video nasty' was defined not as a film which would make children do nasty things, but as one which might give them nasty dreams.

As these observations suggest, discourses about media effects carry a considerable social charge: they provide a powerful means of defining oneself in relation to others, not least in terms of maturity and emotional 'health'. Yet, at the same time, we should beware of assuming that people simply swallow such arguments whole – and hence that campaigns to increase the censorship of media violence necessarily represent the views of the population at large, however much appeal they may have for their elected representatives. In this respect, the complaint that 'there is too much violence on television' – a complaint which is, in fact, much less frequent than is often assumed – should not necessarily be taken to reflect a belief in the widespread existence of 'copy-cat' violence.

## DEFINING 'EFFECTS'

As I have implied, therefore, there is a need to be much more precise about the *kinds* of effect which are at stake here. Violence on television, for example, may have *behavioural* effects – leading to aggression, or encouraging people to take steps to protect themselves. It may have *emotional* effects – producing shock, disgust or excitement. And it may have *ideological* or attitudinal effects – encouraging viewers to believe that they are more likely to be victimised by particular kinds of people, or in particular kinds of situation, and hence that specific forms of legislation or social policy are necessary to prevent this. These different levels of 'effect' might be related – emotional responses might lead to certain kinds of behaviour, for example – but the connections between them are likely to be complex and diverse. And the question of whether any of these effects might ultimately be seen as harmful or beneficial is equally complex, depending upon the criteria which one uses in making the judgement.

In my recent research, I have concentrated specifically on the question of the emotional 'effects' of television on children.[17] In this area, at least, it is clear that television frequently has very powerful effects – and, indeed, that children often choose to watch it precisely in order to experience such effects. Television can provoke 'negative' responses such as worry, fear and sadness, just as it can generate 'positive' responses such as amusement, excitement and pleasure – and, indeed, it often generates 'positive' and 'negative' responses at one and the same time.

Nevertheless, the question of whether these responses are to be seen as harmful or as beneficial is far from straightforward. Emotional responses which are perceived as 'negative' may have 'positive' consequences: for example, in terms of children's learning. Children (and adults) may be extremely distressed by images of disasters or social conflicts shown on the news, but many people would argue that such experiences are a necessary part of becoming an informed citizen – and, indeed, this was an argument that many of the children made on their own behalf. A fear of crime, for example, of the kind that is sometimes thought to be induced by television reporting, can lead to an illogical desire to retreat from the outside world; but it may also be a necessary prerequisite for crime prevention. Likewise, children's fiction has always played on 'negative' responses such as fear and sadness, on the grounds that experiencing such emotions in a fictional context can enable children to conquer the fears they experience in real life. In this respect, therefore, the *consequences* of such emotional responses cannot easily be categorised as either 'positive' or 'negative'.

At the same time, children's perceptions of what is upsetting (or, indeed, violent) are extremely diverse. Many children are certainly frightened by horror movies, and by some explicit representations of crime, particularly where they involve threats to the person. But they can also be very upset and even frightened by what they watch on the news or in documentary programmes. And while they generally learn to cope with fictional material – either by developing their knowledge of the genre, or simply by deciding to avoid it – they often find it much harder to distance themselves from non-fictional material. While Freddy Kruger may be frightening at the time of viewing, children can learn to control such fears by reassuring themselves that he is merely fictional; yet such reassurances are simply not available when one is confronted with images of suffering and violence in Bosnia or Rwanda. As they gain experience of watching *fictional* violence, children may indeed become 'desensitised' to images of *that kind* of violence, or at least develop strategies for coping with it; yet the notion that they are thereby 'desensitised' to *real-life* violence is impossible to sustain.[18] Ultimately, there may be very little that children can *do* in response to non-fictional material in order to come to terms with their responses, precisely because they are so powerless to intervene in issues that concern them.

Within these different forms, children are also learning to make fine distinctions between what they perceive to be realistic and not realistic. 'Violence' should not, in this respect, be treated as a single category that can be seen to have singular effects. A great deal depends upon the nature and context of the violence; and upon children's existing expectations and knowledge of the genre and the medium. *Child's Play III*, for example, was described by many of the children in this research as a comedy (in my view quite accurately); yet other horror movies, such as *Pet Sematary*, and even *The Omen*, appeared to be seen as more plausible, and hence more likely to disturb.

Significantly, however, the text that was often described as the most frightening was one that deliberately set out to play with these distinctions: it was not a 'video nasty' but a television film called *Ghostwatch*, transmitted in the BBC's Screen One slot at Hallowe'en in 1992. This programme apparently featured a real-life ghost hunt being conducted at a house on the outskirts of London; and by using all the conventions of an outside broadcast report, including well-known presenters playing themselves, it appears to have succeeded in fooling many viewers (in spite of various pointers to the fact that it was, indeed, a fiction). Yet, while many children found the programme disturbing, a number of the older ones expressed considerable interest in seeing it again.

Rather than simply condemning such material, it makes sense to begin by asking why people – and children in particular – actively choose to watch it. Horror films do frighten most children, in some cases quite severely – but they also give many of them considerable pleasure. Yet the failure to recognise the ambivalence of this experience, the complex relationship between 'distress and delight', is characteristic of much of the research and debate on these issues.

Indeed, many horror films would seem to be implicitly addressed to children, or at least to 'the child in us all'. They are about the ways in which the physical power of adults threatens children; or they are about childlike figures, or repressed dimensions of childhood, taking revenge on the adult world. This may well be why the figure of Chucky from *Child's Play III* proved to be so offensive to many adults: he represents a direct and highly self-conscious affront to cherished notions of childhood innocence. One might even argue that horror provides a relatively safe opportunity for learning to cope with such anxieties, or for indulging in such fantasies. Far from causing lasting psychological harm, the ultimate effects of horror might even be therapeutic.

**RETHINKING REGULATION**

Particularly since the advent of the domestic video recorder in the early 1980s, the ability of the state to control the traffic in moving images has been dramatically reduced; and with the availability of new technologies such as satellite television and digital multi-media the imposition of centralised regulation is becoming an ever more difficult struggle. On the basis of my own research, there is certainly evidence that substantial numbers of under-age children have seen the kind of material which it is officially illegal for them to watch – and which some would like to ban outright. While they are exceptional, I have interviewed children as young as 6 who have seen films from the *Nightmare on Elm Street* series; and I would guess that a majority of children in their early teens have seen at least one film from this or the *Child's Play* series.

In this situation, much of the responsibility for regulating children's viewing has inevitably shifted to parents, and indeed to children themselves. As I have noted, the debate about media effects has become increasingly tied up with the debate about parenting – a debate which, in the wake of the child abuse cases of recent years, has taken on an increasingly urgent tone.

Nevertheless, the debate about parents' and children's relationship with television has been dominated for much too long by negative arguments. It often seems as though the most responsible thing one can do as a parent is simply to throw out the TV set. Perhaps the most offensive aspect of these debates has been the way in which the blame has been allocated to working-class parents. It is these inadequate parents, living their depraved and aimless lives on council estates up and down the country, who are alleged to have absolved themselves from all responsibility for their children.

Yet, whatever public positions they might espouse, most parents do attempt to control the kind of material their children watch, at least until their middle teens. I certainly do so myself, and throughout several years of research in this field, with children and parents from a whole range of social backgrounds, I have yet to meet or be told about parents who do not. Yet, as I have noted, parents' central concern in relation to so-called 'violent' material is not that they fear their children will become criminals or child-killers. On the contrary, they are seeking to protect their children from material they might find frightening or upsetting. And, at the same time, children are also learning to protect *themselves* from such experiences in a variety of ways.

The problem for parents (and, indeed, for broadcasters) is that it is very hard to predict what children will find upsetting. Many of the children I have interviewed have described very surprising experiences from their early childhood, such as being frightened by *Mary Poppins* or by Fairy Liquid advertisements. Nor is this simply a matter of development: I have interviewed 6-year-olds who blithely profess that they were not frightened by *Nightmare on Elm Street* and 15-year-olds who say precisely the opposite. Individuals are often most disturbed by material that is close to their own experience, although this is bound to be very diverse. For parents, this makes it hard to know when or how to intervene. Simply banning material gives it the attraction of forbidden fruit, and means that children will try that much harder to see it elsewhere. Instinctive responses – turning the programme off when it gets too much, or sending the kids out of the room – may deprive them of the reassurance that is provided at the end of the narrative.

Nevertheless, children themselves generally accept that parents are correct to attempt to protect them from such material, at least in principle. In practice, of course, there is a great deal of negotiation over what is seen as 'appropriate' for children to watch, and many children appear to be extremely successful at evading their parents' attempts at regulation. Yet, in claiming the right to make their own decisions about what should be seen, both groups agree that the responsibility for such regulation should be with the family, and not in the hands of others.

## A MODEST PROPOSAL

My argument, then, is that we need to begin by exploring what children make of the films and television programmes that *they themselves* identify as upsetting or, indeed, as 'violent' – which, it should be emphasised, are not necessarily those that adults would identify for them. In a debate that is dominated by adults purporting to speak on children's behalf, children's voices have been almost entirely unheard. Yet we also have to engage with the genuine concerns of many parents – concerns which, as I have argued, may be rather different from those of politicians, for whom the media have always served as a convenient scapegoat for rising crime or moral decline.

This is clearly one way of beginning to shift the agenda, although I would acknowledge that it hardly begins to engage directly with the question of censorship. As I have suggested, technological changes are increasingly rendering state-controlled censorship difficult to enforce. And yet wholesale libertarianism is, in my view, an inadequate option, particularly in relation to children. A completely unrestricted trade in media images could never be a realistic possibility – as recent moves to police the Internet clearly demonstrate. Societies will always have to 'censor', to control the images that are made available to young people. The question is not *whether* but *how* and *where* this takes place.

I want to argue that what is often termed the 'liberal' distinction between the public and the private – exemplified most clearly in the Williams Report on obscenity and film censorship (Home Office, 1979) – is one that, for all its problems, should be sustained and actively supported. We need to find ways of backing up parents' and children's attempts to regulate their *own* viewing, rather than seeking merely to increase the state's control over the private citizen – an approach which, at least in this case, is likely to prove ineffective anyway.

At the same time, we should be much more precise about what we mean by children. My research would suggest that the legal notion that childhood stops at 18 (which is also enshrined in the categories of film classification) simply does not square with most parents' perceptions, let alone children's. Most parents seem to agree that, by the time they reach 15 (and in many cases before), children should be free to make their own decisions about what they watch. While parents do take note of the classifications – which thus would appear to serve a useful advisory role

– they also frequently dispute them. The notion that stricter censorship legislation would somehow reflect public wishes is, I would argue, highly questionable.

If we are to construct a meaningful alternative to simply increasing censorship, we will need to begin in this way: with children and with parents. We will need to respect their ability to make their own decisions about what is appropriate, and try to support them in doing so. We will need a positive *educational* strategy, rather than a negative one that is based on censorship.

This will mean, first, a more informative and accountable approach to centralised media regulation of all kinds. There should be more objective information for parents (and, indeed, for all viewers) about the content of films, videos and television programmes, particularly where this relates to areas of general concern. Of course, providing such information could well be counter-productive, by identifying forbidden fruit. But we cannot expect parents or children to make informed decisions unless we are prepared to advise them more effectively than we do at present.

Likewise, a great deal more could be done to make the film and video classification system more accountable. The reasons for decisions should be published or made freely available for interested parties (for example, through video shops), and it should be possible for decisions to be challenged by the public and independently reviewed. Steps could be taken to ensure that parents are involved in the decision-making process, or at least consulted – for example, through establishing a representative panel of parents, and by conducting research with children themselves. There is no doubt that decisions such as the granting of a 12 certificate to *Mrs Doubtfire* (a film heavily promoted to a younger audience) brings the system into disrepute among many parents. While there may be good reasons for such decisions, no purpose is served by keeping them secret from the very people on whose behalf they are made.

Second, media education, both for parents and for children, should be regarded as a major priority. It was ironic – and, indeed, really galling – that the Government's plans to increase censorship in the wake of the Bulger case coincided with its attempt to remove media education from the National Curriculum. Yet, if it is to be constructive, media education should be seen not as a prophylactic designed to protect people from things that are deemed to be 'bad' for them; nor, indeed, as something that is solely concerned with 'violence'. On the contrary, it should be regarded as an essential guarantee of an informed and critical audience for all forms of media output.

Third, we need to ensure that the films and television programmes that are produced explicitly for children are both diverse and of the highest quality – while at the same time acknowledging that there are many forms of 'quality'. All too often, the characteristics of films and television programmes for children are defined negatively, in terms of the *absence* of sex or violence or 'negative role models'; as a result, they are often anodyne and conservative. While the Government persistently employs a rhetoric about protecting childhood, and bemoans the negative aspects of children's relationship with the media, it has been conspicuously unwilling to invest in positive alternatives.

## CONCLUSION

These proposals are intended as a modest, practical starting point. Paradoxically, however, I suspect that they avoid what is really at stake. As I have implied, the debate about children and media violence is really a debate about other things, many of which have very little to do with the media. It is a debate that invokes deep-seated moral and political convictions, and it is rooted in people's unsettling experiences of social change and their genuine fears for the future. The issue of 'violence' serves as 'a cipher for some very diverse, but none the less fundamental, anxieties – about the decline of the family and of organised religion, about the changing nature of literacy and contemporary culture, or, indeed, about the shortcomings of capitalism. How we might engage with these bigger issues is, of course beyond my scope here. However, in the short term, there may be some benefit in attempting to address the violence issue on its own terms, rather than seeking merely to avoid it.

## NOTES

1 Newson (1994). I have discussed the debates surrounding the Bulger case at length in Buckingham (1996).
2 This is well documented, for example by Gans (1974), Ross (1989) and many others. It is also explored by Julian Petley in Chapter 6 of this book.
3 This work is reviewed by Young (1990).
4 For an excellent review of effects research in this area, see Durkin (1985).
5 See Neuman (1991).
6 For reviews of this work, see Bryant and Anderson (1983) and Dorr (1986).
7 See, for example, the studies in Brown (1976) and the extensive Swedish study by Rosengren and Windahl (1989).
8 See, for example, Hodge and Tripp (1986) and Buckingham (1993a).
9 For example, Palmer (1986) and the studies collected in Buckingham (1993b).
10 For a further discussion of these points, see Buckingham (1993a) and Liebes and Katz (1990).
11 For a recent example, see Geen (1994).
12 See Segal and McIntosh (1992).
13 The account which follows is based on Buckingham (1993a), Chapter 5, and Buckingham (1996), particularly Chapters 3 and 8. I am grateful to the Broadcasting Standards Council for funding the latter research, and to Mark Allerton for his assistance.
14 For example, Holman and Braithwaite (1982); Buckingham (1993a).

15  In 1987, Michael Ryan murdered sixteen people in the English town of Hungerford, having allegedly been inspired by the film *Rambo* – which it later transpired he had never seen. For an account of the debates surrounding the case, see Webster (1989).
16  See Buckingham (1996), Chapter 2.
17  The material here is based on Buckingham (1996).
18  Of all the popular hypotheses about the effects of television violence, this is the one that is least effectively supported by the available evidence: see Buckingham and Allerton (1996).

## REFERENCES

Brown, R. (1976), *Children and Television*, London: Collier Macmillan.
Bryant, J. and Anderson, D. R. (eds) (1983), *Children's Understanding of Television*, New York: Academic Press.
Buckingham, D. (1993a), *Children Talking Television: The Making of Television Literacy*, London: Falmer.
Buckingham, D. (ed.) (1993b), *Reading Audiences: Young People and the Media*, Manchester: Manchester University Press.
Buckingham, D. (1996), *Moving Images: Understanding Children's Emotional Responses to Television*, Manchester: Manchester University Press.
Buckingham, D. and Allerton, M. (1996), *Fear, Fright and Distress: A Review of Research into Children's 'Negative' Emotional Responses to Television*, London: Broadcasting Standards Council.
Dorr, A. (1986), *Television and Children: A Special Medium for a Special Audience*, Beverly Hills, Calif.: Sage.
Durkin, K. (1985), *Television, Sex Roles and Children*, Milton Keynes: Open University Press.
Gans, H. (1974), *Popular Culture and High Culture*, New York: Basic.
Geen, R. G. (1994), 'Television and aggression: recent developments in research and theory', in D. Zillmann *et al.* (eds), *Media, Children and the Family*, Hillsdale, NJ: Erlbaum.
Hodge, B. and Tripp, D. (1986), *Children and Television: A Semiotic Approach*, Cambridge: Polity.
Holman, J. and Braithwaite, V. A. (1982), 'Parental lifestyles and children's television viewing', *Australian Journal of Psychology*, 34:3, pp. 375–82.
Home Office (1979), *Report of the Committee on Obscenity and Film Censorship*, London: HMSO.
Liebes, T. and Katz, E. (1990), *The Export of Meaning*, Oxford: Oxford University Press.
Neuman, S. B. (1991), *Literacy in the Television Age*, Norwood, NJ: Ablex.
Newson, E. (1994), 'Video violence and the protection of children', *The Psychologist*, June, pp. 272–4.
Palmer, P. (1986), *The Lively Audience*, Sydney: Allen & Unwin.
*Report of the Committee on Obscenity and Film Censorship* (1979), London: HMSO, Cmnd 7772.
Rosengren, K. E. and Windahl, S. (1989), *Media Matter: TV Use in Childhood and Adolescence*, Norwood, NJ: Ablex.
Ross, A. (1989), *No Respect: Intellectuals and Popular Culture*, New York: Routledge.
Segal, L. and McIntosh, M. (1992), *Sex Exposed: Sexuality and the Pornography Debate*, London: Virago.

Taylor, I. (1988), 'Violence and video: for a social democratic perspective', in P. Drummond and R. Paterson (eds) *Television and Its Audience*, London: British Film Institute.

Webster, D. (1989), ' "Whodunnit? America did": *Rambo* and post-Hungerford rhetoric', *Cultural Studies*, 3:2, pp. 173–93.

Young, B. (1990), *Children and Television Advertising*, Oxford: Oxford University Press.

# Living for libido; or, *Child's Play IV*
## The imagery of childhood and the call for censorship

*Patricia Holland*

In late 1993, when two 11-year-old boys were convicted of murdering 2-year-old James Bulger, battering him to death beside a railway line near their home on Merseyside, the popular press blamed (erroneously) their capacity for such incomprehensible violence on their supposed viewing habits. It could well be more than a coincidence that the video which was the focus of this virulent outcry was called *Child's Play III*. That title drew attention to the dangerous ambivalence of play, but it also did something more. Child's play may be threatening enough, but this was not just child's play pure and simple. It was repeated, insistent child's play, child's play for the third time. It was, of course, the 'compulsion to repeat' that first led Freud away from his belief in the dominance of the life-asserting force of the libido and towards his darker accounts of the human psyche – in particular the death drive (Freud, 1984). The title, and the repeated reproduction of the fearsome cover of the video in the press at the time, mobilised a fear of both children and childhood. It insisted that *play* can indeed be a terrible and murderous activity, not subject to adult social limits.

### JESSIE BITES

Within the interweaving discourses of contemporary culture, certain images have gained a particular power. They have the ability to resonate back and forth, repeated in different media, accumulating meanings and values as they go, and coming to stand as a shorthand for shared social judgements. These are the *images* that are mobilised within the potent *narratives* of our contemporary media (Holland, 1992). I am here concerned less with real children and actual events than with the construction and reconstruction of such images and narratives as they relate to real children and actual events. Over the last twenty years or so, images of children have figured with increasing frequency in narratives – both fictional and factual – which express the violence of the contemporary world. Certain images of violent children, and of children as victims of violence, have been reflected back and forth between the small screen and the tabloid press. On the occasion of the James Bulger murder and the fear around *Child's Play III*, a series of new dramatic texts was created which also included the imagined children in the audience. In this secondary drama these new players were the potential and possible viewers of corrupting material, and one of the themes was the fear that they would be drawn into a world in which fantasy and horror were indistinguishable from childish reality.

On the cover of the video of *Child's Play III* is one of those images which has resonated through the media narratives. A terrifying face, superhuman and unreal, yet freckled and somehow childish, glares out at the viewer. This is the face of Chucky, the demonic doll at the centre of the story. In the last months of 1993 the picture was insistently repeated on the front pages of the *Mirror*, the *Sun* and other newspapers, now staring out at a wider public, their millions of readers. In the *Sun* (26 November 1993) the image was shown consumed by flames and the headline was: 'For the Sake of ALL Our Kids . . . BURN YOUR VIDEO NASTY.' But this is by no means the only image whose association with childhood and its uncontrollability has placed it at the centre of public anxiety. I would like to compare a sequence from the first (1988) *Child's Play* film with an image from the controversial series of photographs by the American photographer Sally Mann, published under the title *Immediate Family* (Mann, 1992).

The sequence I have in mind from *Child's Play* is that in which Chucky first reveals himself to the single mother who has risked her job and her safety to buy him for her 6-year-old son, Andy. Chucky is dressed in the same outfit as Andy and is almost his height. Terrible things have happened in the first part of the film, and Andy has been blamed. Now, Andy's mother holds the inert doll at arm's length and shakes it, demanding that it speak to her, just as Andy had claimed it had spoken to him. It is her threat to throw the doll on to the fire if it doesn't respond that elicits a stream of abuse in a guttural adult voice like that of the possessed young girl in *The Exorcist* (1973), that archetypal narrative of diabolical childhood. Suddenly we are watching a struggle between a woman and a figure now ambivalently seen as a recalcitrant, resisting child. It is a struggle which ends only when Chucky sinks his teeth painfully into her arm and escapes. The bruising and the tooth marks remain as a terrifying reminder of the 'real' nature of the innocent doll and of Chucky's viciousness.

For me, this sequence recalls the photograph which impressed me most vividly when I first saw Sally Mann's sultry images of her children at play in their home in the foothills of the Blue Ridge Mountains of south-western Virginia. The black-and-white pictures, showing Jessie, Virginia and Emmett between the ages of about 3 and 10, are heavy with a sensuality normally repressed in the imagery of childhood. Inside the house, on the veranda, or in the immediate rural surroundings, the children occupy their space without inhibition or restraint. They offer themselves to their mother's camera, sometimes naked, sometimes partially dressed or experimenting with clothes and make-up. They may be grubby, bruised by a fall or caught wetting the bed, but they almost never smile at the camera. The picture I have in mind is called *Jessie Bites*. Jessie, aged about 8, lies on a cushion. Her body is partially painted with stripes and dots like the wild young boys in *Lord of the Flies* (1963). A wisp of a feather boa, a remnant from the dressing-up box, rests across her chest. Her expression is intense and remote. Her arm is linked around that of an adult or much older child – the arm and part of a shirt and trousers are all we see of this second person. But on the upper part of the visible arm is a circle of deeply impressed tooth marks.

A mild horror video, certificated as suitable for viewers of 15 and over, and a culturally valued work which has been exhibited on the walls of several prestigious galleries; these two images from very different cultural practices deal in a disturbing territory which is all too easily repressed when narratives are designed only to reassure.

## THE CONFUSION OF TONGUES

The contemporary focus on children as a centre of adult fears frequently expresses what the psychoanalyst Sandor Ferenczi described as a 'confusion of tongues'. In his celebrated 1932 paper on sexual activity between adults and children, Ferenczi described the confusion between discourse that is appropriate for an adult and that for a child, the 'playfulness' of the child and the passionate 'wishes of a sexually mature person'. To protect themselves, abused children may become prematurely adult and both identify with and attempt to protect their aggressor (Ferenczi, 1932, p. 289). Hence Regan in *The Exorcist* and Chucky in *Child's Play* both speak with adult voices.

I would suggest a parallel confusion between the concepts of child*ren* and of child*hood*. Cinematic and video narratives of demonic childhood – from *The Exorcist*, *The Omen* (1976), *Carrie* (1976) through to the *Child's Play* films in the late 1980s – have become interwoven with those narratives in the tabloid press which envisage a child audience caught up in their demonising influence. My contention is that these films are stories about the nature of child*hood*, a state which survives in the submerged memory of every adult, and have very little to do with actual child*ren*. When they become part of a secondary newspaper-based narrative, the confusion between an exploration of childhood and a commentary on the lives and behaviour of real-life children becomes difficult to disentangle. The two interacting sets of narratives both express a deep disappointment and cynicism at the disappearance of the figure of the romantic child. Nearly two hundred years after its inception, the once inspirational vision of the child as an expression of simplicity and purity has become a shallow stereotype. Peter Coveney associates its disappearance with Freud's 1905 essay on infantile sexuality. Yet its shadow remains, even when sneered at and exposed for the damaging fantasy it has undoubtedly been (Coveney, 1967).

The public discourse around childhood has dramatically shifted. The image of innocence lingers only in the most decadent forms – on Christmas cards and in the truncated language of the moral right. Even greetings cards now offer babies dressed in sunglasses and smoking pipes, or little boys and girls in a pre-pubertal kiss, as often as saucer-eyed moppets. Innocence has become an open invitation to corruption. It is not only Sally Mann's Jessie who is no longer inclined to simper.

A call for censorship which centres merely on the *effects* of corrupting materials on children claims hard-headed factuality. However, it can be seen to be deeply implicated in this web of images and narratives, both as spin-off and exacerbating cause of this shift in consciousness. Just as the purity of the romantic child smoothed over the contradictions of the mid-nineteenth century, the darkness of today's world has found expression in the evanescent figure of the corrupted child. I want to argue that it is anxiety about child*hood* – in other words about the uncertainty of adult status – that is evoked by this new popular discourse, as much as an anxiety on behalf of child*ren* themselves. Tabloid outrage could be seen as less about fears for children than about fears of child*hood* projected on to real children. The repetition of the narrative of fear is itself pleasurable. The call for a violent reaction ('BURN YOUR VIDEO NASTY') is in tune with this narrative, whereas carefully thought out measures for child protection remain much less sexy as front-page material. The belief that children will imitate what they see continues to take precedence over the far more likely consequence that they will be traumatised by it, and thus a call for repressive censorship overwhelms arguments for protective – and enabling – regulation (Buckingham, 1996).

## MALE FANTASIES AND CHILDISHNESS

As traumatised children take on a precocious adulthood, so the desire to recapture a libidinous childishness has become newly attractive to adults. Alice Miller's injunction to 'nurture the hurt child within' has won her many followers who feel that their own childishness has been denied to them (Miller, 1987).

The action movie genre which flourished in the 1980s can be read as an invocation of such regressive desires. Jean-Claude Van Damme, Arnold Schwarzenegger and Sylvester Stallone live out male fantasies close to those described as pre-Oedipal by Klaus Theweleit (Theweleit, 1987). Their films are expressions of a childish impatience in which impulsiveness is valued above restraint. In *Rambo III* (1988), to take a striking example, Stallone is chubby-bodied and naked like a baby, disregarding the frosts of Afghanistan. His anger, like that of an infant, appears to carry its own destructive force, while he remains unscathed. This is surely the stuff of infantile fantasy. In *Terminator II: Judgement Day* (1991) the 'father' figure, the muscular all-powerful enemy turned protector, can be seen as both a projection of the child's omnipotent fantasy and an expression of the (young) adult male's refusal to mature: Arnold Schwarzenegger as a modern Peter Pan.

Stallone and Schwarzenegger thus both embody the irresponsibility, the infantile narcissism and the terrifying qualities of play. It is at play – that quintessentially childish activity – that children, and particularly boys, are depicted as turning into little monsters.

Rambo has his toys. In his case they are his armoury of guns and his bullet belt. In *Child's Play* and its two sequels the figure which characterises play is the far more domestic image of a doll. An inert, ambivalent thing, without life of its own, it is charged with significance. Like D. W. Winnicott's 'transitional object' or Julia Kristeva's 'abject', it is neither one thing nor the other, neither subject nor object, potentially monstrous (Winnicott, 1965; Kristeva, 1982). Unlike most dolls, Chucky is not waiting to have life breathed into him by an ever-playful child. With an appearance which can be transformed from the bizarre to the downright terrifying, this doll has a life of its own which threatens to take over its owner. Bringing the urban hell of the outside world into the home, Chucky becomes the expression of his play-master's denials: encapsulating sadism and a drive for destruction and amorality in a horrific contradiction of everything childhood has come to stand for. This cannot be the return of the repressed for, in childhood, repression is not yet effected. This is precisely why 'play' is its quintessential expression. Play takes us back to the margins of childhood, to the border with infancy, to a time of confusion and uncertain identity. D. W. Winnicott in his influential radio talks on *Woman's Hour*, which were themselves part of the optimistic post-war child-centred view of the world, explained to his audience of mothers: 'Playing takes place in the potential space between the baby and the mother figure.' It is only when anxiety is too great that the structure of play breaks down to become 'the pure exploitation of sensual gratification' (Winnicott, 1964, pp. 146, 144).

The anxious narratives of the late twentieth century – both the narratives on the screen and the narratives *about* the screen – also focus on the confusion signified by the concept of play, but this time as a 'potential space' between action for 'real' and action as fantasy. Much comment sets out to keep play neatly in a safe, childish compartment. 'Children are meant to play,' said Stan Golden, president of Saban Entertainment, which produces the much-criticised children's television programme *Mighty Morphin' Power Rangers*, in which ordinary kids metamorphose into fantasy vigilantes, 'and they are always going to be playing with something' (*Independent*, 24 October 1994). Many texts, including videos and newspapers, deal with this potential confusion. The horror comes when 'play' merges into 'reality'. In this discourse it is also the margin between the experience of being a child and that of being an adult which is at stake. Jon Thompson and Robert Venables acted out those confusions in their most horrific form when they murdered James Bulger.

Exploring the romantic image of early-twentieth-century childhood, Jacqueline Rose points to the 'all too perfect presence of the child'. This figure, she claims, was evoked to 'hold off panic' brought on by the infinite instability of language and identity (Rose, 1984, p. 10). Now, at the other end of the twentieth century, the image of the child speaks chiefly of panic. Innocence is recognised as the most deceptive of appearances. We know that, paradoxically, the attack will come from where we least expect it and that the most dreadful violence underlies the gentlest of exteriors.

## IMAGES FOR THE HOME: IMAGES BREAK THE HOME

Observing the changing imagery of childhood, we can detect an increasing tension between a representation of children as central to the home and family, securing its stability, and another image of childhood as *itself* the sign of disruption of the familial social order. My local video shop, Video Forum, used to advertise itself as 'cinema for the home'. The crudely drawn image on its catalogue evoked that withdrawal from a public to a private place. Stately neo-classical pillars reminiscent of a 'picture palace' here enclosed an extended family gathered around a television set in the living room. The grandparents are on the sofa, the young man is inserting the video into the VCR, while the toddler sits on the floor on a cushion. His back is to the set and he is playing with his toes. It is a cohesive image, with children at its centre.

The children of the 1990s may not be part of the workforce, but their economic importance is increasing as the all-consuming market encroaches on this hitherto protected territory. The television-centred, child-centred home is where the economic work of consumption is done, and a popular evocation of the family audience, like this one, insists that this type of work is shown as expressive pleasure. The television set, home entertainment and stories for children *should* secure children's pleasurable presence in that safe environment. They *should* keep them at home and off the streets. But the *content* of that pleasure – the video that this young man is sliding into the machine for his family to watch –

may well reproduce those very fears which will blow the cosy family circle apart. Disruption comes from within, from the centre of the home itself. There's no point in bolting the doors because it's Chucky/Andy who is the murderer. The *Child's Play* films make the link with video culture explicit. Andy wanted the doll so badly because of high-pressure advertising aimed directly at kids from his television set.

The child as the centre of the family remains the most potent, and commercially convenient, of images. 'My greatest satisfaction is to sit in an audience surrounded by happy children and their smiling parents', says the producer of Walt Disney's *World on Ice* (*Independent*, 13 October 1994). But this family-based child is closely controlled by the parents and other adults in the family and may be described as the legitimate target of their anger. In the year of the Bulger murder, some of the noisiest newspaper campaigns revolved around the 'right' of parents to hit their children. (On this subject see Petley in Chapter 9 of this book.) In the context of child abuse and violent parents, Andy's mother's threat to throw the resisting Chucky on the fire takes on an unpleasant new meaning.

Our culture continues to take pleasure in the image of the child as a humiliated individual, subordinated to adult power. One of the most popular posters at the National Museum of Photography, Film and Television at Bradford – which hangs in the ladies' toilet, as if suitable only for women's motherly instincts – is a photograph by Wolfgang Suschitzky, entitled *The Orange*. It shows a baby around 1 year old, full-face to the camera. But her face is screwed up in a mixture of pain and surprise. An orange, clearly bitter to the taste, is clasped in her hand at the bottom of the frame. An adult trick has produced a picture which we have learnt to see as amusing, and which sells posters. In this indirect fashion, hatred for childhood, for the child one once was, for the child within oneself, threads its way through contemporary imagery.

In the news pages of the popular press, a horror story about untamed boyhood has been building up over the last twenty years. This is where the bad boys and little monsters have their space, children who have moved beyond the control of their parents. Since well before the murder of James Bulger, a repertoire of images has portrayed boys who are incomprehensible and uncontrollable, little demons running wild in the streets. An image of chaos was used to characterise the riots of the 1980s. Children on the streets were 'undisciplined, prejudiced and arrogant hooligans'. They were wreckers, young thugs, animals, beasts, 'stunted demons' and a 'threat to our sanity' (Holland, 1992, p. 118). When the James Bulger murder occurred, a vocabulary full of references to the demonic and the monstrous was already in place. In reporting the murder the popular press, to a byline, declared that they were dealing with an elemental force. The boys, it seemed, were not just possessed, like Regan in *The Exorcist*, but, like Chucky, themselves embodied evil.

## REALISM AND FANTASTIC FEARS

In her account of the life of the activist Margaret McMillan, Carolyn Steedman links children's withdrawal from the workforce and from economic activity with their transformation into an object of study (Steedman, 1990). As the century has progressed, a more empathetic study of children has generated its own set of discourses and images, where the very realism of the enterprise, the attempt to capture the lived texture of children's lives – with all the pitfalls that entails – has run parallel to, but sometimes together with, the expression of adult fears. Horrors that are all too real, such as baby-battering, the effects of extreme deprivation, child sexual abuse and playground bullying, have become centres of real concern, as well as enjoyably shocking reading or viewing. Most importantly, there have been an increasing number of spaces for children to make their own voices heard, opening up an embarrassing gap in adult discussions.

In Britain it has been television, produced in a regulated, public-service environment, that has allowed stereotypical definitions to be challenged. From *Grange Hill* (1978–) to Channel 4's *Look Who's Talking* season (1994), a view of childhood from something close to a child's perspective has become part of our regular television fare.

However, despite such advances, the situation remains in which outrage expressed through a frightening image of child*hood* may have the consequence of leaving real child*ren* unprotected. The 'common-sense' solution to the problem of violent movies on television has consistently been that 'the *parent* can always switch off' (or, now, 'use a V chip'), implying a childhood under exclusive parental control. One of the reactionary effects of a resistance to the regulation of television, video and cinema is such a privatisation of childhood. A wider vision would allow children to grow beyond the narrow and over-heated family environment into a diverse public sphere. Regulation is one of the ways in which society as a whole can take responsibility for its children. The 'family viewing policy' reproduced weekly in the *Radio Times* begins, 'Broadcasters expect parents to share responsibility for what children watch,' but continues to outline broadcasting policies in relation to the times at which suitable programmes will be broadcast, in order 'to help [parents] decide'. Without such regulatory structures, ordinary, everyday children will have even less opportunity to speak for themselves.

*Child's Play* will remain horrific as long as children remain silent.

## REFERENCES

Buckingham, D. (1996), *Moving Images: Understanding Children's Emotional Responses to Television*, Manchester: Manchester University Press.

Coveney, P. (1967), *The Image of Childhood*, Harmondsworth: Peregrine.

Ferenczi, S. (1932), 'Confusion of tongues between adults and the child', in J. Masson (1984), *The Assault on Truth: Freud and Child Sex Abuse*, London: Faber.

Freud, S. (1984), 'Beyond the pleasure principle', in *On Metapsychology: The Theory of Psychoanalysis*, Harmondsworth: Penguin.

Holland, P. (1992), *What Is a Child? Popular Images of Childhood*, London: Virago.

Holland, P. (1996), 'I've just seen a hole in the reality barrier! Children, childishness and the media in the ruins of the twentieth century', in Jane Pilcher and Stephen Wagg (eds), *Thatcher's Children? Politics, Childhood and Society in the 1980s and 90s*, Falmer: Falmer Press.

Kristeva, J. (1982), *Powers of Horror*, New York: Columbia University Press.

Mann, S. (1992), *Immediate Family*, London: Phaidon.

Miller, A. (1987), *For Their Own Good*, London: Virago.

Rose, J. (1984), *The Case of Peter Pan, or the Impossibility of Children's Fiction*, London: Macmillan.

Steedman, C. (1990), *Childhood, Culture and Class in Britain: Margaret McMillan 1860–1931*, London: Virago.

Theweleit, K. (1987), *Male Fantasies*, Cambridge: Polity Press.

Winnicott, D. W. (1964), *The Child, the Family and the Outside World*, Harmondsworth: Pelican.

Winnicott, D. W. (1965), *The Family and Individual Development*, London: Tavistock.

# Chapter 4

# I was a teenage horror fan

## Or, 'How I learned to stop worrying and love Linda Blair'

### Mark Kermode (Age 32)

My first introduction to the world of horror and sci-fi came in the early 1970s through watching a regular spot on ITV called 'The Monday X Film'. At around about 11.00, when everyone else was in bed, I would sneak down into the family living room and sit entranced by a selection of creaky (but crucially *always* colour) horror flicks, usually from the Hammer or Amicus stable. No matter that I had to have the volume turned down so far that it was impossible to hear anything that was being said: what was captivating was the electrifying atmosphere, the sense of watching something that was forbidden, secretive, taboo. It was, indeed, my first real experience of discovering something that was uniquely *mine*, something that existed outside the domain of my parents' control and authority.

I also sensed from the very beginning that there was something incomprehensibly significant about the actions being played out on-screen, something which spoke to me in a language I didn't quite understand. Like a novice watching opera for the first time and recognising something in the gestures but nothing of the language, I felt from the outset that beyond the gothic trappings these movies had something to say to *me* about *my* life. I just didn't have any idea what. . . .

Like any enthusiast, I rapidly discovered that there was secondary literature available about my particular obsession. I remember first finding a copy of *Castle of Frankenstein* in a local newsagent, and being both thrilled and terrified, desperate to buy it, but frankly scared of what buying it would *mean*. What would the newsagent think? Would he look at me in a different way from then on? Would he tell my mum? More important, would he actually sell it to me? The bizarre realisation that the newsagent neither noticed nor indeed cared what I was buying soon gave way to a weird sense, first, of anti-climax, then of dawning horror when I finally got to read *Castle of Frankenstein*. What was disappointing was the fact that the magazine didn't talk about any of the movies I had actually seen – although I'd watched only a handful, I just assumed that any horror magazine would deal in detail with the twenty or so movies that I'd stumbled across. Instead, *Castle of Frankenstein* opened the door on a frankly incomprehensible world of films of which I had never heard, people I didn't recognise, from countries I never knew existed.

From furtive but devoted fan, I was suddenly (and terrifyingly) transformed into a know-nothing dilettante who had no right even to profess an interest in horror movies. Here were people who *knew* what they were talking about, grown-up people who had been doing this for *years*, who actually *understood* what these movies were about. (Flicking back through those early issues, I notice that no less a notable than Joe Dante served as assistant editor on *Castle of Frankenstein*.) I still remember vividly the cold, clammy, slightly panicky feeling I got sitting on a wall opposite Christ's College School in Finchley, realising that I was simply never going to get up to speed with the back catalogue of horror which stretched back to the 1930s and beyond. I was *never* going to be able to remember Boris Karloff's real name, pick out Elsa Lanchester in a line-up, or name any of the directors, writers and cameramen who had steered Hammer through the hey-day of the 1960s. I was completely at sea, drowning in the realisation that the scab I had been gently picking had suddenly fallen away to reveal a vast, gaping, chasmic wound.

The second event of real significance in my education as a horror fan came with the British release in 1974 of *The Exorcist*, William Friedkin's ground-breaking shocker which sparked off an international wave of media-fuelled hysteria. My first knowledge of the movie came via a feature on the early-evening BBC magazine programme *Nationwide*. In a three-minute segment, Sue Lawley quickly recapped the film's plot (a young girl becomes demonically possessed), recounted Stateside tales of audience hysteria, questioned the involvement of teenage actress Linda Blair, and wondered whether the film shouldn't be banned in the UK. I was transfixed. Unlike the classic gothic horror fantasies which had played on late-night TV, here was a movie set in the present day, with everyday people, apparently based on real-life experiences, which (if the reports were to be believed) was literally driving viewers insane. The idea of such a movie scared the living daylights out of me and, oddly, drove me straight back to the safer pastures of Karloff, Lugosi and Lee, in whose company I now began to feel profoundly safe. Reading about (and even watching) the classic chillers began to seem almost a respectable pastime, compared to the ground-shaking horror that lurked out there in the form of *The Exorcist*.

I began to pursue a pseudo-scholarly interest in pre-1970s horror, deceiving myself that I had no interest in the shocking turn which the genre had taken in the wake of *The Exorcist*. What I really wanted to know about, I told myself, was how much nice, avuncular Vincent Price or Peter Cushing could remember about the good old days of horror. Yet whenever any of my older friends (I was 11 or 12 by now) claimed to have seen *The Exorcist* I would pump them mercilessly for information about it, demanding that they recount each scene as if they were witnesses to some appalling crime. And all the time I insisted that I *really wasn't interested* in it at all.

What was infuriating was that, for the most part, neither were they. They hadn't sat there (as to my mind they should have done) taking notes, drinking in every scrap of information on-screen, studiously committing to memory every image that passed before their eyes. Maddeningly, they had seen the film, been scared by it, then wandered out of the cinema and back into the mundanity of their everyday lives. It had not had any profound impact upon them whatsoever. And they really weren't that interested in talking about it. They generally wanted to talk about girls and football, both of which seemed to me as alien as the blob-headed monsters in *This Island Earth*.

For the second time, I was made profoundly aware of the absolute divide between horror fans and everybody else in the world; only by now I knew absolutely which side of the divide I was on. Finally, frustrated by the inability of anyone else to tell me what I needed to know in the kind of depth and detail that I needed to know it, I succumbed, and turned back to the new breed of horror and fantasy magazines that were arriving from the States to fill the gap. I first fell into the company of *Cinefantastique* through a newsagent in Muswell Hill which had clearly stocked it by mistake. Inside its pages I found interviews with the writer, director, cast and crew of *The Exorcist*, along with sombre under-stated stills (any graphic material was fiercely defended by the film's distributors), and a series of in-depth readings of the film. Unable to trace any further copies of the magazine locally, I began to venture into central London, where a series of vintage magazine and movie memorabilia stores sat cheek-by-jowl with seedy-looking strip-clubs and porn vendors. Going up to Soho on a Saturday became a regular quest to track down back issues of *Castle of Frankenstein*, *Famous Monsters*, *C.F.Q.* and *Quasimodo's Monster Magazine*.

Then, in 1979, the new bible of hard-core horror fandom, *Fangoria*, began to arrive in the UK, bringing with it a garishly modern approach to horror which seemed oddly in tune with the post-punk nihilism blighting British youth culture. It wasn't for nothing that *Fango* earned the affectionate nickname 'Exploding Heads Monthly'. For all its up-market production values, *Fango* was the Sex Pistols of horror fanzines, loud, noisy, visually graphic and absolutely guaranteed to send your parents apoplectic with righteous indignation. It was terrific! At around the same time I started frequenting the Phoenix cinema in East Finchley which every Friday and Saturday night played late-night double bills of the sort of culty horror and fantasy films that I'd by now read so much about.

From around the age of 15 (1978 or so) it was possible to get into X-rated movies with ease, particularly late-nighters, and I began to spend every weekend either at the Phoenix or at the Scala, losing myself in *Night of the Living Dead*, *Rosemary's Baby*, *The Possession of Joel Delaney*, *The Crazies*, *Eraserhead*, and of course *The Exorcist*.

Going to see these movies was essentially a lonely pursuit since no one at school shared my enduring enthusiasm for horror. Most of them would go and see a current mainstream horror picture maybe once a year – *Halloween*, *Friday the Thirteenth*, *Carrie* and so on – and considered it something to be endured, a test of machismo, an instantaneous thrill (and often a great way to cop off) but nothing more. Only at the late-nighters would I find myself surrounded by other 'loners' who, like me, weren't there to impress anybody but themselves, and who were clearly getting more out of the movies than passing scares, watching them again and again, learning them, studying them.

Although I almost never said anything to any of these people (one thing we seemed to have in common was that we were all lousy conversationalists) an odd bond was formed by seeing the same faces at the same cinemas, watching the same movies, time after time. In fact, there was something profoundly 'conversational' about the act of watching the movies, something that joined us together as a group in our increasingly knowing reactions to what was happening on-screen.

A prime element in this was the fact that the movies themselves seemed acutely aware of their audience. More than any other genre, horror movies play to and feed upon the knowledgeability of their fans. Directors, writers, actors, even special-effects men, all become recognisable to devotees who provide the hard-core fan-base for the genre. Through the pages of *Fangoria* – and later *Gore Zone* – we had met these people in their natural surroundings, seen photographs of them goofing around with severed latex heads, and read their behind-the-scenes accounts of how the movies got made. We understood that when special-effects maestro Tom Savini popped up on-screen as 'third bystander from the left' (as he did with increasing frequency) it was the film-makers' way of winking at the fans in the audience, to which the correct response was a knowing laugh. I remember forming a fleeting bond with a fellow movie-goer at a screening of *The Fly* at the Manchester Oxford Road Odeon in the 1980s when an on-screen doctor preparing to abort Geena Davis' insect foetus turned out to be director David Cronenberg. While everyone else cringed, the two of us chuckled smugly from opposite sides of the auditorium, like ships signalling each other in deep fog. I don't know who the other person was, but I bet they had a stackful of *Fango*s under their bed.

Just as film-makers' faces are familiar to the horror fans, so generic conventions of plot, narrative, character and dialogue become the playthings of writers and directors well versed in the genre, as do recurrent visual motifs and archetypal images. While Quentin Tarantino litters his hugely popular movies with nods and winks to the films which inspired him, so horror has a tendency endlessly to recycle its own history. Like the climactic sequence from Joe D'Amato's *Anthropophagous* in which the ravenous cannibal disembowels himself only to begin chomping upon his own intestines, so horror movies have habitually found sustenance from devouring their own flesh. For the horror fan, the recognition of these recycled elements is a crucial part of the enjoyment and appreciation of the movies.

At its most basic, this is merely a rarefied form of 'getting the joke', of feeling 'in the know', of understanding that a knife is never just a knife. Produce a chainsaw on-screen in a horror movie, and the devoted fan will automatically click into a celluloid history dating back to Tobe Hooper's ground-breaking *Texas Chainsaw Massacre*, and marauding to the present day via the parodic excesses of *Motel Hell, Hollywood Chainsaw Hookers, Bad Taste, The Evil Dead* and, of course, *Texas 2, 3* and *4*. To the genre fan, a chainsaw is not a threatening weapon – it's a magical talisman, conjuring up a heritage of horror.

Gory special effects, constantly the target of attacks by the censors and media pundits alike, work upon disparate audiences in a similarly polarised manner. A key problem in persuading non-horror fans that genre devotees are not a pack of marauding sadists hell-bent on destruction (I wish!) lies in the recurrent inability of untrained viewers to see past the special effects, puncture the gaudy surface of the movies, pull apart their rubbery rib-cages and grasp their dark thematic hearts. Essentially a surrealist genre, contemporary horror demands to be read metaphorically rather than literally. Throughout the 1980s, advanced latex special-effects processes allowed directors like David Cronenberg, Brian Yuzna and Clive Barker to stretch the envelope of on-screen surrealism with a previously impossible ease.

Yet the work of all these directors is meaningless if taken at face value. The bizarre physical mutations of *Videodrome*, the body 'shunting' of *Society*, the skin-flailing tortures of *Hellraiser* – none of these on-screen wonders are intended to be read as depictions of 'real' physical possibilities. Instead, each film uses body-based special effects to address a range of issues (the power of the televisual image, the nature of inter-class conflict, the sadomasochistic allure of desire) which have little or nothing to do with actual bodily contortions. The horror fan understands this, and is thus not only able but positively compelled to 'read' rather than merely 'watch' such movies. The novice, however, sees only the dismembered bodies, hears only the screams and groans, reacts only with revulsion or contempt. Being unable to differentiate between the real and the surreal, they consistently misinterpret horror fans' interaction with texts which mean nothing to them. Just as, to me, all opera is basically fat people shouting at each other, many opera fans clearly believe that all horror is crazy people torturing and killing each other. Neither of us has an effective take on the chosen fetish of the other. The only difference is, I don't go round calling for opera to be banned.

One clear example of the way in which fans' knowledge affects their viewing of a movie is the case of Sam Raimi's *The Evil Dead*. A gruesomely satirical first feature, *The Evil Dead* is in essence a horror farce, a violent comedy which strives to elicit a response of startled hilarity from its audience. The movie was shot in America in the early 1980s using finance raised from local shop-keepers, dentists and hardware store owners by a group of enthusiastic young film-makers, equally well versed in the traditions of horror and slapstick. Praised in the horror press for its feisty verve, *The Evil Dead* scored a major hit with fans, but ran into trouble with British censors. In UK cinemas, the movie was cut by forty seconds by the British Board of Film Classification, who recognised its ghoulish flair, but couldn't countenance its self-parodic excesses. In February 1983 (before the introduction of the Video Recordings Act) Palace Video released this cut version on to the video rental market, unfortunately coinciding with the rise of press-fuelled hysteria about 'video nasties'.

In the panic that followed, *The Evil Dead* was cited by the Director of Public Prosecutions as potentially likely to deprave and corrupt, and a number of video dealers stocking the title were prosecuted (with varying results) under the Obscene Publications Act. In courts up and down the country, juries utterly unfamiliar with the horror genre or the audience which it attracts, were asked to respond either to key scenes from the movie or to written check-lists of the violent acts depicted therein. Unsurprisingly, their reaction tended to be one of shock – to them, the catalogue of on-screen dismemberment which the movie offered was nothing more than unashamed sadism, designed to delight those who would revel in pain.

Crucially, this is not how the movie plays to horror fans. It's not just that the juries who considered this sadistic pleasure to be the primary function of *The Evil Dead* were over-reacting to the on-screen atrocities; it's that they were literally seeing an entirely different movie from that which had delighted *Fango* readers the world over. To the uninitiated viewer, *The Evil Dead* was a gruelling horror picture in which human bodies were mercilessly hacked to pieces. To erudite horror fans, it was *The Three Stooges* with latex and ketchup standing in for custard pies, a knockabout romp in which everything is cranked up to eleven, and in which pain and suffering play no part. As James Ferman rightly observed: 'With *The Evil Dead*, the name of the game is excess.'

The reason for this disparity of opinion between jurors and genre-hounds is not (as is sometimes suggested) that horror fans have become hardened or insensitive to violence through years of exposure to sadistic material. The truth is simply that the experienced horror fan understands the on-screen action in terms of a heritage of genre knowledge which absolutely precludes the possibility of sadistic titillation. Nowhere in *The Evil Dead* does the horror fan see the actual torture, mutilation or violation of the human form (as they *would* do in a movie like John McNaughton's solidly unfunny *Henry: Portrait of a Serial Killer*). What they do see is the playful trashing of a tradition of special-effects work, in which the refining of various latex additives has opened up vistas of possibilities for enthusiastic amateur film-makers everywhere. To the horror fan, *The Evil Dead* is about as threatening as a pop group smashing up their guitars on stage – it's stupid, but it's huge fun none the less. And just as it's impossible for any modern pop group to ram a guitar through the front of a vast Marshall stack without invoking the ghost of axe-wielding legend Pete Townshend, so it is impossible for any horror fan to see the chainsaw sequence in *The Evil Dead* without indulging in a knowing laugh. They're not laughing at pain, they're laughing at the movie. Or, more precisely, they're laughing *with* the movie.

This is not to say that all horror movies rely upon humour. Far from it – there is clearly very little to find funny in films as diverse as *The Haunting, Night of the Living Dead, The Exorcist, Dead Ringers, The Vanishing, Cronos* or *Henry: Portrait of a Serial Killer*. These are movies which work because they are *deadly* serious, and horror fans understand absolutely the difference between these brutal masterpieces and the upbeat buffoonery of *The Evil Dead*. Yet, crucially, those ill-versed in the genre generally have no means of distinguishing between these wildly different strands. To the average bleary-eyed juror, there is simply no difference between the gory goings-on of the farcical *Brain Dead* or the bleaker-than-bleak *Dawn of the Dead*. But, to the horror fan, these movies are as unlike as *Apocalypse Now* and *Whoops! Apocalypse*.

Similarly, experience has taught me that only those who have dutifully ploughed through hour upon hour of indescribable European dreck tend to have any truly valid concept of the difference between a good and bad horror movie. And, as the fans know only too well, even within the infinite sub-divisions of the horror genre there are vast differences between the good and the bad, whether it be cannibal movies (*Cannibal Holocaust* vs *Cannibal Ferox*), serial killer movies (*Manhunter* vs *The New York Ripper*), zombie movies (*Dawn of the Dead* vs *Zombie Flesh Eaters*), latter-day vampire movies (*Near Dark* vs *Innocent Blood*), demonic kids movies (*The Omen* vs *The Good Son*), psycho-automobile movies (*Duel* vs *Christine*), or even Freddy Krueger movies (*Nightmare on Elm St. Parts 1, 3* and *7* vs *Parts 2, 4* and *6*).

Knowing, understanding and arguing about the difference between these movies is an integral part of horror fandom. And the place where these debates rage is across the pages of the current horror magazines, the direct descendants of *Famous Monsters* and *Castle of Frankenstein* which themselves owe a hereditary debt to EC comics and their ghoulish predecessors. What is most encouraging about the best of these publications is their international dimension, the fact that no self-respecting horror magazine (unlike the majority of mainstream cinema mags) is considered complete without in-depth coverage of the works of European film-makers like Mario Bava, Dario Argento, Lucio Fulci, Michele Soavi, Guillermo del Toro, even the irredeemably tiresome Jess Franco. It's not for nothing that Britain's own *Shivers* accurately described itself (before its disappointing relaunch) as 'The Global Magazine of Horror'. Nor would any self-respecting horror fan be unprepared to discuss in detail the often minute dissimilarities between English, French, Italian, German and Japanese versions of the same horror movie. In fact, I can think of no other cinematic genre in which internationalism is so genuinely championed, and in which linguistic boundaries are so nimbly overstepped.

The watch-word of horror fans is 'completist', and it is in this arena that publications such as Tim Lucas' indispensable *Video Watchdog* really come into their own. Only a die-hard horror devotee such as Lucas could have made internationally viable a magazine whose primary purpose was to document the tiny differences between versions of movies available across the world. And, unlike the mainstream film magazines which can blithely pass over the small factual blips and inconsistencies which litter their pages, *Video Watchdog* is subject to the sort of intense scrutiny usually afforded only to legal documents. Horror fans *need* to know this kind of detailed information, and they are very unforgiving of inaccuracy. As director Joe Dante has said, *Video Watchdog* is less a film magazine than a survival manual – it simply cannot get things wrong. Indeed, in a market-place in which there is no legal requirement for a distributor to declare that a film may have been abridged from its original format, *Video Watchdog* is often the only source of product information which in other areas would be strictly monitored by trading standards and weights-and-measures laws. If only such publications existed for all areas of cinema!

A logical extension of the on-going consumer dialogue pioneered by horror fanzines is the horror film festivals which flourished in Britain in the late 1980s, and which have a healthy tradition throughout Europe and the States. In Britain, the ground was broken by the indefatigable 'Shock around the Clock', which brought together spotty adolescents from around the country to pig out on twenty-four hours of international terror. Organised by Alan Jones and Stefan Jaworzyn, the mercurial talents behind the UK horror magazine *Shock Xpress*, 'Shock around the Clock' paved the way for subsequent festivals like 'Black Sunday' (a

Northern riposte to the capital-based 'Shock'), 'Splatterfest' and, ultimately, 'Fantasm' at the National Film Theatre, an up-market affair which
continues to delight audiences with its varied range of international
shockers. (The fact that the air in the 'Fantasm' auditorium is generally
breathable and that the projectionists usually put the reels through in the
right order also adds a charm often lacking in other such gatherings.)

In Europe, the horror festival brand-leader for many years was Milan's
currently dormant 'Dylan Dog' festival, an absolute riot of an event in
which thousands of screaming kids greeted each new chiller with a rock
star's reception, chanting, cheering, whooping and whistling. And here's
a bizarre thing – for some unfathomable reason, the teenage horror
devotees who roamed the streets of Italy and crowded out the 'Dylan
Dog' enormodrome *weren't* the malnourished, acne-ridden pasty-faces
that we know and love in Britain. On the contrary, they were sparkling
young things, dashingly elegant in their designer jeans and logo-blasted
T-shirts, hair cut *à la mode*, and generally paired off in a manner that
suggested sexual achievement. In a frankly inexplicable biological quirk,
Italy has somehow managed to breed good-looking movie geeks, a fact I
find more profoundly shocking than anything I have ever seen in a horror
movie. Elsewhere in Europe, Sitges and Oporto continue to play host to
popular annual horror festivals (and public entrance to these tends to be
on the increase); while, in America, *Fangoria*'s annual conventions get
bigger each year. For British fans, cut ever deeper by the UK's censorious
scissors, these festivals are becoming increasingly important. Where else
can British fans see these movies as they were intended, and not in the
BBFC-approved bastardised versions, which have been slashed to pieces
by people who have neither any affection for, nor understanding of, the
horror genre?

And here is perhaps the greatest irony of horror fandom in the UK.
For here an obsession which absolutely demands rigorous attention to
detail, which thrives upon intense research and the patient devotion of
the true completist, is utterly thwarted from the outset by the clumsy
bludgeoning of genre-illiterate censors. If there were ever a genre in
which cutting and banning could do nothing but harm to both the movies
and their audience, then it is the horror genre. It is perhaps unsurprising
that, of all the issues which recur through the pages of British horror
mags past and present such as *Samhain, Fear, The Dark Side, Shivers,
Eyeball, Ungawa!* and *Shock Xpress*, censorship has generally commanded
more column inches than any other subject. Personally, I look forward to
the time when European trading laws make a legal mockery of the
senseless snippings and belligerent bannings which blight so many horror
films in the UK. In the mean time, as I slip my uncut copy of *Texas
Chainsaw Massacre 4* into the video machine, I remember the illicit thrill
I got as a child sneaking downstairs to ogle 'The Monday X Film' unde-

tected by my parents. It doesn't matter if the movie isn't any good (and, believe me, *Texas 4* is no good at all). It's the fact that you're not supposed to be watching it which makes it fun.

# Chapter 5

# Reservoirs of dogma

## An archaeology of popular anxieties

*Graham Murdock*

On the morning of Wednesday, 13 March 1996, Thomas Hamilton, a middle-aged man with no criminal record, walked into the primary school in the small Scottish town of Dunblane, shot sixteen children and a teacher and then killed himself. It was a deeply disturbing incident and, although there was no evidence that he had a particular interest in watching screen violence, it prompted a rash of commentary condemning the morality of popular film and television. Here is Andrew Neil, writing in the *Sunday Times*:

> There are some crimes so horrific that they make us all wonder what kind of country we have become. ... It should be cause for concern that, in the values and mores of modern society, we have created a quagmire from which monsters are bound to emerge ... far too much of what passes for popular entertainment pollutes our society and creates a new tolerance in which what was thought to be beyond the pale becomes acceptable. Young minds are particularly vulnerable.
> (Neil, 1996, p. 5)

An almost identical catalogue of complaint followed two other traumatic events of recent years: Michael Ryan's random shootings in Hungerford and the brutal murder of 2-year-old James Bulger by two boys of 10. Again, although there was no firm evidence of direct 'effects' in either case, screen violence was singled out as a major contributory cause. In recent discussions, a small number of films containing scenes of violence have come to stand for the state of contemporary cinema. Quentin Tarantino's début feature *Reservoir Dogs* has been a particular target. One popular cartoon, which appeared in the wake of the intense debate on the James Bulger case, showed two children sitting in front of a television set displaying the film's title. One is turning to the other saying: 'Let's go and drown some puppies.'

This simple image of direct effects draws its power from a deep reservoir of social fear and dogma which first formed in the mid-nineteenth century as commentators began to link the social costs of modernity with the proliferation of new forms of popular entertainment. Then, as now, the perceived disorders of the present were often counterposed against an idealised image of the past.

> Once upon a time, so the story runs . . . violence and disorder were unknown in Britain. . :. But now all that is no more. Now violence and terror lurk in the once-safe streets. The family no longer holds its proper place and parents have abandoned their responsibilities.
>
> (Pearson, 1983, p. 3)

Here is Andrew Neil again:

> There was a time, within my memory, when popular culture sought to lift our spirits and encourage what was good, honourable and just in our society. We aspired to what we saw on our screens, and evil was generally given a bad press.
>
> (Neil, 1996, p. 5)

This is a startling case of selective recall. Though Neil grew up in the 1950s he has conveniently forgotten the moral panics about media 'effects' which greeted the American 'horror comics', the hard-boiled pulp thrillers of Mickey Spillaine and Hank Janson, and the 'Teddy Boy riots' in cinemas showing early rock 'n' roll films. For a newspaperman, he also displays a woeful ignorance of the long history of condemnation that has accompanied popular media throughout the modern age.

By the 1850s the core patterns of modern social life had begun to crystallise, and popular fictions, dramas and journalism were assuming their familiar contemporary forms. The blood-soaked melodramas playing in the 'penny gaffs', the lurid stories carried by the 'penny dreadfuls' and the sensationalised coverage of crime in the populist Sunday newspapers established traditions of representation which are still very much with us. Violence and lawlessness were one of their principal stocks-in-trade. They paraded the dark side of modernity's promise of progress, the monstrous doubles of order and respectability, the animalistic potentials that continually elbowed and jostled sobriety and rationality. Commentators were quick to see them as both a potent symptom of moral decline and a powerful new incitement to anti-social behaviour. Because they supposedly lacked an adequate training in moral and social restraints, young people were widely seen as particularly open to suggestion. As the critic who reviewed a series of recent publications on juvenile crime for the *Edinburgh Review* in 1851 lamented:

> One powerful agent for depraving the boyish classes of our population in our towns and cities is to be found in the cheap concerts, shows and theatres, which are so specially opened and arranged for the attraction and ensnaring of the young . . . when our fear of interfering with per-

sonal and public liberty allows these shows and theatres to be training schools of the coarsest and most open vice and filthiness – it is not to be wondered at, that the boy who is led on to haunt them becomes rapidly corrupted and demoralised, and seeks to be the doer of the infamies which have interested him as a spectator.

(*Edinburgh Review*, 1851, p. 409)

This attractively simple notion, that what young people watched was directly linked to what they later did, rapidly moved to the centre of debate. Despite the serious reservations that have been lodged against the research evidence claiming to 'prove' these connections (e.g. Murdock and McCron, 1979; Cumberbatch and Howitt, 1989; Gauntlett, 1995) studies in this tradition are still routinely cited by commentators arguing for more stringent controls on film and video. According to Melanie Phillips of the *Observer*, for example:

The remarkable fact is that there is a vast amount of evidence, more than 1,000 studies carried out in the United States and elsewhere, demonstrating a link between screen violence and aggressive behaviour in children. . . . True, there are problems with this kind of research. . . . But there are simply too many studies all pointing the same way to be ignored.

(Phillips, 1994, p. 25)

Anyone who questions this conclusion is presented as an arrogant, self-opinionated member of 'the progressive, libertarian intelligentsia', out of touch with the justified concerns of ordinary people.

The attraction of these 'many studies' is not simply that they offer the illusion of strength in numbers, but that they fit perfectly with the common-sense assumption that, since 'it stands to reason' that there must be a link, responsible research is simply confirming what reasonable people already know, and that refusing to accept this is patently unreasonable.

As we shall see, this circular relationship between empiricist science and common-sense thinking was built into academic work on media 'effects' from the outset. The dominant research tradition adopted the definition of the 'problem' already established in popular and political commentary. The result was banal science, which failed to ask awkward questions, to pursue other possible lines of inquiry or to place 'effects' in their social contexts. But because its investigative procedures corresponded to common-sense notions of what 'proper' science was – the image of controlled experimentation being particularly central – its 'findings' seemed to offer strong confirmation of popular assumptions and anxieties. These, in turn, were anchored in a deep-rooted formation of fear about the precarious balance between anarchy and order in the modern age.

As nineteenth-century observers knew very well, the dynamics of modernity called all pre-existing moral and social relations into question. As Marx put it in 1848, in one of his most lyrical passages, there was an 'uninterrupted disturbance of all social conditions . . . all fixed, fast-frozen relations are swept away. . . . All that is solid melts into air, all that is holy is profaned' (Marx and Engels, 1968, p. 38). What Marx celebrated as a liberation others mourned as a loss. They saw established social restraints crumbling away. They were haunted by the spectre of moral decline amidst material plenty. Many worried about the loosening grip of religious faith, and drives to 'purify' popular entertainment were often linked to campaigns to re-Christianise society.

As Andrew Neil's piece illustrates, anxieties about the moral and spiritual costs of social and cultural change remain central to present debates. They establish potent connections between concèrn about media violence and more general fears for the future. If we are to develop a more comprehensive analysis of the interplay between popular media and everyday thinking, feeling and behaviour, and to argue convincingly for expressive diversity in film, television and the new media, we need to challenge popular fears. Retracing the intellectual and political history that has formed them is a necessary first step. This is a substantial task. What follows is simply a very bald sketch of an embedded structure of feeling which will, hopefully, suggest some lines for future inquiry.

## DANGEROUS ASSOCIATIONS

The civic culture of high modernity was increasingly based around the social contract of citizenship. Every adult was entitled to participate fully in social and political life. In return they were expected to behave responsibly. Citizens were model Enlightenment individuals. They made rational choices on the basis of careful reflection and disinterested evidence. But the fact that the French Enlightenment had also produced the French Revolution and the Terror left an indelible impression on contemporary observers. As the great British constitutionalist Walter Bagehot warned in 1876: 'Such scenes of cruelty and horror as happened in the great French Revolution . . . we now see . . . were the outbreak of inherited passions long repressed by fixed custom, but starting into life as soon as that repression was catastrophically removed' (quoted in McClelland, 1989, p. 162). From the outset, the imagination of citizenship was shadowed by the fear of the elemental power of the crowd and the mob waiting to be detonated just below the surface of routine social life. As the journalist Charles Mackay put it in his highly successful book *Extraordinary Popular Delusions and the Madness of Crowds*, first published in 1841, men 'go mad in herds, while they only recover their sense slowly, and one by one' (Mackay, 1956, p. xx).

The packed tenements and slums of the major cities offered the most visible image of the crowd, and depictions of the 'mass' as a physically dense body continually on the edge of unpredictable motion played a central role in the formation of respectable fears. They constituted what Matthew Arnold called, in a memorable passage written after a crowd broke down the railings around Hyde Park during a demonstration protesting at the defeat of the Reform Bill of 1866, a 'vast residuum', a murky mass left at the bottom of the decanter after the drinkable wine had been poured off (Arnold, 1966, p. 105). This notion of a population at the bottom of the pile, disconnected from the mainstream, finds powerful contemporary expression in the notion of an urban 'underclass'. Mackay, however, was careful to stress that 'the madness of crowds' was a psychological rather than a physical phenomenon, and he set out to explore a variety of 'moral epidemics which have been excited, sometimes by one cause and sometimes by another, and to show how easily the masses have been led astray, and how imitative men are, even in their infatuations and crimes' (Mackay, 1956, p. xvii). These ranged from the fashion for beards to the craze for magnetism and a spate of slow poisonings.

The idea of the 'psychological crowd', physically separated but united by shared experiences, regularly surfaced in debates throughout the second half of the century and, by the time the Chicago sociologist and former journalist Robert Park came to write on the subject in 1904, the view that 'it is the psychological conditions rather than the spatial relationships of individuals which forms the essential content of the concept of the crowd' (Park, 1972, p. 12) was widely accepted. It found its most forceful and widely quoted formulation in Gustave Le Bon's massively influential 1895 book, *The Crowd*.

Crowds were the beast within, the absolute antithesis of a public composed of citizens. As Le Bon argued, 'by the mere fact that he forms part of a crowd, a man descends several rungs in the ladder of civilisation. Isolated he may be a cultivated individual, in a crowd he is a barbarian – a creature acting by instinct' (Le Bon, 1960, p. 32).

Where citizenship relied on rational debate and respect for evidence, psychological crowds, Le Bon argued, were formed by images. They worked with emotional associations rather than sequential arguments.

Crowds being only capable of thinking in images are only to be impressed by images. It is only images that attract them and become motives for action. . . . Nothing has a greater effect on the imagination of crowds than theatrical representations. . . . Sometimes the sentiments suggested by the images are so strong that they tend, like habitual suggestions, to transform themselves into acts.

(Le Bon, 1960, p. 68)

This argument appeared eminently plausible since it coincided with a major shift towards a more visually oriented popular culture. The Lumière Brothers' first film performance in Paris in 1895 ushered in the age of commercial cinema, and the rising generation of press enterpreneurs (such as Alfred Harmsworth who launched his *Daily Mail* in 1896) were pioneering new styles of popular journalism in which visual illustrations had a much more central role to play.

It was almost universally assumed that the seductions of imagery operated particularly powerfully among groups who were either pre-literate or semi-literate. Children were seen as particularly vulnerable to suggestion and exploitation. In a fierce attack on the 'penny dreadfuls', James Greenwood, one of the leading muck-raking Victorian journalists, pictured the publishers as vampires preying on the innocent, and urged 'careful parents' to beware: 'already he may have bitten your little rosy-cheeked son, Jack. He may be lurking at this very moment in that young gentleman's private chamber, polluting his mind and smoothing the way that leads to swift destruction' (Greenwood, 1874, p. 168). Children were vulnerable but they were not regarded as a threat to social order. Dangerousness lay with adolescents. They were not only suggestible, but capable of acting out what they had seen.

The new psychology of adolescence, pioneered by writers like Stanley Hall, argued that, because puberty unleashed physical and emotional potentials which young people did not have the moral and mental maturity to cope with, they were in constant danger of 'descending the ladder of civilisation'. As Frank Lydston, a professor of medicine in Illinois, put it in 1904:

> The pubescent is in the greatest danger ... the emotions are keyed to the highest pitch; centres of ideation are plastic. As the psychic twig is bent at this time, the cererbral tree is indeed inclined. Many a life has been ruined by psychic wounds – wounds from infected and infective ideas at this critical period.
>
> (Lydston, 1904, p. 101)

Working-class adolescent boys were a particular focus of respectable fears. They were highly visible on the streets of the cities, they regularly featured in press reporting, and they figured prominently in the official crime statistics. Moral entrepreneurs believed that they were locked in an uphill battle for young hearts and minds. As one prominent expert on 'Boy Life' put it:

> the boy's mind is in many respects a blank sheet at fourteen, and the writing that will be engraved upon it is dependent on the influences through which the boy passes. The senses of the adolescent, now open at their widest, are opened not to Art, but to cheap and tawdry panto-

mime, his emotions are fed, not with gracious and elevating influences, but with unnatural excitements.

(Freeman, 1914, p. 151)

These 'excitements', many observers believed, had turned young men into 'hooligans'. As *The Times* complained in 1900:

Our 'Hooligans' go from bad to worse . . . they hustle and waylay solitary old gentlemen with gold watches; they hunt in packs too large for a single policeman to cope with. . . . At best they will be bad citizens. They are an ugly growth on the body politic . . . a hideous excrescence on our civilisation.

(Quoted in Schwarz, 1996, p. 104)

The figure of the hooligan (and the parade of later folk devils) comprehensively undermined the idealised image of the citizen and condensed 'with great power a cluster of anxieties . . . around masculinity and youth, read through the lens of class' (Schwarz, 1996, p. 119).

Within this framework of concern, censoring 'infective ideas' or trying to keep them out of adolescents' reach (as in systems of film classification) was not simply an expression of aesthetic judgement but a social duty designed to repair the rents in the body politic. However, because these measures cut across two of the most cherished values of capitalist democracy, freedom of artistic expression and freedom of consumer choice, their supporters were obliged to look for plausible proofs to support their demands for action.

## PERSUASIONS AND PANICS

Some commentators seized upon the substantial sums of money being spent on advertising by the turn of the century to argue that, since marketing seemed to work in the world of goods, as shown by sales figures, images of crime and violence probably promoted anti-social behaviour in the same way. They saw the sensationalist popular press as a potent agent of both kinds of persuasion. As W. I. Thomas, the Chicago sociologist, argued in 1908:

[A]n article in commerce – a food, a luxury, a medicine or a stimulant – can always be sold in immense quantities if it be persistently and largely advertised. In the same way the yellow journal by an advertisement of crime . . . in a way that amounts to approval and even applause, becomes one of the forces making for immorality.

(Thomas, 1908, p. 496)

This argument still features regularly in contemporary comment, as in the editorial carried in the *Independent on Sunday* after the Dunblane shootings:

the modern, liberal mind is strangely resistent to cause and effect. . . . Yet millions of pounds are spent annually on advertising and the entire media industry strains over presentation, using music, visual effects, camera, lighting, to put audiences in the right mood. How can we possibly believe that the film shoot-out never has an effect?

*(Independent on Sunday*, 1996, p. 20)

At first sight, this is an attractive argument, but it ignores the fact that popular representations of crime organise pleasures, fears and excitements in complex combinations that can be responded to at a number of levels. Some readers may be attracted to the aggressor but many more are likely to identify with the victim and to support calls for tougher policing and sentencing.

As *The Times* leader quoted earlier illustrates, by the turn of the century 'hooligan' had become a handy popular label that was liberally applied by the press to all kinds of youthful street disorder. And, as one London magistrate of the period remembered, this continual labelling prompted a response out of all proportion to the threat.

Southwark and Bermondsey were famous for some years as the head-quarters of hooliganism . . . the press had so boosted the heroes of it that it was quite dangerous at one time for a group of youths to walk together down a street. They were sure to be charged with insulting behaviour and to be reported with the words 'more hooliganism in the Borough'.

(Chapman, 1925, pp. 11–12)

As a number of commentators observed at the time, the popular press had played a leading role in orchestrating concern. The educationalist John Trevarthen, for example, was quick to castigate sensationalist reporting for prompting an over-reaction:

Gangs of young roughs and thieves are no new thing in London and other large towns . . . though something like a scare has been produced by paragraphs in popular newspapers. . . . The result has been numerous leading articles in various papers, with reports of speeches and sermons on the subject, followed as usual by letters from people, some of whom are evidently very imperfectly informed on the subject.

(Trevarthen, 1901, p. 84)

This argument was pursued more systematically in one of the pioneering works of critical criminology, an inquiry into the workings of the criminal justice system in Cleveland, Ohio, published in the early 1920s. The authors noted that 345 crimes were reported in the city's newspapers in the first half of January 1919, and 363 in the second half, but that the amount of news space devoted to issues of crime and justice jumped dramatically over the same period, from 925 column inches to 6,642. As they argued, although there had been no appreciable change in the situation on the ground, the press had set in motion an escalating cycle of public fear, leading to calls for tough action that placed order above law or civil liberties. They went on to provide a very clear outline of the main stages in this cycle of response:

> News treatment tends to create . . . the belief that all crimes committed at such a time are part of some phenomenon that constitutes a 'crime wave' and can be cured by some quick panaceas [and stimulates] a tendency to demand summary action and quick reportable 'results' on the part of police, prosecutors, and judges . . . officials responsive to popular whims will, at least unconsciously, care more to satisfy popular demands than to be observant of the tried process of law.
>
> (Pound and Frankfurter, 1922, pp. 545–6)

This pioneering anatomy fits the career of later 'moral panics' about the possible links between popular media and social violence almost exactly.

## UNRELIABLE ACCOUNTS

As public reactions to the Hungerford killings, the James Bulger murder and the Dunblane shootings illustrate, moral panics are often sparked off by one particularly dramatic and newsworthy event that crystallises and distils a range of latent social fears and concerns. The practice of generalising from single cases has a long history; but, as sceptics were quick to point out in the nineteenth century, miscreants hoping to appeal to notions of diminished responsibility had every reason to try to blame their actions on allegedly corrupting influences from outside. As one commentator observed at the height of the nineteenth-century panic over 'penny dreadfuls':

> It often happens, we are aware, that some juvenile till-robber is found to be a reader of 'penny dreadfuls'. Nevertheless, we cannot agree with the conclusion usually taken for granted in these cases, that the reading and the robbery stand in the relation of cause and effect. Young gentlemen 'in trouble' are ready enough to avail themselves of this plea when it is put into their mouth.
>
> (Wright, 1881, p. 35)

The problem of putting convenient words into young men's mouths surfaced again and again. In their eagerness to establish a secure link between misdirected reading and subsequent misdeeds, interviewers often asked leading questions designed to elicit the response they were looking for.

In the spring of 1875 the American publisher James T. Fields visited the adolescent murderer Jesse Pomeroy in prison. The case, which had involved the killing of children, had received enormous publicity, and Fields was concerned to discover what had prompted Pomeroy's actions. As his memoir records, in the course of their conversation he asked him about what he liked to read:

*Fields* 'Were there any pictures in the books?'
*Pomeroy* 'Yes, Sir, plenty of them, blood and thunder pictures, tomahawking and scalping.'
*Fields* 'Do you think these books were an injury to you, and excited you, and excited you to commit the acts you have done?'
*Pomeroy* 'Yes, Sir, I have thought it all over, and it seems to me now they did.'

Unfortunately for Fields, the reliability of Pomeroy's testimony is immediately undermined by his next remark: 'I can't say certainly of course, and perhaps if I should think it over again, I should say it was something else' (quoted in Hawes, 1971, p. 112).

## DISEASED IMAGININGS

One response to the unreliability of individual witnesses was to assemble a large number of cases, on the grounds that there might be safety in numbers. Doctors, lawyers and other professionals working in the proliferating institutions set up to maintain surveillance and control over the urban poor and the youthful population could draw on their practical experience and invest their hunches and prejudices with claims to an expertise won in the rough-and-tumble of investigation.

Hence William Wadsworth could in 1911 write to the American Academy of Medicine claiming that:

After years of observation of a stream of crime, in one of the largest centres of population in our country, and a careful professional study of the details of a very large number of cases of crimes, I have no hesitation in pointing out the fact that newspaper accounts of crimes influence those who commit crimes.

(Wadsworth, 1911, p. 316)

Wadsworth, who practised as a coroner's physician in Philadelphia, worked with a medical model which presented media influence as a contagious disease attacking the mentally and morally unfit. This powerful metaphor was deeply attractive to many commentators. As Frank

Lydston, a professor of genito-urinary surgery, argued in his book *The Diseases of Society*:

> There is a moral or psychic contagium in certain books that is as definite and disastrous as that of the plague. The germs of mental ill-health are as potent in their way and, as things go nowadays, as far-reaching in evil effects as syphilis or leprosy.
>
> (Lydston, 1904, p. 101)

From this vantage point, the new popular media appeared as open sewers of the imagination, carrying a continuous flow of infection. The sensationalist newspapers were seen as a 'gutter press'. As the Italian criminologist Corre put it: 'Infectious epidemics spread with the air or the wind; epidemics of crime follow the line of the telegraph' (quoted in Tarde, 1912, pp. 340–1). The metaphors changed later, the image of a hypodermic needle injecting drugs into an unresisting body being a particular favourite, but the basic elements of the medical model remained remarkably stable.

But the new professionals were by no means unanimous. Those with other claims to expertise frequently rejected the medical model's argument for direct effects and emphasised more tangible environmental causes. As Newcastle's Director of Education, Percival Sharp, told a British inquiry into the influence of cinema in 1917:

> I have not during the last three years of investigation (covering 186 cases of committal) had a single case brought to my notice in respect of which it has been alleged or even suggested by police, school attendance officer or head-teacher that the genesis of the wrong-doing was to be found in the cinema show, EITHER IMMEDIATELY OR REMOTELY.
>
> (National Council of Public Morals, 1917, p. 284; emphasis in the original)

Other critics, like the American author Horace Kallen, went further, insisting that

> Investigation discovers no ground for the belief that any one of the arts ... has in and by itself any important influence at all on conduct. ... The fact is that crowded slums, machine labour ... barren lives, starved emotions ... are far more dangerous to morals, property and life than ... any motion picture.

On the contrary, he argued, in a version of what later came to be called the catharsis theory, films 'are substitutes for more elaborate and more serious overt actions, not inciters to them' (Kallen, 1930, pp. 50–1)

Faced with their critics, supporters of imitative effects could appeal to one further source of evidence: they could try to establish strong correlations between the details of well-publicised court cases and subsequent 'copy-cat' crimes. Gabriel Tarde, one of the leading early criminologists, was happy to support his case for contagious imitation by drawing on Corre's argument about the effects of press reporting of the notorious Whitechapel murders:

> What more striking example of suggesto-imitative assault could there be . . . ? The newspapers were filled with the exploits of Jack the Ripper, and, in less than a year, as many as eight absolutely identical crimes were committed in various crowded streets of the great city. This is not all; there followed a repetition of these same deeds outside of the capital and very soon there was even a spreading of them abroad . . . the Hamburg murder accompanied by disembowelling of a little girl; in the United States disembowelling of four negroes.
>
> (Quoted in Tarde, 1912, p. 340)

Leaving aside the view, widely held at the time and since, that Jack the Ripper was a serial killer, this argument rests on a classic conflation of correlation and causality. It is possible to see the cases cited as similar only by removing them from their contexts and ignoring all other possible situational causes. At a time when racist attacks were a constant feature of black life in America and the 'bitter fruits' of lynchings hung from trees across the South, there were many more obvious places than London's East End to look for an explanation of a mass murder in Alabama.

Despite the obvious flaws in Corre's case, and in other similar forms of anecdotal and impressionistic evidence, the argument that there was a direct, cause-and-effect relationship between images and actions continued to dominate common-sense thinking. Much of the work undertaken by university-based researchers, from the turn of the century onwards, simply took over this agenda. It was a marriage of convenience. Academics seeking to establish new disciplines could bolster their claims to utility, relevance and research grants. In return, commentators and politicians could draw on seemingly 'scientific' evidence to support their calls for greater controls over popular entertainment.

## BANAL SCIENCE

The search for factual support took two main forms. First, there were content-analysis studies which set out to provide statistics on the prevalence of violent imagery by painstakingly counting the space taken up by stories or incidents featuring violence. Second, there were studies designed to isolate direct links between imagery and behaviour. Some of these relied on experiments conducted under laboratory conditions. Others used quasi-experiential designs in real-life settings or applied statistical controls to the results of questionnaire surveys in an effort to eliminate other possible causes. The 'findings' of these inquiries over the years have provided the 'scientific' evidence that is ritually cited in support of claims for direct 'effects'.

Although commentators had been attacking representations of violence in popular literature and journalism more or less continually since the 1850s, it was not until the century's turn that researchers set about calibrating sensationalism more precisely. Delos Wilcox's extensive content study of American newspapers, published in 1900, was a pioneering effort. He used his calculations to show that newspapers defined by critics as 'yellow' tended to feature materials thought likely to activate the mob spirit – advertisements, illustrations, and news of crime and vice (Wilcox, 1900, pp. 77–8). But, unlike most commentators, he was reluctant to draw firm conclusions about effects, arguing that 'the great mass of information we get in reading the papers affects our action only vaguely and remotely, if at all' (Wilcox, 1900, p. 87). Other writers, like Frederick Peterson, writing in 1906, were rather less restrained, however:

It is not overstating it to say . . . these newspapers represent in the domain of culture and enlightenment the mob spirit, a vast, impersonal, delirious, anarchic, degenerating and disintegrating force. And it is this force which, acting upon the minds of the masses, sways them irresistibly in its own direction, making chaos where there should be order.
(Peterson, 1906, p. 13)

This same basic argument was pursued in another important early study, Frances Fenton's 'The influence of newspaper presentations upon the growth of crime and other anti-social activity', which appeared in 1910–11. This combined a content analysis and a close reading of selected news stories with a model of influence which drew heavily on current writings on imitation and suggestion. After reviewing the evidence, Fenton concluded that 'On the basis of the psychology of suggestion . . . a direct causal connection may be established between the newspaper and crime and other anti-social activities' (Fenton, 1910–11, p. 370).

Gabriel Tarde had already assigned a central place to imitative effects in his influential work on crime. In *Penal Philosophy*, which first appeared in 1890, he had no hesitation in arguing that:

All the important acts of social life are carried out under the domination of example. . . . One kills or does not kill, because of imitation. . . . One kills oneself or one does not kill oneself, because of imitation. How can we doubt that one steals or does not steal, one assassinates or does not assassinate, because of imitation.
(Tarde, 1912, p. 322)

But how did imitation work? In searching for an answer Fenton and a number of other analysts turned to fashionable theories of subconscious suggestion. These shared a number of the overlapping oppositions which made up the structure of respectable fear: rationality versus emotion, progress versus degeneracy and the crowd versus the citizen. As Boris Sidis put it in 1898, in his book *The Psychology of Suggestion*: 'the subpersonal, uncritical social self, the mob self, and the suggestible sub-conscious self are identical' (Sidis, 1927, p. 364).

Sidis' book carried a foreword by William James, one of the influential central figures in the struggle to establish psychology as an independent discipline in America. But the theory, though attractive, presented formi-dable problems of evidence. As Fenton pointed out, because people are unaware of 'unconscious suggestion', cases cannot be analysed by getting them to reconstruct their experiences and motivations through introspec-tion (the standard procedure in psychology at the time) and, as a result, 'it is not possible to measure this influence quantitatively' (Fenton, 1910–11, p. 61, p. 370).

This presented a serious problem for a fledgling science attempting to establish its ability to produce firm factual evidence on pressing social issues. One solution was to build on Freud's techniques for unlocking the dynamics of the unconscious mind. The other was to reject the notion of the subconscious altogether and to focus on what people actually did rather than on what they claimed or thought had happened. This line of inquiry was pursued with great vigour by John Watson in his enormously influential theory of behaviourism.

Freud's central ideas first became widely available in America in 1910 when the talks he had given at Clark University were published as *Five Lectures on Psycho-analysis*. Watson, who had been working with his notion of behaviourism since 1903, dismissed them out of hand, claiming that they could 'never serve as a support for a scientific formulation' (Watson, 1924, p. vii). He not only rejected the idea of the unconscious but also set out to make 'a clean break with the whole concept of consciousness' and the prevailing methods of introspection (Watson, 1924, p. viii). He argued that if psychology was to become a true 'science' and to contribute to 'the prediction and control of human action' (ibid., p. xiii) it had to focus on observed behaviour. He claimed that, providing the relevant stimuli were correctly identified, it was possible to explain all forms of behaviour 'from jumping at a sound' to 'having babies, writing books, and the like' as simple, predictable responses (Watson, 1930, p. 6). Unlike Freud, who argued that experiences (particularly in childhood) may only affect action years later, Watson insisted that the relations between stimulus and response were immediate and direct. This made them eminently suitable for investigation by laboratory experimentation, or by studies that followed the basic logic of experimentation.

Laboratories commanded pride of place in popular conceptions of 'science'. They were the spaces where important discoveries were made and conjectures subjected to rigorous testing. Hence any discipline claiming to be a 'science' had to have laboratories. Even so, Watson initially had strong reservations about their relevance to social issues. In the first edition of his major work on behaviourism, published in 1924, he conceded that 'Certain important psychological undertakings probably can never be brought under laboratory control. Reference here, of course, is made to the social problems which psychology sometimes has to study. There are many problems of this character that yield only a little at the hands of a laboratory man' because key influences in the outside environment are 'not under the immediate control of the observer' (Watson, 1924, p. 28). By the time the revised edition of the book came out in 1930, however, he had become more assertive, arguing that behaviourism 'is basal to the organisation of society' and expressing the hope that 'sociology may accept its principles and re-envisage its own problems in a more concrete way' (Watson, 1930, p. 44).

By then sociological researchers were themselves deeply divided, however. Some shared Watson's enthusiasm for hard-nosed empiricism and set out to gather 'social facts' using large-scale, relatively impersonal sample surveys. But others argued that the human sciences should be concerned with understanding the close-grained textures of everyday experience and not with prediction and control. They saw them not as 'an experimental science in search of law but an interpretive one in search of meaning' (Geertz, 1973, p. 5).

These divergent traditions of inquiry produced two major research literatures on the possible relations between popular imagery and social violence. One followed the general model of experimentation and attempted to isolate the impact of screen violence, using an array of physical and statistical procedures designed to rule out 'all extraneous influences that might produce the observed effect' (Eysenck and Nias, 1978, p. 66). This approach has produced research practices which single-mindedly neglect 'questions about the social construction of meaning', relegating them to 'on the one hand, technical problems in Content Analysis and, on the other, taken-for-granted views of the general cultural context' (Tudor, 1995, p. 87). The concerted search for statistical proofs of strong effects has led its enthusiasts to make some odd claims. In January 1995, for example, the respected Swedish researcher Karl-Erik Rosengren wrote an article for *Dagens Nyheter*, one of the country's most influential newspapers. In it he claimed that 'one can say that 10–20% of all kicks and smacks in our school yards, and also with time, on our streets and squares, can be explained as direct or indirect effects of media violence' (quoted in Linne, 1995, p. 8). As critics were quick to point out, there was absolutely no way that he could make these calculations on the basis of the evidence he had collected. They were pure guesswork masquerading as 'scientific' precision.

In opposition to this euphoric dream of certainty, the interpretive tradition has developed a range of qualitative techniques – depth interviewing, focus groups, ethnographic observations of everyday life – designed to explore the myriad ways in which the experience of violence (as a reader, viewer, witness, victim or aggressor) is woven into personal identities and everyday thinking and action. Where empiricist approaches depend on a 'transportation' model of media, which sees popular forms as simple vehicles for moving meaning from one place to another, interpretive studies work with a 'translation' model (Murdock, 1994). This views popular representations as complex ensembles of meaning that can be interpreted and responded to in a variety of ways and, in its more critical variant, insists that people's relations with them can be properly understood only in the context of the networks of social relations and forces that envelop and shape them (Murdock, 1989).

Interestingly, Watson's own research experience had presented him with a perfect illustration of the dynamics of 'translation' and the limits of behaviourism. In 1919 he was asked to assess the effect of an anti-VD film on the sexual behaviour of young people. The film, a modified version of *Fit to Win* which had originally been shown as a warning against the dangers of loose living and venereal disease to American troops being shipped to the Western Front, was released for general viewing against the background of a rising tide of concern about the 'loose' morals of 'Flaming Youth'. Watson and his team observed screenings around the country, and attempted to measure any subsequent changes in the sexual behaviour of members of the audience over a period of up to three months. After sifting through the results, Watson reluctantly concluded that 'no lasting effects were found' and that 'there is no indication that behaviour is modified significantly' (Lashley and Watson, 1922, p. 216). However, he did note that observations made during screenings of the film suggested that 'The manner in which the picture presents prostitution and other material tends to break down the sense of reserve, modesty or shame' (ibid., p. 203). He was particularly concerned about the responses that greeted the appearance on the screen of captions such as 'I wouldn't touch a whore with a ten foot pole' and 'Ain't yous afraid you'll have a wet dream tonight?' (ibid., p. 209), warning that flippant banter 'readily slips to the indecent, and the step from indecent in word to indecent in act is short' (ibid., p. 203). He had inadvertently discovered a classic 'boomerang' effect.

The instability of anti-VD propaganda films as bearers of meaning was recognised by a number of social purity campaigners at the time. They applauded their message, but saw problems in the way they spoke to popular audiences through the conventions of narrative cinema. They viewed the pleasures of the screen as, themselves, intrinsically erotic. As one campaigner complained: 'instead of affecting the mind [film dramas] affect the nerves and, above all, the sexual instincts. . . . In that lies the mysterious secret of the astonishing success of the cinemas' (quoted in Kuhn, 1985, p. 127).

Ironically, in the year that the report on *Fit to Win* was published, Watson was accused of misbehaviour with a female student and forced to leave his professorship at Johns Hopkins. He moved to the country's leading advertising agency, J. Walter Thompson, where he rose to become vice-president, a position that provided the perfect platform from which to sell his behaviourist theories and to experiment with the promotional stimuli that might prompt a swift purchasing response.

Although Watson has long since fallen from intellectual favour, his single-minded search for simple, direct links between stimulus and response has continued to underpin almost all later work on violent imagery in the effects tradition. This represents an unbroken line of banal science that succeeds in its own terms only because it fails to acknowledge that the making and taking of meaning in everyday life is never as straightforward as it first appears. Before we can understand how popular representations are woven into popular thinking and action, we need to restore a proper sense of complexity and context.

## ADDRESSING EXCLUSION

As I have sought to show, the dominant 'effects' tradition has proved so resilient partly because it chimes with a deeply rooted formation of social fear which presents the vulnerable, suggestible and dangerous as living outside the stockade of maturity and reasonableness that the 'rest of us' take for granted. 'They' are the 'others', the ones 'we' must shield or protect ourselves against. As Horace Kallen noted when the new censorship began to bite in Hollywood at the beginning of the 1930s, 'When a censor proclaims that a state of danger has been created by . . . a motion picture . . . whose is the danger? His own? Never. Ostensibly, he is secure, he is beyond the reach of any subversive influence, an untouchable' (Kallen, 1930, p. 30). He was thinking of commentators like William Wadsworth, who was careful to stress that he was calling for tighter controls over popular entertainment not

> for the better care of the smug lawns and pretty garden plots, but for . . . a very real and deadly mischief lurking in our waste places. . . . It is for the protection of those accidentally potential ones and for the help of those congenitally defective ones that we plead for methods of prevention.
>
> (Wadsworth, 1911, p. 321)

This bifocal vision remains at the centre of contemporary debate. As *Independent* columnist Bryan Appleyard argued, Tarantino's *Reservoir Dogs* might well be a 'brilliant' film but 'I would prefer [it] not to be seen by the criminal classes or the mentally unstable or by inadequately supervised children with little else in their lives' (Appleyard, 1993, p. 33).

The easy exclusions of these cavalier common-sense labels signal not simply a failure of the respectable imagination. They also have a hard material edge. If we are to understand and respond constructively to social violence in contemporary Britain we need to place it in the context of the massive social and psychic disruptions set in motion by mass unemployment, the decay of communal life and public space, and the evaporation of hope. It is unreasonable to expect 'hooligans' to become upright citizens unless they are offered the full range of resources required for social participation. These include not only jobs, decent living standards and a stake in the future, but also access to the information, arguments and representations that enable people to understand their situation and to recognise and respect the claims of others. Diversity of expression and debate is a precondition for dismantling exclusion. Increased censorship is a precondition for its reinforcement and for the reproduction of the violence it generates.

British controls over the content of films, television programmes and videos are already among the most restrictive of any advanced society. There is no reliable research evidence to suggest that they should be tightened further and, indeed, there are good arguments for encouraging greater openness. The justifications are not to do with the rights of media professionals but with the rights of citizenship.

## NOTE

I first used this title for an earlier version of the present paper, presented to a seminar on 'Expression and Censorship' organised by the Institute for Public Policy Research. It was later used by the organisers (with due acknowledgement) as the title for the seminar's published proceedings (see Collins and Purnell, 1996, p. 1).

## REFERENCES

Appleyard, Bryan (1993), 'Making a killing in videos', *Independent*, 1 December, p. 33.
Arnold, Matthew (1966), *Culture and Anarchy*, ed. with introduction by J. Dover Wilson, Cambridge: Cambridge University Press.
Chapman, Cecil (1925), *The Poor Man's Court of Justice: Twenty-Five Years as a Metropolitan Magistrate*, London: Hodder & Stoughton.
Collins, Richard and Purnell, James (1996), *Reservoirs of Dogma*, London: Institute for Public Policy Research.

Cumberbatch, Guy and Howitt, Dennis (1989), *A Measure of Uncertainty: The Effects of Mass Media*, London: John Libbey.

Edinburgh Review (1851), 'Juvenile delinquency', 94, October, pp. 403–30.

Eysenck, H. J. and Nias, D. K. B. (1978), *Sex, Violence and the Media*, London: Maurice Temple Smith.

Fenton, Frances (1910–11), 'The influence of newspaper presentations upon the growth of crime and other anti-social activity', *American Journal of Sociology*, 16, pp. 342–71, 538–64.

Freeman, A. (1914), *Boy Life and Labour*, London: P. S. King & Son.

Gauntlett, David (1995), *Moving Experiences: Understanding Television's Influences and Effects*, London: John Libbey.

Geertz, Clifford (1973), *The Interpretation of Cultures: Selected Essays*, New York: Basic Books.

Greenwood, James (1874), *The Wilds of London*, London: Chatto & Windus.

Hawes, Joseph M. (1971), *Children in Urban Society: Juvenile Delinquency in Nineteenth-century America*, New York: Oxford University Press.

Independent on Sunday (1996), 'They deserve our answers', 17 March, p. 20.

Kallen, Horace (1930), *Indecency and the Seven Arts: And Other Adventures of a Pragmatist in Aesthetics*, New York: Horace Liverlight.

Kuhn, Annette (1985), *The Power of the Image: Essays on Representation and Sexuality*, London: Routledge & Kegan Paul.

Lashley, Karl S. and Watson, John B. (1922), *A Psychological Study of Motion Pictures in Relation to Venereal Disease*, Washington, DC: Interdepartmental Social Hygiene Board.

Le Bon, Gustave (1960), *The Crowd: A Study of the Popular Mind*, New York: Viking Press.

Linne, Olga (1995), 'Media Violence research in Scandinavia' *The Mordicom Review of Nordic Research on Media and Communication*, 2, pp. 1–11.

Lydston, G. Frank (1904), *The Diseases of Society (The Vice and Crime Problem)*, Philadelphia, Pa: J. B. Lippincott Company.

McClelland, J. S. (1989), *The Crowd and the Mob: From Plato to Canetti*, London: Unwin Hyman.

MacKay, Charles (1956), *Extraordinary Delusions and the Madness of Crowds*, London: George Harrap.

Marx, Karl and Engels, Frederick (1968), *Selected Works in One Volume*, London: Lawrence & Wishart.

Murdock, Graham (1989), 'Critical inquiry and audience activity', in Brenda Dervin *et al.* (eds), *Rethinking Communication, Vol. 2, Paradigm Exemplars*, London: Sage Publications, pp. 226–49.

Murdock, Graham (1994), 'Visualising violence: television and the discourse of disorder', in Cees J. Hamelink and Olga Linne (eds), *Mass Communication Research: On Problems and Policies*, Norwood, NJ: Ablex Publishing Corporation, pp. 171–87.

Murdock, Graham and McCron, Robin (1979), 'The television and delinquency debate', *Screen Education*, 30, Spring, pp. 51–67.

National Council of Public Morals (1917), *The Cinema: Its Present Position and Future Possibilities*, London: Williams & Norgate.

Neil, Andrew (1996), 'Shots straight to the heart of our sick society', *Sunday Times News Review*, 17 March, p. 5.

Park, Robert (1972), *The Crowd and the Public and Other Essays*, Chicago, Ill.: University of Chicago Press.

Pearson, Geoffrey (1983), *Hooligan: A History of Respectable Fears* London: Macmillan.

Peterson, Frederick (1906), 'The newspaper peril: a diagnosis of a malady of the modern mind', *Collier's*, 1 September, pp. 12–13.

Phillips, Melanie (1994), 'Mediocrity's fight against violent truth', *Observer*, 17 April, p. 25.

Pound, Roscoe and Frankfurter, Felix (1922), *Criminal Justice in Cleveland*, Cleveland: The Cleveland Foundation.

Schwarz, Bill (1996), 'Night battles: hooligan and citizen', in Mica Nava and Alan O'Shea (eds), *Modern Times: Reflections on a Century of English Modernity*, London: Routledge, pp. 101–28.

Sidis, Boris (1927), *The Psychology of Suggestion: A Research into the Subconscious Nature of Man and Society*, New York: D. Appleton.

Tarde, Gabriel (1912), *Penal Philosophy*, London: William Heinemann.

Thomas, W. I. (1908), 'The psychology of the Yellow Journal', *American Magazine*, March, pp. 491–6.

Trevarthen, J. (1901), 'Hooliganism', *The Nineteenth Century*, 49, pp. 84–9.

Tudor, Andrew (1995), 'Culture, mass communication and social agency', *Theory, Culture and Society*, 12:1, pp. 81–107.

Wadsworth, William S. (1911), 'The newspapers and crime', *American Academy of Medicine Bulletin*, 12:5, pp. 316–24.

Watson, John B. (1924), *Psychology from the Standpoint of a Behaviourist*, Philadelphia, Pa: J. B. Lippincott Company.

Watson, John B. (1930), *Behaviourism*, Chicago, Ill.: University of Chicago Press.

Wilcox, Delos F. (1900), 'The American newspaper: a study in social psychology', *Annals of the American Academy of Political and Social Science*, 16, July, pp. 56–92.

Wright, Thomas (1881), 'On a possible popular culture', *Contemporary Review*, July, pp. 25–44.

# Chapter 6

# Us and them

*Julian Petley*

Debates about media effects tend to focus on how children and young people are supposedly affected – usually for the worse. But lurking behind these fears about the 'corruption of innocent minds' one finds, time and again, implicit or explicit, a potent strain of class dislike and fear. The object is often the spectre of the working class in general – at other times it is more specifically defined as an 'underclass', an ideologically loaded version of what used to be called (equally ideologically) the redundant population, the relative surplus, the residuum, the *lumpenproletariat*, the social problem group, the dangerous classes, the undeserving poor and so on.

There is nothing new about such fears and dislikes, and nothing new about attempts to locate the causes of working-class 'hooliganism' in the allegedly malign effects of various forms of popular entertainment. As Orwell put it: 'the genuinely popular culture of England is something that goes on beneath the surface, unofficially and more or less frowned on by the authorities' (Orwell, 1968a, p. 78). Geoffrey Pearson (1983) has made a seminal study of the history of middle-class disapproval of working-class culture, in which he concludes that:

> popular entertainments of all kinds have been blamed for dragging down public morals in a gathering pattern of accusation which remains essentially the same even though it is attached to radically different forms of amusement: pre-modern feasts and festivals; eighteenth-century theatres and bawdy houses; mid-nineteenth-century penny gaffs; the Music Halls of the 'Gay' Nineties; the first flickering danger signs from the silent movies; the Hollywood picture palaces between the wars; and then television viewing in our own historical time. Each, in its own time, has been accused of encouraging a moral debauch; each has been said to encourage imitative crime among the young.
>
> (Pearson, 1983, p. 208)

Nor are such attitudes unique to Britain. Herbert Gans (1974) has argued that dislike of popular culture frequently stems from 'a marked disdain for ordinary people and their aesthetic capacities'. He also quotes with approval the conservative sociologist Edward Shils to the effect that 'fictions about the empirical consequences of mass culture' are based partly on a dislike of those that consume it, and also stem from the fact that 'the objects of mass culture are repulsive to us' (Gans, 1974, p. 61).

Chief amongst these 'repulsive objects' are films, whether on cinema or television screens. From its inception the cinema has been regarded by moral entrepreneurs as a cause of decline and deterioration, and as a veritable textbook of bad examples to the young, the easily influenced, the working class. Nowhere was this more clearly the case than in Britain, which, consequently, had by the 1920s and 1930s built up one of the most strict and elaborate systems of film censorship in Europe. Although cinema-going was hugely popular by then, 'highly educated people saw in it only vulgarity and the end of old England' (Taylor, 1970, p. 392). Indeed, Rachel Low, the leading historian of the early British cinema, has suggested that this snobbish and fearful attitude hampered British cinema's development as an industry, making it unable to attract the necessary talent and capital. She concludes that

> in Britain the film had to overcome the resistance of a particularly inelastic social and intellectual pattern. In France and Italy the film might be a younger sister of the arts, in America art itself. In England it was a poor relation, and, moreover, not a very respectable one.
>
> (Low, 1949, pp. 137–8)

Evidence for this view is not hard to find. Pearson (1983, p. 32) quotes H. A. Secretan's 1931 account of youth work, *London below Bridges*, to the effect that 'every boy's sympathy goes out to the lithe and resourceful crook. . . . Occasionally a weak-minded youth may be urged by the exploits of a Chicago gangster to essay a feeble imitation.' Meanwhile Hugh Redwood's *God in the Slums* (1932) infantilises the working class thus:

> the boys of the slums are wonderful training material for good or evil. They are children in their love of pictures and music. Hollywood's worst in the movie line has recruited hundreds of them for the gangs of race-course roughs, motor-bandits, and smash-and-grab thieves.
>
> (Pearson, 1983, p. 32)

The Second World War brought its quotient of fears about 'spivs' and 'Blitz kids', and the arrival of the Americans in Britain in large numbers served only to fuel the anti-Americanism which was to become an increasingly prominent feature of attacks on working-class popular culture. Thus, for example, George Orwell in his essay 'Raffles and Miss Blandish', comparing English and American crime fiction:

the common people, on the whole, are still living in the world of absolute good and evil from which the intellectuals have long since escaped. But the popularity of *No Orchids* and the American books and magazines to which it is akin shows how rapidly the doctrine of 'realism' is gaining ground.

This was something which Orwell viewed with alarm:

> in Mr Chase's books there are no gentlemen and no taboos. Emancipation is complete, Freud and Machiavelli have reached the outer suburbs. Comparing the schoolboy atmosphere of the one book [*Raffles*] with the cruelty and corruption of the other, one is driven to feel that snobbishness, like hypocrisy, is a check upon behaviour whose value from a social point of view has been underrated.
>
> (Orwell, 1968b, pp. 259–60)

By the late 1940s, in spite of the efforts of the British Board of Film Censors (BBFC), the American style had found its way not only into British crime novels but into British crime films, too, such as *Noose, They Made Me a Fugitive, Brighton Rock*, the Diana Dors vehicle *Good Time Girl*, and a version of the aforementioned *No Orchids for Miss Blandish*. These 'spiv' films, with their working-class settings, then rather unusual in the overwhelmingly middle-class British cinema, aroused considerable concern on the part of society's self-appointed moral guardians, including the film critics of the national press. Thus we find Fred Majdalany of the *Daily Mail* complaining of *They Made Me a Fugitive* in the same terms that nineteenth-century critics had lambasted stories about Dick Turpin:

> I deplore the picturesque legend that is being created round that petty criminal fashionably known as the spiv. The spiv as stylised by the writers and caricatured by the actors seems to be a mixture of delightful Cockney comedian and pathetic victim of social conditions. For myself, I find the activities of sewer rats – in or out of a sewer – of strictly limited interest.
>
> (Quoted in Murphy, 1986, pp. 294–5)

Meanwhile *Miss Blandish*, even though heavily interfered with by the British Board of Film Censors, was the object of a quite extraordinarily hysterical campaign of vilification by the press, which led MPs to allege that it would 'pervert the minds of the British people', local councils to ban it and, eventually, the President of the BBFC, Sir Sidney Harris, to apologise to the Home Office for having 'failed to protect the public'!

By the early 1950s the first of the major working-class folk devils of the post-war period had appeared – the Teddy Boy. Inevitably the media were blamed, in this case music (the newly emergent rock 'n' roll) and the cinema. An early victim of this particular panic was the Marlon

Brando film *The Wild One* which, it was thought, would encourage anti-social behaviour among the young, and specifically the working-class young. Thus the BBFC told the film's distributor, Columbia, that

> having regard to the present widespread concern about the increase in juvenile crime, the Board is not prepared to pass any film dealing with this subject unless the compensating moral values are so firmly presented as to justify its exhibition to audiences likely to contain (even with an 'X' certificate) a large number of young and immature persons.
>
> (Quoted in Mathews, 1994, p. 128)

This attitude was to persist. In 1959, on the occasion of one of the film's periodic rejections by the BBFC, its then Secretary John Trevelyan stated that

> the behaviour of Brando and the two gangs to authority and adults generally is of the kind that provides a dangerous example to those wretched young people who take every opportunity of throwing their weight about. . . . Once again we have made the decision with reluctance because we think it is a splendid picture. I only hope the time will come, and come soon, when we do not have to worry about this kind of thing.
>
> (Quoted in ibid., p. 130)

In other words, the film is fine for us middle-class intellectuals who will judge it on 'aesthetic' grounds, but it can't be shown to the plebs in case it gets them worked up.

The Board were equally worried about the potential effects on the young of the film *The Blackboard Jungle*, which they rejected out of hand when it was first submitted, complaining, as in the case of *The Wild One*, that 'the moral values stressed by the film' were not

> sufficiently strong and powerful to counteract the harm that may be done by the spectacle of youth out of control. . . . We are quite certain that *Blackboard Jungle*, filled as it is with scenes of unbridled, revolting hooliganism, would, if shown in this country, provoke the strongest criticism from parents and all citizens concerned with the welfare of our young people and would also have the most damaging and harmful effect on such young people.
>
> (Quoted in Robertson, 1989, p. 114)

In the event the film was passed with heavy cuts; the occasional trouble in the audience was not because of the effects of the scenes of 'unbridled, revolting hooliganism' but because the soundtrack contained Bill Haley's 'Rock around the clock' and teenagers, long denied proper access to rock 'n' roll by a censorious and nannyish BBC, got over-excited!

The alleged ill effects of rock 'n' roll, whether on film, record or in clubs, filled acres of column space in the press. According to a 1956 edition of the *Daily Sketch* 'rhythm-crazed teenagers terrorised a city last night', and in the same year the *Daily Mail* actually printed a front-page editorial entitled 'Rock 'n roll babies' in which it claimed that the music is 'often known now as rock, roll and riot' and has 'led to outbreaks of rowdyism'. It links this 'music of delinquents' with the picket-line troubles which, then as ever, were obsessing the British press, concluding that both were 'manifestations of the primitive herd instinct'. But at least the pickets were British, whilst the music 'has something of the African tomtom and the voodoo dance. . . . We sometimes wonder whether this is the negro's revenge' (quoted in Pearson, 1983, p. 24). Nor were such sentiments confined to the Conservative daily press. The same year, the *Melody Maker* described rock 'n' roll as 'one of the most terrifying things to have happened to popular music' and featured a review by Steve Race of Elvis Presley's 'Hound dog' which concluded that 'I fear for the country which ought to have had the good taste and the good sense to reject music so decadent' (quoted in Chambers, 1985, pp. 19, 30).

By the late 1950s fears about disaffected working-class youth, media effects, Americanisation, crime and national decline had become thoroughly sedimented in British 'common sense' and had formed a pervasive mythology which could routinely be wheeled out to 'explain' each and every new object of panic. In 1957 these feelings found their most comprehensive expression, up until that time, in Richard Hoggart's celebrated *The Uses of Literacy*. Whilst it needs to be stressed that Hoggart does not draw a causal connection between crime and the consumption of popular culture, his strictures on the negative effects on working-class consumers of 'Americanised' culture are unremitting. An important section of the book is devoted to 'The juke-box boys'. According to Hoggart, these are particularly symptomatic of the general trend whereby the working class has been 'culturally robbed' and fed on an ersatz diet which

> is surely likely to help render its consumers less capable of responding openly and responsibly to life, is likely to induce an underlying sense of purposelessness in existence outside the limited range of a few immediate appetites. Souls which may have had little opportunity to open will be kept hard-gripped, turned in on themselves, looking out 'with odd dark eyes like windows' upon a world which is largely a phantasmagoria of passing shows and vicarious simulations.

Thus the juke-box boys, 'living to a large extent in a myth-world compounded of a few simple elements which they take to be those of American life'. Furthermore (and this is particularly important in the present context), although the whole of the working class is exposed to the 'debilitating mass-trends of the day', certain sections are more prone than others to surrender to their blandishments. Hoggart notes that if the juke-box boys

seem to consist so far chiefly of those of poorer intelligence or from homes subject to special strains, that is probably due to the strength of a moral fibre which most cultural providers for working-class people are helping to de-nature. The hedonistic but passive barbarian who rides in a fifty-horsepower bus for threepence to see a five-million dollar film for one-and-eightpence, is not simply a social oddity; he is a portent.

(Hoggart, 1957, pp. 246–50)

In the 1960s the debate about the effects of the media, especially upon the young (implicitly or explicitly working class) tended to shift its focus on to the television, and it would take a book in itself to map the features of this particular, and on-going, debate. Such a book urgently needs to be written; but, for the moment, I want to cite a couple of other cinematic instances which illustrate the class basis of many fears about media effects before going on to a more detailed study of two key 'moments' in the history of domestic video in the UK which prove the point only too clearly.

Both examples come from 1972. That was the year that the British Board of Film Censors looked as if it were going to ban the Warhol/ Morrissey film *Trash* and thus confine it, like its predecessor *Flesh*, to the limbo of the specialist film club. In the end the film was passed with cuts, but not before the furore had elicited the immortal remark from a BBFC chief censor to the *Guardian's* film critic, Derek Malcolm, to the effect that 'it is all very well for sophisticated, educated people like you to go to the ICA cinema and see Warhol's *Trash*. But think of its effect on your average factory worker in Manchester' (quoted in Malcolm, 1984). (I myself was present at a National Film Theatre screening of *The Texas Chainsaw Massacre* in the late 1970s when the current BBFC Director, James Ferman, made a similar remark, except that the 'average factory worker in Manchester' became the 'car-worker in Birmingham'.)

Nineteen seventy-two was also the year that *A Clockwork Orange* was released. Even before it had appeared, the Labour MP Maurice Edelman was writing in the *Evening News* that 'when *Clockwork Orange* is gener- ally released it will lead to a clockwork cult which will magnify teenage violence' (27 January 1972). Needless to say, within weeks of the film's release the press was full of stories about 'copy-cat crimes' and wild denunciations of both Kubrick and his creation. The *Evening News* dug out a former chaplain to Pinewood Studios to denounce this 'celluloid cesspool' and allege that 'it is the weak, the impressionable and the immature which such a film helps to destroy' (4 July 1973). Needless to say, the stories of 'copy-cat crimes' don't bear up to investigation, but this hasn't stopped them passing into effects mythology (see Martin, 1995; Petley, 1995; Wistrich, 1978, pp. 129–30).

As Tom Dewe Mathews has argued (1994, p. 2), in Britain censorship is governed by the 'long-serving, silently spoken rubric: the larger the audience, the lower the moral mass resistance to suggestion'. In other words, the more popular the cultural form, the more likely it is to be seen by members of the working class, the more heavily its content is likely to be regulated and, if necessary, censored. The whole attitude is perfectly summed up by the prosecution's famous question at the start of the Lady Chatterley trial in 1960 – 'Is it a book that you would even wish your wife or your servants to read?' – but it is often overlooked that an important part of the prosecution's closing speech rested on a quite explicit contrast between the way in which the defence's academic and literary experts would read the book and the way in which 'the ordinary man in the street' would do so. Thus, for example, the film critic Dilys Powell's reading is explicitly contrasted with how 'the young men and boys leaving school ... at the age of 15, going into their first jobs this last September' would supposedly read it; the Bishop of Woolwich with 'the girls working in the factory'; Rebecca West with 'the average reader'; and all of these witnesses with the 'ordinary, common men and women' (Rolph, 1961, pp. 214–19).

No one should be in the least surprised, therefore, given the prevalence of such attitudes, that the prospect of unregulated, uncensored videos being freely available to the British public at the start of the 1980s was greeted with such horror and dismay from certain quarters, and that draconian censorship was soon imposed (for the full story of this process see Barker, 1984; Petley, 1984; Martin, 1993). What concerns us here are the threads of class dislike and fear that weave their way through this particular saga. Admittedly, most of the concern expressed about the original so-called 'video nasties' was about their supposed effects on children and young people, but from time to time the class dimension of the perceived problem rose visibly to the surface.

For example, in the *Mail* on 28 June 1983, Lynda Lee Potter complained of 'the impact that this sick, beastly, money-making corruption is having on illiterate minds', whilst in the *Telegraph* of 2 November 1983 the Prime Minister's daughter Carol Thatcher quoted the NSPCC's director Dr Alan Gilmour as describing

> the experience of a senior social worker in a deprived area of Greater Manchester who, making a call on a family at 9.30 a.m., had to wait until the whole family had finished watching the rape scene in *I Spit on Your Grave*.

Mathews (1994, p. 250) also quotes a revealing remark by Ken Penry, the deputy director of the BBFC, about one of the most notorious 'nasties', *Driller Killer*:

> now and again, you get clever dicks who say, 'Ah, this is art. This is bigger than it seems'. But I think of Joe Bloggs who's going to the Odeon on Saturday night who's not on that wavelength. He's going along seeing it literally and I always keep that in mind. Joe Bloggs is the majority and film censorship is for the majority.

The issue of class also crops up in the *Video Violence and Children* report which played such a major role in the passing of the 1984 Video Recordings Act. This is not the place to recount the story of the report (see Barker, 1984) but it is important to note what it has to say about social class and exposure to 'video nasties'.

Thus, for example, apropos children's alleged exposure to 'nasties', the report says that 'social class seems to be a relevant variable . . . working-class children, especially those from large families, appear most at risk in watching the "nasties" ' (Hill, 1983, p. 15). There's a suggestion that this remark is based on a questionnaire sent out to parents, but the only problem is that this had not been analysed at the time the report was published. The remark appears in the section entitled 'Reactions of children', but the report itself makes clear that this is not based directly on answers to questionnaires which were handed out to schoolchildren but was 'compiled from data supplied to us by teachers who conducted the survey and subsequently led discussions and had conversations with individual children' (Hill, 1983, p. 14). In a later document (Barlow and Hill, 1985, p. 14) it is explained that the purpose of these discussions was

> to provide additional data relating to the children's viewing patterns and to act as a check upon the accuracy of the answers provided in the questionnaires. . . . Further data was obtained from head teachers who often gave an overview of the situation in their school with age groups other than those included in the sample obtained from their school. Hence a dossier of anecdotal data was produced to go alongside the statistical data derived from the analysis of questionnaire returns.

Clearly, then, a good deal of the report is based on teachers' *perceptions* of their pupils' viewing habits. In responding to criticisms of the report's methodology, Hill (1983, p. 164) offers a rather unfortunate hostage to fortune by stating that 'children are notoriously unreliable respondents. But so are adults!' In this respect it is extremely difficult to take seriously those sections of the report which seem to have been strained through a sieve of intense teacherly disdain for popular culture – not to mention for their pupils as well. For example, this is a teacher in a South London comprehensive with a mixed fourth-year class of boys and girls:

this is quite a 'nice' class by this school's standards. In discussion afterwards I was quite surprised. They nearly all prefer the horror films. They like the blood and they didn't think that 'video nasties' should be banned. For most there was no parental control over television or video viewing. Most parents would allow younger children to watch violent videos.

(ibid., p. 143)

In the earlier document we find that:

One headmaster of a school in the Surrey commuter belt said that even those children who come from home backgrounds where they are highly protected and where parents take them and fetch them from school are nevertheless being affected by the values of violence and horror that are being transmitted in the playground from children from less protected home backgrounds.

(Hill, 1983, p. 15)

Nor were such attitudes confined to the Home Counties:

the headmaster of a primary school in a mixed social class London suburb said that the reaction of middle class children to hearing the playground stories of those who were allowed to watch violent videos was often one of 'suppressed envy'. He spoke of the great danger facing the children through the permissive attitude of the playground that reinforces the values of violence and impresses them upon the children despite the values they derive from their home and family backgrounds.

(ibid., p. 16)

Teachers' observations also led them to conclude that

among many boys, especially from working class backgrounds, watching the 'nasties' has become a test of manliness. . . . For working class boys, especially those who are unable to achieve educationally, knowledge of the most intimate details of violent video films carries with it a kind of 'butch kudos'.

(ibid., p. 16)

As Michael Tracey put it at the time: 'it is very difficult to see what can be claimed for such information, which of its nature can have no real social scientific significance' (Tracey, 1984) – except as, one might add, a depressing indicator of the degree of paedophobia and snobbery amongst teachers. To be asked to regard such people as reliable rapporteurs of young people's viewing habits – particularly in the midst of a lurid press blitz on 'video nasties' – is quite frankly preposterous.

Such sentiments would matter less if they had remained firmly in the staff room; but, unfortunately, if entirely predictably, they were massively amplified by the way in which the report was treated by the press – often as the lead story on the front page, no less. Such stories build on the already-existing repertoire of class dislike which, as we have seen, has a long history. They, in turn, then enter the mythology: witness Harry Greenway, the Conservative MP for Ealing North, in a debate on the Video Recordings Bill on 16 March 1984, who argued that videos 'are often a higher priority in the homes of people who are not particularly articulate, and who do not read books or listen to music very much. In some homes videos even take priority over food and furniture.' Clearly, the Sturdy Beggar was alive and well and stalking the streets of West London in 1984.

By the time of the next most significant 'moment' in the seemingly never-ending 'video nasty' débâcle in Britain – the aftermath of the murder of James Bulger, and the efforts of the press to blame it on the effects of *Child's Play III* on his killers (see Petley, 1993) – the discourse of class had become even more evident in the 'debate' (and this in spite of John Major's rhetorical evocations of the 'classless' society). More specifically, the 'video nasty' issue was deliberately and explicitly used as an illustration of the dangers of the so-called 'underclass'.

Broadly speaking, there are two versions of 'underclass' theory. The liberal version, of which Frank Field's *Losing Out: The Emergence of the British Underclass* is a clear example, holds that increasingly uneven economic growth, the restructuring (or destruction) of manufacturing industry, poor education, poor childcare facilities and the general failure of the 'flexible' economy to create a sufficient number of decently paid jobs have detached a growing number of people from society and from citizenship. The Conservative version of this theory, best represented by Charles Murray's *Losing Ground* and *The Emerging British Underclass*, and L. M. Mead's *Beyond Entitlement: The Social Obligations of Citizenship*, is really little more than an updating of the notion of the 'undeserving poor'. Its more recent antecedents can be traced at least as far back as the 'Cycles of deprivation' project initiated by Sir Keith Joseph when he was Secretary of State for Education, to the 'moment of the mugger' (Hall *et al.*, 1978), and above all to the great 'scrounger-phobia' outbreak of 1976 so brilliantly analysed by Golding and Middleton (1982).

In the Conservative version of 'underclass' theory 'the term has acquired a sense both pejorative and threatening', as Lydia Morris (1994, p. 1) has put it. Here the 'underclass' is represented as a sub-section of the poor, living off mainstream society (either via welfare benefits or crime) whilst not only refusing to participate in it but actively rejecting its dominant norms and values. The real problem, according to this point of view, is that benefits have created a 'dependency culture' or 'culture of poverty', in which no stigma or disadvantage is attached to being unemployed and/or a single mother. Indeed, since the State will provide, either or both may well have distinct advantages. If members of the 'underclass' are unemployed it is because their attitudes exclude them from the labour market, not because there are no jobs. An absence of proper role models (that is, the two-parent family), parental irresponsibility, early school leaving and poor socialisation have combined to produce entirely unemployable people trapped in a 'cycle of dependency'.

Such a theory obviously has enormous attraction to the right, and there are no prizes for guessing which version of the theory has been overwhelmingly favoured by the British press, especially *The Times*, *Sunday Times* and *Mail*, which have regularly provided a highly uncritical platform for the ideas of Murray and his followers. Let me conclude by illustrating this by reference to press coverage of the aftermath of the murders of James Bulger and Suzanne Capper (another young person whose murder was pinned by the press, without a shred of justification, on *Child's Play III*).

The link between videos, violence and the 'underclass' during this particular 'moment' was first made, interestingly, not in a Conservative paper but in the *Independent*, by Brian Appleyard on 1 December 1993, in which he asked rhetorically: 'Would you allow an ill-educated, culturally deprived, unemployable underclass unlimited access to violent pornography?' Ignoring the inconvenient fact that *no one* in Britain has unlimited access to such material anyway, he blithely continues that if you abolish censorship (which most certainly has *not* happened in the UK)

> you don't just get Mapplethorpe for the connoisseur, you also get vicious drivel for the masses. More painfully, you also get unarguably fine films such as *Taxi Driver* and *Goodfellas*, which, if you are honest, you would rather were not watched by certain types of people.

*Reservoir Dogs* is also singled out as a 'brilliant, bloody film that I would prefer not to be seen by the criminal classes or the mentally unstable or by inadequately supervised children with little else in their lives'.

Even more up-front was an editorial in the *Mail* on 18 December in the wake of the just-concluded trial of the murderers of Suzanne Capper. Noting that the police had commented on the murderers' 'ordinariness' the paper went into ideological overdrive, proclaiming that

> they are the product of a society which tolerates petty crime, the breakup of families and feckless spending. It subsidises and, in many cases, encourages them. It is interesting to note that most of Suzanne's tormentors were on social security. But then those in society who are

genuinely out of work but who have savings, do not receive income support. Thus are the prudent penalised while the negligent are nurtured. . . . All this reflects a society showing reckless disregard for the survival of its own decency. An underclass is being created today which is a grave threat to Britain's future. If it is not countered, then we will continue a decline towards lawlessness and degeneracy.

What kind of mind makes ideological capital out of a particularly brutal murder? One that is so demented that it appears to think that sadistic killers are created, if not by 'video nasties', then by what's left of the welfare state.

In the *Telegraph*, 20 February 1984, the inner-city GP and Fleet Street regular Theodore Dalrymple also bemoans the condition of a section of the population, although not from the *Mail*'s grotesque viewpoint nor with any direct reference to the 'underclass'. However, it is clear to whom he is referring. This is a terrible sphere in which 'children are growing up without any spiritual or cultural framework whatever', a world of 'degraded rootlessness and desolate isolation', in which mothers appear not to know that parental control is either 'desirable or necessary' and 'fathers, except in the biological sense, are generally unknown or, if known, are violent, arbitrary, abusive and uncouth'. In this void of 'quotidian savagery' 'there are no positive moral influences [but] there are plenty of negative ones, chief among which are those of television and, worse still, of video'. Whilst 'liberals in Hampstead' and the 'intellectual classes' pooh-pooh the effects of video, from which they are anyway immune, 'the effect on minds which are entirely empty of a moral framework' is likely to be devastating.

Entirely unsurprisingly, the connection between the 'underclass' and 'video nasties' came very much to the fore at the time of the Alton amendment to the Criminal Justice Bill, aimed at tightening video censorship still further. Thus in the *Sunday Times* of 3 April 1994 we find one Margaret Driscoll arguing that 'the children most likely to be damaged are those being brought up in sink estates where family values no longer hold sway – the products of the "anything goes" society', whilst a *Times* editorial of 11 April 1994 held forth that 'horror-video addiction is part of a socially-disadvantaged sink culture in which lack of parental supervision is endemic'. Meanwhile, two days later the inevitable Lynda Lee Potter in her *Mail* column shrieked that

> there are thousands of children in this country with fathers they never see and mothers who are lazy sluts. They are allowed to do what they want, when they want. They sniff glue on building sites, scavenge for food and, until now, they were free to watch increasingly horrific videos. By 16 they are disturbed and dangerous.

Again, it's worth pointing out that such views are not confined to the Conservative press. In the *Guardian* of 16 April, Edward Pearce argues that, as far as the sale and renting of videos is concerned,

it won't do just to restrict juveniles. Let's be plain. In an underclass family where books are unknown, where dynastic unemployment has brought all restraints to a base level, who do we suppose buys the nasty – uncontrolled kids or indifferent father? The law must aim at all sales of injurious goods to anyone.

And in the following day's *Observer* Melanie Phillips, in the course of a polemic against media researchers who have the temerity to disagree with her, confidently states that 'video violence is merely a part of that culture of material and emotional disadvantage which gives rise to young delinquents'.

The most sustained attempt to link 'video nasties' to the 'underclass', however, is to be found in Barbara Amiel's column in that day's *Sunday Times*. Curiously, the article takes an anti-censorship line, arguing that 'while much ails the nation, it is not the viewing of *Child's Play III*, no matter how wretched that video' and that 'time and again we enact cosmetic legislation rather than deal with the real issues'. Quite. However, it rapidly becomes clear that what Amiel means by this is knocking the hell out of what she revealingly calls the 'residium' (sic). This entails that we 'revise immigration policies' and 'stop further reform of our divorce laws'. In more general terms we have to stop trying to create an 'inclusive culture', and

we can segregate the underclass and forget about egalitarian principles. We should try to reintroduce the best of our values while getting rid of the worst. We must stop ruining our free society by enacting rules appropriate for a zoo. Just because some of the rooms in our house have been taken over by pigs and donkeys does not mean that we should turn the entire kingdom into a place appropriate for the housing of animals – which is what we do when enacting blanket legislation for everyone, such as the new censorship rules. . . . We cannot even console ourselves that we are doing something useless that is at least not injurious. We are injuring everything.

In other words, thanks to the presence of the 'underclass', who can't be entrusted to watch violent videos without running amok, the freedom of the middle class to do what it wants has been unreasonably curtailed.

This chapter has attempted to demonstrate, across a wide time-scale and range of media, the remarkable prevalence and persistence of certain quite specific views of the effects of the media on members of the working class. We started off in the pre-modern era and ended up in 1994, though readers of Barbara Amiel may have thought it was 1794. It's depressing how little has changed in the way of attitudes, both to popular culture and to the working class. Of course, it could be argued that these are not the attitudes of ordinary people but, for the most part, of the moral entrepreneurs and of a notoriously conservative (and Conservative) press. None the less, it *is* disturbing that, in the on-going controversy about 'video nasties', the tone of class dislike and, in some cases, hatred should be so much more pronounced, unashamed and *naked* in 1993/4 than in 1983/4.

It could also be argued that these attitudes have remained so constant for so long because they are rooted in actuality and based on fact. In other words, people believe that working-class people are more likely than middle-class ones to be adversely affected by media messages because it's true, they are! The answer to that, however, is: prove it. Anybody who tries to read through the literature on this subject will encounter a great deal of confident assertion and bluff 'common sense', but precious little in the way of social scientific research. *Video Violence and Children* attempted to penetrate this particular thicket but, as we have seen, its assertions about the links between social class and video viewing are really little more than that. Other than that, what are we left with – except the huffings and puffings of a few Fleet Street pundits, a hideously reactionary bunch at the best of times, and hardly an informed or authoritative source of reliable knowledge on this or any other matter. Of course, to lay bare the lengthy history of a particular claim or belief is not sufficient to expose it as a myth, but it does begin to look dangerously threadbare when no reliable evidence can be adduced with which to back it up.

Our main concern in this chapter has been with how films, television and videos have been regarded as affecting working-class people 'worse' than middle-class ones. In our discussion of the 'underclass', however, and of the way in which ultra-Conservative versions of the theory have been assiduously pedalled by sections of the British press, we have ended up by touching on one of the most poisonous legacies of the Thatcher–Major years – the deliberate exclusion of a growing number of people from being considered as members of society. Oh, I quite forgot – there's no such thing.

## REFERENCES

Barker, M. (ed.) (1984), *The Video Nasties: Freedom and Censorship in the Media*, London: Pluto Press.

Barlow, G. and Hill, A. (eds) (1985), *Video Violence and Children*, London: Hodder & Stoughton.

Chambers, I. (1985), *Urban Rhythms: Pop Music and Popular Culture*, London: Macmillan.

Field, F. (1989), *Losing Out: The Emergence of the British Underclass*, Oxford: Basil Blackwell.

Gans, H. (1974), *Popular Culture and High Culture: An Analysis and Evaluation of Taste*, New York: Basic Books.

Golding, P. and Middleton, S. (1982), *Images of Welfare: Press and Public Attitudes to Welfare*, Oxford: Martin Robertson.

Hall, S., Critcher, C., Jefferson, T., Clarke, J. and Roberts, B. (1978), *Policing the Crisis: Mugging, the State and Law and Order*, London: Macmillan.

Hill, C. (1983), *Video Violence and Children: Children's Viewing Patterns in England and Wales*, London: Oasis Projects.

Hoggart, R. (1957), *The Uses of Literacy*, London: Chatto & Windus.

Low, R. (1949), *The History of the British Film, 1906–1914*, London: Allen & Unwin.

Malcolm, D. (1984), 'Stand up to the new censorship', in the *Guardian*, 15 March.

Martin, J. (1993), *The Seduction of the Gullible: The Curious History of the British 'Video Nasty' Phenomenon*, Nottingham: Procrustes Press.

Martin, J. (1995), 'Curse of the copycat people', in *The Dark Side*, 50, October.

Mathews, T. D. (1994), *Censored: What They Didn't Allow you to See and Why: The Story of Film Censorship in Britain*, London: Chatto & Windus.

Mead, L. M. (1986), *Beyond Entitlement: The Social Obligations of Citizenship*, New York: Free Press.

Morris, L. (1994), *Dangerous Classes: The Underclass and Social Citizenship*, London: Routledge.

Murphy, R. (1986), 'Riff-raff: British cinema and the underworld', in C. Barr (ed.), *All Our Yesterdays: 90 Years of British Cinema*, London: British Film Institute.

Murray, C. (1984), *Losing Ground*, New York: Basic Books

Murray, C. (1990), *The Emerging British Underclass*, London: Institute of Economic Affairs.

Orwell, G. (1968a), *The Collected Essays, Journalism and Letters of George Orwell, Vol. 2, My Country Right or Left*, London: Secker & Warburg.

Orwell, G. (1968b), *The Collected Essays, Journalism and Letters of George Orwell, Vol. 3, As I Please*, London: Secker & Warburg.

Pearson, G. (1983), *Hooligan: A History of Respectable Fears*, London: Macmillan.

Petley, J. (1984), 'A nasty story', *Screen*, 25:2, pp. 68–74.

Petley, J. (1993), 'In defence of "video nasties" ', *British Journalism Review*, 5:3, pp. 52–7.

Petley, J. (1995), 'Clockwork crimes', *Index on Censorship*, 24:6, pp. 48–52.

Robertson, J. C. (1989), *The Hidden Cinema: British Film Censorship in Action, 1913–1975*, London: Routledge.

Rolph, C. H. (ed.) (1961), *The Trial of Lady Chatterley: Regina v. Penguin Books Limited*, London: Penguin.

Taylor, A. J. P. (1970), *English History 1914–1945*, London: Penguin.

Tracey, M. (1984), 'Casting cold water on the ketchup', *The Times*, 25 February.

Wistrich, E. (1978), *'I Don't Mind the Sex It's the Violence': Film Censorship Explored*, London: Marion Boyars.

Chapter 7

# Television violence redux
## The continuing mythology of effects

*Willard D. Rowland, Jr*

## THE AMERICAN EFFECTS TRADITION

The growth of the predominant style and content of social research in the United States is directly related to a deep-set pattern of American attitudes toward intellectual activity and about accommodations among public and private interests. From the earliest days of the Republic, and even well before, the American intellectual tradition was constituted of a strong inter-mixture among moral philosophy, political theory and applied scientific research. The Enlightenment origins of the American experience established it as a series of practical experiments to be carried out across the range not only of the vast uncharted continent, but also of all human political and social activity. These experiments were seen spatially, as an opportunity to map, settle and control the new frontier, but they were also imagined as an opportunity to extend temporal control, to be able to build the New Jerusalem and to have in place the means for continuing to discover and reveal it over the course of a grand and lasting future. The constitutional provisions for separation of powers, the emerging system of private enterprise in agriculture, manufacturing and trade, the country's developing transportation and communication systems, its various forms of religious and secular organization, and its new institutions of education and training were all seen as wide open to testing, tinkering and progressive improvement.

From the beginning Americans invested those progressive values in their expectations for science and the role of an applied academy. The 'founding fathers' were not only statesmen and men of letters, they were practical scientists, and from them sprang a persistent veneration of applied, useful science and a pragmatism that consistently has remained dominant over concerns about theory and epistemological self-reflection. Clearly apparent in the natural and engineering sciences, such utilitarianism helped define the transformation of moral philosophy into the social sciences.

Simultaneously, there emerged an early unquestioned association among government, private enterprise and academic interests in scientific pursuits. The faith in the positive benefits of those associations and in the values of practical application reflected the heritage of a country that imagined itself as a laboratory for social and political experiments to be conducted over time in a process of competitive individual entrepreneurship.

This environment of beliefs and structural accommodations set the framework within which the dominant forms of communication research would emerge. During the turn-of-the-century period, roughly 1880–1920, co-operation among government, industry and academy became particularly well institutionalized, through various Populist and Progressive-era mechanisms in state and federal governments, public and private universities and philanthropic organizations. It was in this period that the modern forms of telecommunications and mass media moved to the center of American social and economic life, and it was in response to the various hopes and anxieties about them and the pre-existing forms of public and private accommodation that the pragmatic social sciences began to consider their significance.

The co-operative, applied ethic of social science was particularly well demonstrated during the 1920s with the rise of the joint private–public study commission mechanism and calls by leading politicians, industrialists, journalists and intellectuals for establishment of elite centers or institutes for advanced research and public policy guidance, what Walter Lippmann (1922) called 'the intelligence bureau'. The Depression and New Deal experiences enhanced the development of such structures and the belief in their efficacy. As the mass media, particularly broadcasting and film, grew in importance, the lens of applied social and behavioral science and the instrumentality of 'bureau research' began to focus on them.

The Payne Fund studies of film's impact in American life (Charters, 1933) were the first examples of organized media research, involving a variety of private and public interests addressing what was perceived as a major social problem. Paul Lazarsfeld's Bureau of Applied Social Research, eventually established at Columbia in the late 1930s, was the prototype of the research centers that were to take up aspects of communication inquiry on a more continuous basis. Thereafter, and particularly during the decade after the Second World War, the establishment of advanced communication research in a number of midwestern university centers followed that model. Those universities were usually the major state land-grant research institutions that had been founded on the basis of their applied service potential in agriculture and engineering. It was in such universities that the new programs in communication were first established. Typically those programs were closely associated with professional schools of journalism and speech which were influenced by the ancient rhetorical traditions of public speaking and debate, and which in their emerging new forms were closely affiliated with state press and broadcasting associations. Intellectually, then, communication study began with a decidedly pragmatic, even vocational purpose.

That purpose was reflected in the strong administrative research characteristics of the university communication research institutes. Their agendas were driven by the marketing and audience circulation research needs of their various private industry and government agency clients. Those practical agendas were decisively set, first by the competitive struggles among the media, and then by the domestic and international political exigencies of the Second World War and the Cold War.

That administrative bias in the work of the initial communication research institutes had important intellectual consequences for the field. It encouraged American communication studies to become captured early by positivistic debates about media effects and to let itself be drawn unwarily into the politically loaded mass culture debate. Its association with journalistic and broadcast training also reinforced in it relatively shallow, industry-oriented renderings of issues involving press and individual freedom, social responsibility and professional ethics.

As a result, the emerging mid-century model of communication was essentially an amalgam of organic and mechanical images, of behavioristic/ stimulus-response and transportation/transmission processes (Carey, 1989). In the immediate post-war period those images were explicitly married to the analogous sender-receiver models then emerging in systems theory, leading to the formulation of a simplistic, yet highly heuristic, S-R model of communication that was to dominate the next generation of US research. From those perspectives communication and culture were simply products of an industrial, commodity process, and for a considerable period that orientation led American communication research to forget or ignore much of its own more interpretive social science and humanistic heritage, leaving it with very little to say about meaning, ideology or power.

It is important to stress that there were other traditions of communication inquiry. The land-grant university journalism, speech and communication faculties also often were constituted of scholars whose work followed various paths which stemmed from earlier, albeit atrophied, traditions of progressive social and political inquiry. Throughout the 1950s and 1960s there were neo-idealist strains of constitutional and press history and social psychological constructivism that fostered patterns of social and political inquiry that in turn encouraged the recovery of symbolic interactionist, interpretive and more broadly cultural studies (Blumer, 1969; Siebert, 1952). Likewise there were unbroken, if often slender, lines of critically materialist inquiry into questions of media ownership, economics, power and performance that eventually shaped broad-ranging traditions of institutional and content criticism (Skornia, 1965; Smythe, 1957). Those traditions reflected a diversity of social and cultural discourse in the broader American academy that is much older than is commonly recognized and that has frequently been overlooked, at home and abroad. None the less there can be no doubt that the normal science, empiricist tradition, shaped by a congruence of industrial, governmental and university needs, predominated throughout mid-century American communication research. It reflected a strong techno-cratic tendency in American intellectual life and established the general context for the debates about television in society that steadily shaded toward the behavioral effects questions.

## PREVIOUS CRITIQUES OF VIOLENCE EFFECTS RESEARCH

By the late 1970s, in response to a series of critical discourses across the entire face of the humanities and social sciences, communication research itself began to be much more introspective and within that process began to examine the entire effects tradition. In that light it became possible to reinterpret the violence effects tradition specifically (Rowland, 1981, 1983).

The new critique had four principal elements:

### The research and the legitimation of communication

At its core the critique was deeply skeptical of the effects research findings, particularly of the causal linkage claims. The critique noted how the official research regularly confounded laboratory experiments with field settings, how it tended to rely heavily on correlational statistics, even in longitudinal studies, and how it never succeeded in separating television from other environmental influences when trying to account for aggression.

Such factors were regularly written off by the proponents of the direct linkage argument. Faced with the regularly cautious conclusions over many years of congressional committees, the proponents, particularly those associated with the Surgeon General's Advisory Committee (Comstock and Rubinstein, 1972; Surgeon General's Scientific Advisory Committee on Television and Social Behavior, 1972), explained them away as merely the result of the politics of broadcast industry involvement in the process and of deliberate political efforts to downplay the evidence. They worked hard to use the National Institute of Mental Health (NIMH) report (1982) and subsequent hearings (US House, 1983; US Senate, 1984) to overturn the impression of inconclusiveness. None the less, any dispassionate, truly independent review of the research up through the late 1970s was hard pressed to discover the firm, conclusive evidence that would support the sort of popular representations of the situation that became prevalent in the wake of the intensive research efforts during the 1968–76 period.

But the independent critique of the research led to an even more important argument.[1] Grounded in non-administrative traditions within the wider field, and supplemented now by the more widespread critical social science theoretical ferment of the 1970s, it came to the issue with a deep understanding of the way in which the research was a social construct. Working from the traditions of the sociology of knowledge and cultural interpretation, it was able to analyze the manner in which the research had been shaped not only by the interests of the media industries, but also by those of the reform groups, politicians and even portions of the academy itself. It demonstrated how theoretical constructs, methods and conclusions had been influenced by cultural, political and economic factors in the debates about television and how, with historical changes in those understandings, the models and even the research findings them- selves had changed.

Moreover, the critique went a step further, suggesting that the very process of the research, the political act of resorting to it in the first place, had been fraught with important meaning. The critique found in the communication effects tradition a quintessential American cultural attribute, namely the tendency to see social issues as a series of problems to be solved and to imagine that there was a scientific instrumentality that would guide that solution. It noted that the great accomplishment of twentieth-century American behavioral science had been to take scientific rationalism to positivist extremes and bully the study of society and culture into a posture of formalism and what C. Wright Mills (1959) once called 'abstracted empiricism'. The result had been to deprive much American social inquiry of a capacity for interpretation and the investigation of meaning, to contribute to typically US pragmatic instincts that nearly always tended to ignore questions of class, power and conflict.

### The industry

Much of the critical literature in the 1970s began to take note of the role of the broadcast industry in the more recent phases of the violence inquiry, particularly in the process leading up to the Surgeon General's report (Cater and Strickland, 1975; Cowan, 1979). Telling questions were raised about the stacking of the Advisory Committee and its internal workings, and dark suggestions were made about how those conditions might have affected the official interpretations of the results. A popular conclusion from those accounts was that without such industrial participation the 'true' version of the results would have been reported, with conclusions much more inimical to the interests of the broadcasters.

The media interests in the matter were, of course, manifest. There is no doubt that the broadcasters had managed to muddy the waters through their own in-house social research offices, academic funding programs and direct political influence. But much of the reformist research failed to notice how much more profoundly structural the entire industry question had been. Closer attention to the deeper history of broadcasting and of the communication policy process demonstrated how, since well before the dawn of television, the networks had carefully constructed a diversionary administrative research capacity that had been not only systematically confounding the policy review process for decades, but also actually helping change scholarly accounts of the very theoretical models in communication research, principally on the question of the shift from direct to limited effects hypotheses (see, e.g., Lazarsfeld and Stanton, 1941, 1944, 1949; Klapper, 1960).

Less apparent, too, was a further structural conclusion, namely that in spite of the seemingly profound debate between the effects models the industry-sponsored research process had contributed precisely to the reinforcement of a behaviorist understanding of television that worked against a substantively critical perspective (Rowland, 1983, pp. 52–86, 295–7). In failing to understand the deeper nature of their own epistemology the proponents of the strong, causal linkage school were unable to see how the industry's carefully cultivated two-step, limited effects model and its association with functionalist perspectives in US social science and consumer models in market research, had drawn them into a long pattern of either/or inquiry that never allowed them to address more basic issues of control, power and motive in broadcasting and communications generally.

## Media reformers

The critique of the violence effects tradition also paid careful attention to the arguments and role of the media reform movement, particularly those parties characterized as the citizens' or public interest groups. The critique was partially muted because so much of the reformers' agenda was still caught up in the use of the effects approach. The reformers tended to rely on the dominant direct effects findings and to subscribe to similar expectations that social science could be used to guide matters of control and improvement in broadcasting.

The critique demonstrated that the citizens' movement in broadcasting was firmly a prisoner of its own progressive heritage. That heritage was a contradictory tradition of liberalism that, in spite of deep-seated concerns about large, private corporate enterprise and a social agenda designed precisely to overcome its depredations, had never been able to develop a coherent public policy that could confront the fundamental capitalist libertarianism of American society. That constraint had been particularly felt in communications where First Amendment consider- ations, with their close association of free speech and free enterprise commitments, strictly limited the capacity to introduce significant public- service alternatives into the nation's broadcasting culture, with its firmly private, market orientation. Reflecting these contradictions, US communi- cations policy rested in a neo-libertarian public interest ideology that imagined it could work within the dominant structure to effect reforms that could lead to changes such as improved news and public affairs, high-quality cultural, educational and children's programming, and, of course, restricted violence.

It had taken nearly half a century of limited accomplishments in that policy to exact anything approaching a substantial response, and it was only with the social movements of the late 1960s and early 1970s that such responses began to emerge. A few successful challenges to existing private, commercial television licensees and the rise of support for a newly re-energized and federally supported public service broadcasting enterprise appeared to herald a new era, and it was in that context that the violence inquiries had become so seemingly important and potentially powerful. Yet in the end, for all the traditional reasons associated with the compromises in American social and economic policy, those reforms were individually and collectively limited. Indeed, the very threat of their initial success helped engender a reaction against reregulation that soon led to sweeping deregulation in communications, principally around the introduction of competition in cable television and telecommunications.

The irony of that result is that it was inspired in part precisely because, although still limited, broadcast reforms appeared to have the potential of building into something much more substantial. The system of 'public interest' regulation through the Federal Communications Commission (FCC) had been acceptable as long as it did not truly threaten the dominance of private-enterprise, market-driven broadcasting. The FCC had served more to protect the existing industry than to reform it. When the contradictions of that system began to be more apparent, but more crucially when the opportunities for change began to deliver actual reforms, and not just their promise, a structural adjustment was required. Therefore, at the very moment of the broadcast reform movement's greatest success, it was undercut by a fundamental policy shift, a decision to change the rules of regulation so as to provide for a more explicitly competitive technological market-place. This adjustment provided for one type of reform (industrial competition) and closed the emergent openings in the system for the others (content service requirements and major new public-service structural alternatives).

## The political process

The critique of the violence debate began to focus on the symbolic nature of the political process. Elements of the critique examined the long history of congressional investigations into television violence and discovered that there was a strongly repetitive, ritualistic character to the process. The issue was found to reappear every few years, almost on a regular schedule. In fact the ritual extended back nearly to the turn of the century, well before the arrival of television, to the early days of pulp fiction, comic books and film. The critics of media violence would periodically find a fresh political champion who would engage the issue as if it were brand new and who would follow a regular script that included expressions of outrage and condemnation, calls for research, highly public hearings at which industry figures would be tongue-lashed and exhorted to better performance, fulminations of frustration and anger at the inconclusive research evidence, proposals for new legislation or regulation, and ultimately, in the wake of both the contradictory research and the rediscovery of First Amendment concerns, no major public policy change.

This symbolic use of the process in the television violence investigations was well documented, particularly over the course of the successive Kefauver, Dodd and Pastore committee eras. It demonstrated the full richness and well-rehearsed character of the ritual. It also revealed how thoroughly successful the process was in giving a strong, national appearance of serious political concern, while yet managing in the end to accomplish very little by way of either legislative or regulatory change.

## VIOLENCE EFFECTS RESEARCH UPDATED

### The new communication research environment

After Senator Pastore retired in 1976, there initially were no obvious new congressional champions to take up the struggle. The reasons for this were several.

First there were the embarrassments of the Surgeon General's experience. Regardless of the differential judgments about the merits of the research fostered by the Advisory Committee, there was a widespread awareness of the way that the project had been caught up in the political struggle over television regulation. The strong effects proponents complained about the industry influence in the Committee, and the limited effects camp perceived a scientific disingenuousness that was willing to shade the results in favor of a predetermined position motivated by a dislike of television and mass communication. The new critical perspective threw up its hands, declaring a plague on both houses, arguing that the political motivations were manifest on both sides, but that in any case the more serious underlying lessons about the politics and epistemology

of the question, and the way in which the American debate about television had been narrowed in the Surgeon General's project, were being
ignored. As a result, there was no clear consensus on how, let alone
whether, there should be some effort to re-engage the violence issue
through a federal sponsor.

Meanwhile, as reflected in the critique itself, communication research
in the US was becoming increasingly less comfortable with the terms of
its own theoretical debates. Among other things, the concerns emanating
from American and British cultural studies, the rise of more critical strains
of social and political thought across the face of the humanities, social
sciences and professional fields, and the development of increasingly
meaning-oriented, constructivist views of the audience all began to define
a new stage of theoretical discourse in the field. At the same time, the
empirical patterns in the field were shifting. Qualitative methods courses
found a new, increasingly popular place in graduate curricula, and the
study of the 'active audience' came to be more consciously shaped by
ethnographic sensibilities. All this gave pause to the violence effects
question in the broader communication research community.

## The new technological and economic policy context

Meanwhile, there was a series of developments in the technologies and
industries of communications themselves that seemed to offer a way out
of the political impetus toward the effects questions.

Much of the vulnerability of the broadcast industry to formal, official
investigation of its social impact had been afforded by the Radio Act of
1927 and the Communications Act of 1934 with their adoption of the
fiduciary principle from previous state and federal administrative law.
That principle called for regulation of broadcasting in light of 'the public
interest, convenience and necessity'. There had always been considerable
debate about the meaning of that mandate, particularly about how much
authority it provided for rules involving content.

But the potential of such sanctions persisted, and during the rise of
television it had given authority to major congressional investigations
such as those about the quiz show scandals, the fairness doctrine and the
violence question. The media policy debates during the late 1960s and
early 1970s had been marked by increasing controversy over broadcasting
performance, and many of the policy tendencies in those years (the first
major federal support for public broadcasting, a few commercial television
station license renewal denials, judicial endorsement of the fairness doctrine and a number of content-based radio station investigations) seemed
to be signaling a new era in which program service considerations were
finally coming forward as major regulatory values.

Whatever their different and often overlapping interests, the various parties began to search for a policy and regulatory escape. They found that release in a dramatically changing set of technological and economic conditions in communications. During the 1970s cable television, satellite transmission and common carrier telecommunications were developing to the point of appearing to be able to provide a broadband 'television of abundance', and much more.

The possibility of an end of spectrum scarcity began seriously to disrupt the communications policy assumptions that had dominated broadcasting and telephone regulation for the preceding half-century. Apathy toward the fiduciary principle was encouraged by attacks from within the FCC itself and particularly in the formal declaration by the then FCC chair Mark Fowler that television was nothing more than a toaster with pictures and that the public interest is only that in which the public is interested (Horwitz, 1989, p. 245; Fowler and Brenner, 1982). Situating itself squarely in line with the general appeal to market-based forms of economic and social regulation sweeping across US and global public policy considerations, that approach came to dominate communications policy debates throughout the 1980s.[2]

Under new conditions, there was less confidence in the ability of policymakers and regulators to appeal to examinations of programming and its social impact in determining whether broadcasting, let alone cable and telecommunications, were operating in the public interest. This situation, coupled with rising doubt about the merits of the scientific evidence, and their increased understanding of the political and ritualistic nature of the debate, led many in communication research to abandon the violence effects inquiry.

**Behavioral science persistent**

However, at least one set of interests in the academy had not given up the chase. That cadre of behavioral scientists who had been drawn to and worked together in the National Science Foundation (NSF) and Surgeon General's projects had developed substantial intellectual and professional commitments to the linkage cause. Most of them were predisposed to such positions by virtue of training in the liberal behaviorism and functionalism of the post-war academy, a social engineering tendency that was comfortable with the possibilities of political power for the social sciences, a hope for something akin to the position that the natural and engineering sciences had achieved so firmly by mid-century.

This perspective had successfully fought its way to the NSF table in the early 1950s and had offered its services in the social and educational programs hanging over from the New Deal that were being transformed into the domestic and international projects of the New Frontier and the Great Society.

This group was part of the academic subset of the New Class (Bazelton, 1967; Gouldner, 1979). It had a strong orientation toward analyzing social problems related to communication and trying to fix them, as for instance in various applied projects in educational television, public information and political communication at home and abroad under the aegis of the US Office of Education, Agency for International Development and other federal agencies.[3] They were hardly uncritical of existing institutions, and much of their effort was dedicated to what they saw as progressive social change. But their origins in psychology, educational psychology and rural sociology had been marked by lacunae in precisely the more critical and cultural areas which came to the fore in US social science and communication studies in the 1970s.

Over the decades of inquiry about media effects, behavioral psychologists had been the most persistent proponents of the direct, causal effects arguments. Even with the rise of cognitive theory, their models of behavior were less troubled by questions about confounding social phenomena, and they therefore still tended toward a transmission model of communication. That paradigmatic orientation dominated the staff of the Surgeon General's Advisory Committee and their contract researchers. It remained the predominant perspective as the post-Pastore process emerged.

### The initial effort to effect a policy impact recovery

By the early 1980s the causal effects proponents had reason to be concerned. Senator Pastore had retired and there had been virtually no legislative ·or regulatory action on the basis of the Surgeon General's project. Meanwhile under the reregulation and deregulation policies of the Carter administration (1976–80) there was a growing interest in market-place solutions to the questions of communication policy. At the same time there was considerable confusion about congressional leadership in communications policy. The Republicans had seized the majority in the Senate in 1978, and in the House the post-Watergate Democratic freshmen from 1974 were now coming into increasing power and were jockeying for position among themselves and with the administration on a whole range of issues. In keeping with the new view, the House communication subcommittee efforts to rewrite the Communications Act in the late 1970s, under then chairman Lionel Van Deerlin (Democrat, California), had focused on introducing new technologies and opening up all of electronic communications to more competition.

The effects scientists had never given up on their quest to have their work be more determinative in the policy process. At least as early as mid-1979 they began lobbying for renewed congressional attention to the Surgeon General's report and to the additional work that had been commissioned by NIMH since. With the election of Ronald Reagan later that year, their interest in reawakening the issue was increased. The impetus toward communication deregulation would be even greater in the new administration, as was soon reflected in its appointments to the FCC and the National Telecommunications Information Administration (NTIA) and in the position of its Justice Department toward the AT&T monopoly issue then working its way through the federal courts. None of that augured well for proponents of regulation based on behavioral science findings.

But there was an even more serious concern within the research community. The new administration would be looking for budget cuts, and the more socially oriented programs of agencies such as NSF and NIMH were prime targets. If the violence effects project was to continue, it would require substantial renewed publicity and the protection of Congress. To those ends the NIMH scientists prevailed upon the outgoing Surgeon General to encourage their agency to reconvene a working group of research scientists to review once again the status of the literature and to reprovoke the public debate. Directed by and drawn principally from those on the former Advisory Committee staff and those among the contract researchers who had been disappointed in the cautious tone of the results under Pastore's supervision, the new project group issued a report (National Institute of Mental Health, 1982) that provided precisely their resurgent call to arms. Meanwhile they found in Representative William Hughes (Democrat, New Jersey) and Senator Arlen Specter (Democrat, Pennsylvania) the initial congressional sponsors they needed. In the traditional fashion the NIMH report was accorded at least two public hearings, by the House and Senate Judiciary Committees (1983 and 1984).

The House effort was carefully staged. The news media, and particularly television, were strongly encouraged to cover the 1983 proceedings. Daniel Schorr, a well-known broadcast journalist then working for CNN and who had considerable, albeit justified, animosity toward the networks, was presented as the lead-off witness. Nearly four dozen behavioral scientists, virtually all of whom were associated in some way or another with the Surgeon General's project or the subsequent NIMH studies, were enlisted for an endorsement statement. The networks' social scientists were permitted to testify, but no other academics were involved, ensuring that the smooth flow of the bipolar behavioral discourse leaning toward the causal linkage side would be uninterrupted.

There is not space here to analyze all aspects of those initial hearings, but if one pays special attention to one of its elements it is possible to observe the gist of what was occurring. The example in question is the summary testimony by the NIMH study director, David Pearl. His initial message was familiar:

The unanimous consensus embodied in the report was that the conver-
gence of findings from a sizable number of studies, on balance, indicated
a causal connection between televised violence and later aggressive
behavior. The conclusions reached in the 1972 Surgeon General's report
thus were strengthened by the more recent research.

(US House, 1983, p. 34)

In keeping with the organized aspect of the campaign this testimony was
careful to anticipate several of the major criticisms of the research. Here
is how it addressed the issues of field studies vs experimental work and
the singular nature of television in cultivating aggressiveness:

Now, the majority of both experimental and the more naturalistic field
studies coalesce and are mutually supportive in indicating that there is
a linkage between the viewing of televised violence and aggressive
behaviors. Most behavior [sic] scientists who have studied the question
agree in this regard. . . .

It is important here to stress that the empirical support for a causal
linkage does not mean that all aggressive or violent behaviors in the
real world are television-influenced. Some critics of the NIMH report
have misunderstood this. The causes of behavior are complex and
determined by multiple factors. No single factor, exclusively by itself,
probably makes a person seriously aggressive or antisocial. Under some
psychological, social or environmental circumstances, television may
exert little or no influence. But, with other conditions, it can play a
very highly important role in shaping behavioral style when and how
violence, aggressiveness or other antisocial behavior gets expressed.

(ibid., pp. 34–5)

This testimony contains all the elements of confidence, assertiveness,
compromise and evasiveness that characterize the official behavioral
science position on the matter for the next decade.

Virtually all the political debate in subsequent years refers back to and
builds on this representation of the issue, principally because it seems to
make the case so strongly, creating an impression that there had a been
a great deal ('sizable number of studies') of closely co-ordinated new
work ('over 2,500') that has significantly advanced the issue
('strengthened') and brought all the research, experimental and field
work, together in one grand, solid project ('coalesce' and 'mutually
reinforce'). It also promotes the idea that there was considerable consensus among the relevant expert research community ('most . . .
scientists . . . agree'), and that the critics were simply uninformed.

The argument is powerful, but in light of all that had gone before in
broadcast policy deliberations about violence effects it bears scrutiny. The

number of actual empirical studies closely focused on common violence effects issues is greatly exaggerated, apparently lumping together all sorts of television research, much of which could be considered only marginal to the central questions, and suggesting far more new work after the Surgeon General's report than had in fact been conducted. The image of experimental and field work supporting one another suggests a level of co-ordination and integration that likewise simply did not exist. For the most part these projects were not conducted in any joint, mutually cross-referenced fashion. The image of 'coalescence' was only a *post hoc* construct; it did not inhere in the actual research.

The oral testimony also left out an important qualifier, namely that correlational statistics represented the predominant form of data among the studies reviewed. There was a reference to correlations in the more formal prepared statement in the hearings record (ibid., p. 40), and witnesses always have the problem of needing to condense their longer presentations into oral testimony. However, there is much in Pearl's remarks that is verbatim from the prepared report. Inclusion of the reference to correlations would have been quite easy.

Leaving out the correlation reference bespeaks a general tactic. Even in the longer report the reference is fleeting and not dwelt upon ('there is a significant positive correlation between television viewing and aggressive behaviors', ibid., p. 40). Later in that same passage the reference is changed – 'a significant positive correlation' becomes 'the positive relationship'. One can read through this long, complex statement and readily miss these nuances as well as the significance of what is being done. First, the paper is sliding around the fact that what it calls the 'causal inference' is based principally on non-causal measures. Second, it reduces and subtly transforms the meaning of the reference. What begins as a correlation ends up as a definitive relationship with implications of causality. Additionally, while the formal statements are careful to include other qualifiers ('under some circumstances', 'television may'), those cautions tend to be dropped in the summary statements. In this and later versions of reports on the 1982 study, the reference to the NIMH findings being an 'inference' of a causal connection, as opposed to a firm conclusion, also drops away.

The 1984 hearings appear to have been a bit more balanced. Again a noted media figure, in this case Robert Keeshan, 'Captain Kangaroo', is employed to draw publicity. David Pearl also testifies, providing a reprise of his House testimony in 1983 on the NIMH report, and he is accompanied by another former Surgeon General's project colleague, John Murray, who testifies on behalf of the American Psychological Association. Their presentations are countered by an industry representative, Philip Harding, the CBS/Broadcast Group vice-president for social and policy research, and Jib Fowles, a professor of human sciences and humanities at the University of Houston.

The last appearance is particularly interesting because it is one of the few times in the post-Pastore recovery effort that a dissenting academic is permitted to testify in opposition to the official NIMH position. Citing the argument from his then recent book (1982), Fowles calls effects research 'one of the greatest travesties in the uneven history of social science', and suggests that the research agenda 'is not to understand why children are drawn to television . . . but instead to revile a medium which they see as plebeian when they want to think of themselves as patricians' (US Senate, 1984, p. 59). Fowles also uses his testimony to reintroduce the Feshback work on catharsis which the behavioral scientists had been attacking for many years and which had been dismissed by the NIMH report. That reference led to a bitter colloquy with Pearl and Murray who were quick to try to rebury the Feshback argument and claim that he had recanted (ibid., pp. 60–5). Fowles disputes that conclusion, and in an odd, unexplained gesture the subcommittee staff inserts a copy of an undated Feshback paper in the hearing's appendices. That paper tends to support Fowles' interpretation of the Feshback position.

**A legislative result: Simon says**

In keeping with the old pattern the matter should have expired, particularly in the political climate of the Reagan administration. But the wheel had turned a bit further. Congress had created just enough space to permit the causal linkage argument to be used more forcefully, even in the face of deregulation. A large enough cadre of interested academics now existed, some in federal agencies, to be able to keep the matter alive at the subgovernment level somewhat independently of the leadership conditions in the White House and Congress. And, perhaps precisely because there was so much frustration at other losses, a concerted effort developed to establish some broadcast reform in an arena where it appeared that public anxiety and outrage could be linked to a scientific justification.

Beginning in 1986, Senator Paul Simon took up the mantle that had lain unclaimed since John Pastore's retirement a decade before. In Senator Simon the causal linkage proponents found the sponsor they had been seeking, someone with a willingness to adopt the mission and pursue it single-mindedly. The focus now became the attempt to pass legislation that would provide limited immunity from the antitrust laws, so that the television industry could co-operate in developing voluntary standards to reduce violent content. Although seen as novel to many, this idea went back nearly twenty-five years, to a proposal by then FCC chairman Newton Minow. Now in an era of increasing deregulation, the waiver was perceived by the reformers as better than nothing. In the face of a continuing lack of impact and the general erosion of the traditional fiduciary basis for regulation, it had become imperative to achieve some tangible policy result.

This renewed effort took four years. Annually between 1986 and 1990 the judiciary committees of both the House and the Senate held regular hearings on the antitrust exemption legislation. The justification for the law was the social science research evidence adduced during the NIMH campaign and the 1983–4 hearings, with Senator Simon serving as the primary political advocate of the causal effects argument.

Initially the broadcasting industry resisted this initiative on constitutional grounds, arguing in traditional fashion against any measures that could be construed as regulating content. The counter-argument was that no direct restrictions were being proposed, merely a means for permitting the broadcasters to work together in establishing standards for reducing violence.

Through it all Senator Simon was the congressional leader, often operating almost single-handedly. He had powerful support from such professional constituencies as the American Psychological Association, the American Psychiatric Association and the National Education Association. These groups represented a range of clinical interests in the academy, medicine and education. They managed to promote a discourse of television as pathology, and in taking up the cry against television violence they had joined a cause that continued to garner press attention for themselves and their congressional sponsor. Although the effort did for the first time lead to a piece of legislation dealing with violence on television, it is unclear how popular it was within Congress, and it appeared to be the almost exclusive interest of just one Senator.

Meanwhile, during the years of the antitrust debate (e.g., US House, 1988, 1992; US Senate, 1986), the networks' firm resistance to depictions of the research as so thoroughly conclusive began to soften. This tactic reflected less a judgment about the research than a calculation by the broadcasters about how to regain more policy favor in Congress. The 1984 Cable Act had demonstrated that cable was to be considerably strengthened through favorable federal legislation, and there were concerns about growing policy opportunities for a range of other technologies. Already, with the growth of cable, the networks' high market share had begun to slip. Against these threats the broadcasters hoped to encourage improved policy considerations for themselves.

Under the general deregulation mood the FCC had extended the terms for broadcasting licenses from seven to twelve years, and it had eliminated the Fairness Doctrine.[4] These were considerable victories for the broadcasters, who now hoped to encourage Congress not to overturn those provisions. Similarly it was hoped that Congress and the FCC might work together to reshape the various measures that directly affected the broadcasters' financial interests. At the same time, the networks and others had been severely cutting costs. Those efforts had reached deeply into important, prestigious, publicly visible arms of the industry, such as the network news and programming standards and practice divisions. Under these conditions maintaining expensive offices of social (as opposed to marketing) research was no longer seen to be as important, politically or financially, as in the Stanton days.

During the early 1990s Representative Edward Markey, chair of the House subcommittee on telecommunications, began sponsoring legislation authorizing an electronic decoding device, the V-chip, that would permit the blocking of programs encoded with violence warnings. Because that technology could be used to block all other programming as well, including commercials, it initially had strong opposition in many quarters, including the broadcasters.

Meanwhile, by 1993, the cable television industry, continuing to look for marketing and policy advantages over the broadcasters, indicated a willingness to accept the V-chip (US House, 1993). It also suggested that it would be open to accepting independent monitoring of its programming for violence. The broadcasters had strongly opposed any such monitoring process; but now, in the face of the cable defection and continuing threats from Senator Simon and others to consider stiffer measures, the broadcasters capitulated. As a result, in mid-1994 the cable and broadcasting industries announced the funding of separate violence monitoring projects. To establish these systems the networks turned to an academic organization, the UCLA Center for Communication Policy, for a two-year, $400,000–500,000 project, and for its part the National Cable Television Association (NCTA) contracted (for $3.3 million) with a television study organization, Mediascope, which in turn subcontracted a research team from four universities (California-Santa Barbara, North Carolina, Texas and Wisconsin) to conduct a three-year content analysis of television programming. Both projects promised a much more qualitative orientation toward violence analysis, paying attention to matters of context, motivation and consequence, and the Mediascope project was designed to study attitude changes among viewers and to examine their interpretations and understanding of such things as advisory messages and program ratings schemes.

The broadcasting and cable industries became more willing to make accommodations on the violence matter, while pursuing much more important policy considerations for themselves that addressed considerably expanded economic opportunities and profitability. Their major concerns came to lie with such matters as elimination of cross-ownership restrictions, protections for video markets in and against the telephone industries and securing access to the 'information superhighway'. For assurances from Congress in these areas broadcasters and cablecasters became willing to make concessions in what in the larger scheme of things appeared to be relatively minor program matters.

The Clinton administration, Congress and the reformers focused on reductions in violence, but little attention was paid to the major structural matters of ownership and commercial purpose. Privatization and ever-increasing commercialization were the dominant policy tendencies for both conventional television and the new Internet aspects of telecommunication, and those commitments were stronger in the wake of the fall 1994 elections with the seizure of both houses of Congress by the Republicans. The continuing emphasis on violence therefore amounted to a sideshow, while the central tendencies of capital and entertainment purpose steadily worked themselves out.

It is in that light that one must see the Telecommunications Act of 1996. That law was driven through by the new Republican Congress and acquiesced in by an administration eager in an election year to demonstrate some ability to accomplish some legislation. It was also a major sign of the fascination by the administration and the new Congressional leadership with matters technocratic.

The law seemed to be a great victory for anti-violence interests. It provided for the V-chip in television set manufacture and it forced the broadcasting and cable industries to develop a program rating system. But the act was also largely concerned with eliminating barriers to competition and inter-penetration among the electronic media, and in its only other content-related provisions it attempted to ban indecency on the Internet. Apart from being very difficult to enforce, that latter provision was of dubious constitutionality and was immediately the object of serious court challenge. But its ideology was almost entirely that of the marketplace and the saving grace of technology. It failed to provide any protection for structural alternatives to the purely commercial exploitation of the new media. In fact, not only did the 1996 law provide no public dividend (as in the use for public service institutions of some of the proceeds from spectrum auctions or in taxes on commercial license sales, and the increased profits of the telecommunications industries), the Congress had been at great haste to reduce severely or even eliminate all federal funding of public broadcasting.

The principal significance of the act in relationship to violence is that, as reflected in President Clinton's meeting with industry executives on 29 February 1996 (*New York Times*, 1996), the entire matter was once again reduced to matters of image and symbol. The social results were relatively hollow.

## Status of the research and federal policy

The matter of the research base for the entire argument continues to be controversial. Ironically, at just that point where the repeated assertions of the causal link proponents appeared to have reached a hegemonic status, a much stronger stream of critical literature had grown up. But very little of that literature appeared in the hearings records. In what seems to have been a consistent effort to ignore countervailing evidence, the hearings throughout the late 1980s and into the 1990s featured only those parties – the behavioral researchers, the industry research leaders and reformers – who had always been part of the debate, and who tended to be locked into one another's positions. There were a few exceptions to this exclusionary behavior, as in the citations (US Senate, 1987; US House, 1989) of the work of Freedman (1984, 1986, 1988) and Milavsky, et al. (1982), but by and large those were only passing glances. The hearings systematically failed to examine carefully the extent of the critical literature, domestically and abroad, exhibiting little willingness to engage with that research in the breadth and depth that it deserved (Cumberbatch and Howitt, 1989). In the rush to the 1996 law other more recent critical literature was likewise ignored (Bowman, 1993; Gauntlett, 1994; Gitlin, 1994; Linne and Hamelink, 1994; Siano, 1994).

In the late 1990s most aspects of the old policy ritual remained. The research was widely touted as being conclusive, when in fact the increasing strength of the counter-analyses made it quite clear how tenuous those claims were. Simultaneously Congress labored mightily and brought forth the mice of the antitrust exemption, the V-chip and the 'volunteer' monitoring projects. In timeworn fashion, Congress and a succession of presidential administrations avoided doing anything truly significant by way of structural policy change for US broadcasting. They provided for increasing cross-ownership and technological inter-penetration among the communications industries. But they failed to strengthen the sorts of public-service structural alternative funded outside the market-place that would lead to significant program choice and thereby stand against the violent content purveyed by commercial enterprise.

The reform process continued to wring its hands and indulge in the research mystique, but proved to be unwilling to invest communications policy with any more support for the public service institution in the US or any other positive action that, far from censoring existing broadcasters, would provide other means for realizing pro-social aspects of broadcasting and telecommunications.

As for the communication research community, much of it now seemed to be well beyond the violence debate. Most of the field had recognized the charade for what it was, no longer allowing its epistemological debates to be captured by what was essentially a political issue.

The mid-1990s monitoring projects threatened to restate the issue in the hoary old positivistic fashion. The question would be whether the new research and the related press attention would be able to overcome the traps of the previous generations of television violence debate. The opportunity for communication research at large was to restate the issue in light of the newer models of socially constructed content, audience and process, thereby permitting it to reclaim the debate from the clinical schools that had tended to see television as pathology and that yet had led to no significant reform.

All further behavioral and social science discussions of television violence were going to have to take account of its symbolic, political history. They would have to address the question of how to open up the policy debates on television violence research to reflect the diversity that exists in the field. Otherwise they would continue to be part of a longstanding, ritualistic political process that has always had as its core purpose the avoidance of the truly major structural policy changes that would in fact provide the very improvements in television that were ostensibly being sought.

## NOTES

1 The definition of 'independent' in this context is itself a controversial issue. Proponents of the causal linkage argument have regularly portrayed themselves, and have been so characterized by their congressional sponsors, as independent, making a distinction between themselves and those researchers employed or commissioned by the broadcast networks. That characterization ignores the way in which that cadre of behavioral psychologists and communication researchers were themselves closely involved in, and highly dependent upon, federal grant programs (NSF and NIMH) inspired by the congressional inquiries. For the purposes of this chapter 'independent' refers to the critiques that emanate from neither camp and that tend to see both industrial and governmental sponsorship as part of the political problematic of the television violence debate.
2 It continues to remain arguable how truly different that policy was from the dominant tendency in the prior fifty years of communications regulation. But, whatever the differences, the contemporary doctrine seemed to cut away whatever was left of the previous regime and its assumptions, however ultimately inaccurate (Rowland, 1989, 1993), that there had been an ability to appeal to content performance considerations in communications regulation.
3 In the socially epistemological spirit of this chapter it should be noted that the author's initial training in communication research and his early field experience in applied communication change was exactly in this tradition. He benefited intellectually and professionally from association with several of the individuals, and their mentors, identified as leaders in the US violence effects movement.
4 The 'Fairness Doctrine' was a policy of the FCC from 1949 to 1987 requiring that, in their programming, broadcast licensees (1) cover controversial issues of public importance and (2) that such coverage be fair, defined as attending to all significant sides of the issues.

## REFERENCES

### General

Bazelton, David T. (1967), *Power in America: The Politics of the New Class*, New York: New American Library.

Blumer, Herbert (1969), *Symbolic Interactionism*, Englewood Cliffs, NJ: Prentice-Hall.

Bowman, James (1993), 'The media: the use and abuse of violence', *The New Criterion*, 12:1, September, pp. 71–4.

Carey, James W. (1989), *Communication as Culture: Essays on Media and Society*, Boston, Mass.: Unwin Hyman.

Cater, Douglass and Strickland, Stephen (1975), *TV Violence and the Child: The Evolution and Fate of the Surgeon General's Report*, New York: Russell Sage Foundation.

Charters, W. W. (1933), *Motion Pictures and Youth: A Summary*, New York: Macmillan.

Cowan, Geoffrey (1979), *See No Evil: The Backstage Battle over Sex and Violence on Television*, New York: Simon & Schuster.

Cumberbatch, Guy and Howitt, Dennis (1989), *A Measure of Uncertainty: The Effects of the Mass Media*, London: John Libbey.

Fowler, Mark S. and Brenner, Daniel L. (1982), 'A marketplace approach to broadcast regulation', *Texas Law Review*, 60:2, 1982, pp. 207–57.

Fowles, Jib (1982), *Television Viewers vs. Media Snobs: What TV Does for People*, New York: Stein & Day.

Freedman, Jonathan (1984), 'Effect of television violence on aggressiveness', *Psychological Bulletin*, 96:2, pp. 227–46.

Freedman, Jonathan (1986), 'Television violence and aggression: a rejoinder', *Psychological Bulletin*, 100:3, pp. 372–8.

Freedman, Jonathan (1988), 'Television violence and aggression: what the evidence shows', in Stuart Oskamp (ed.), *Television as a Social Issue*, Newbury Park, Calif.: Sage.

Gauntlett, David (1994), 'Panic Station: Understanding Television's Influences and Effects', unpublished manuscript, Institute of Communications Studies, University of Leeds.

Gitlin, Todd (1994), 'Imagebusters: the hollow crusade against TV violence', *American Prospect*, 16, Winter, pp. 42–9; excerpted in the *Utne Reader*, May/June 1994, pp. 92–3.

Gouldner, Alvin W. (1979), *The Future of Intellectuals and the Rise of the New Class: A Frame of Reference, Theses, Conjectures, Arguments, and an Historical Perspective on the Role of Intellectuals and Intelligentsia in the International Class Contest of the Modern Era*, New York: Seabury Press.

Horwitz, Robert Britt (1989), *The Irony of Regulatory Reform: The Deregulation of American Telecommunications*, New York: Oxford University Press.

Klapper, Joseph T, (1960), *The Effects of Mass Communication*, New York: Free Press.

Lazarsfeld, P. F. and Stanton, F. N. (eds) (1941), *Radio Research, 1941*, New York: Duell, Sloane & Pearce.

Lazarsfeld, P. F. and Stanton, F. N. (eds) (1944), *Radio Research, 1942–3*, New York: Duell, Sloane & Pearce.

Lazarsfeld, P. F. and Stanton, F. N. (eds) (1949), *Radio Research, 1948–9*, New York: Harper & Brothers.

Linne, Olga and Hamelink, Cees J. (eds) (1994), *Mass Communication Research:*

*On Problems and Policies: The Art of Asking the Right Questions*, Norwood, NJ: Ablex.

Lippmann, Walter (1922), *Public Opinion*, New York: Harcourt.

Milavsky, J. Ronald *et al.* (eds) (1982), *Television and Aggression: A Panel Study*, London: Academic Press.

Mills, C. Wright (1959), *The Sociological Imagination*, New York: Oxford University Press.

*New York Times* (1996), 'TV executives promise Clinton a violence ratings system by '97' (p. A1); 'Top TV executives agree, and disagree, on ratings system' (p. A7), 1 March.

Rowland, Willard D., Jr (1981), 'The symbolic uses of effects: notes on the television violence inquiries and the legitimation of mass communication research', in Michael Burgoon (ed.), *Communication Yearbook 5*, New Brunswick, NJ: Transaction, pp. 385–404.

Rowland, Willard D., Jr (1983), *The Politics of TV Violence: Policy Uses of Communication Research*, Beverly Hills, Calif.: Sage.

Rowland, Willard D., Jr (1989), 'The meaning of "the public interest" in communications policy: Part I: Its origins in state and federal regulation', International Communication Association, annual conference, San Francisco, 28 May.

Rowland, Willard D., Jr (1993), 'The meaning of "the public interest" in communications policy: Part II: Its implementation in early broadcast law and regulation', Presentation to the Communication and Law Policy Session 'Rethinking the public interest', International Communication Association, annual conference, Washington, DC, 28 May.

Siano, Brian (1994), 'Frankenstein must be destroyed: chasing the monster of TV violence', *The Humanist*, 54:1, January/February, pp. 20–5.

Siebert, Fred S. (1952), *Freedom of the Press in England, 1476–1776*, Urbana, Ill.: University of Illinois Press.

Skornia, Harry (1965), *Television and Society: An Inquest and Agenda for Improvement*, New York: McGraw Hill.

Smythe, Dallas (1957), *The Structure and Policy of Electronic Communication*, Urbana, Ill.: University of Illinois Press.

### Government documents

Comstock, George A. and Rubinstein, Eli A. (eds) (1972), *Television and Social Behavior: Reports and Papers*, vols 1–5, Washington, DC: Department of Health, Education and Welfare.

National Institute of Mental Health (1982), *Television and Behavior: Ten Years of Scientific Progress and Implications for the Eighties*, vols 1–2, Washington, DC: Department of Health and Human Services.

Surgeon General's Scientific Advisory Committee on Television and Social Behavior (1972), *Television and Growing Up: The Impact of Televised Violence*, Washington, DC: Government Printing Office.

US House (1983), *Committee on the Judiciary: Subcommittee on Crime: Crime and Violence in the Media: Hearing* (98, 1) 13 April.

US House (1988), *Committee on the Judiciary: Subcommittee on Monopolies and Commercial Law: Television Violence Act of 1988: Hearing* (100, 2), 5 October.

US House (1989), *Committee on the Judiciary: Subcommittee on Economic and Commercial Law: Television Violence Act of 1989: Hearing* (101,1), 10 May.

US House (1992), *Committee on the Judiciary: Subcommittee on Crime and Criminal Justice: Violence on Television: Hearing* (102, 2), 15 December.

US House (1993), *Committee on Energy and Commerce: Subcommittee on Telecommunications and Finance: Violence on Television: Hearings* (103, 1), May, June, July, September.

US Senate (1984), *Committee on the Judiciary: Subcommittee on Juvenile Justice: Media Violence: Hearing* (98, 2), October.

US Senate (1986), *Committee on the Judiciary: TV Violence Antitrust Exemption: Hearing* (99, 2), 20 June.

US Senate (1987), *Committee on the Judiciary: Subcommittee on Antitrust, Monopolies and Business Rights: Television Violence Antitrust Exemption: Hearing* (100, 1), 25 June.

Chapter 8

# The dangerous psycho-logic of media 'effects'

*Ian Vine*

That the mass media affect their audiences is a truism. The whole point of communicating is to influence one another by conveying information, whether transmission is reciprocal or uni-directional. Thus it may appear paradoxical, even perverse, if this chapter aims to demonstrate how certain allegedly potent media influences are not what they seem. Even so, when media pessimists send out messages of doom concerning 'dangerous' films and TV programmes, and seek our endorsement of their typically censorious demands, we do have every reason to doubt whether the imagery actually exerts 'effects' of the conceptually peculiar and coercive sort which the critics' rhetoric implies.

The ghost of Behaviourism which still haunts the laboratories of media psychologists can be blamed for mechanistic fairy-tales about how audiences process messages. It encourages pessimism about the insidious power of morally transgressive images, and stirs up pervasive agitation about how these corrupt the young. Few of the academics who promote 'harmful effects' mythologies regard their theorising as Behaviourist. Yet their methodologies reveal assumptions which are both obsolete and deeply insulting to the intelligence of the 'subjects' who participate in their investigations. They conclude confidently that the 'causal' impact of levels of exposure to screen violence upon people's aggressive attitudes and conduct is now proven beyond any doubt. One eminent American authority, Leonard Eron, is fond of insisting to an innocent public that the 'strength of the relationship is the same as cigarettes causing lung cancer' (Anon., 1994, p. 6). Such rhetoric will profoundly mislead and frighten anyone scientifically ill-equipped to counter its errors.

The pessimists' capacity to demonise the media, making transgressive imagery seem all-powerful, hinges upon variants of the tacit assumption that audiences function as passive automatons when responding to screen messages. In contrast, I shall develop a model of our *biased rational agency* as actively intelligent viewers. My priority will be partly with how audiences engage with violent programmes, but also with how the prevailing 'psycho-logic' of *thinking about* media 'effects' is subject to politically significant mental distortions.

## WHAT'S THE PROBLEM WITH 'EFFECTS'?

Exposing the paradox that lurks behind popular and academic understandings of the media's 'effects' requires an informal and selective excursion into philosophical conceptions of causality. Since media messages evidently do influence audiences, why should there be conceptual dispute about whether any lasting impact on beliefs and dispositions has inescapably been 'caused' by the information received? Even if we set aside all-important questions about how we actually *assign* meanings to the coded signals, the mere fact that we *choose to attend* to messages highlights how the recipient's active mind also enters into the causal side of the equation.

Certainly, mediated information does sometimes induce significant attitudinal adjustments, which in turn affect behavioural choices. According to the free-speech pressure group Article 19's *Bulletin* (January/February 1995), 'the power of radio in Africa is chillingly illustrated by the example of Rwanda' – where before the 1994 upheavals a private station linked to the Hutu tribe's regime 'helped organize genocide against the Tutsi minority and the murder of dissenting Hutu'. More routinely, businesses clearly have no doubts about whether advertisements can raise sales of their products. And large-scale consumer panics have periodically been triggered in the UK by media coverage of health scares like that over salmonella in eggs, and most recently the spread of 'mad cow' disease to eaters of beef products. Nor are activating effects upon audiences by any means confined to factual or exhortatory messages. After viewers of the Liverpool soap-opera *Brookside* saw a woman and her daughter found guilty of murdering their brutal husband/incestuous father, we know that Channel 4 itself, women's refuges, and relevant charities were all 'deluged with calls from outraged and despondent women' (*Independent*, 18 May 1995). For some individuals the consequences of becoming highly agitated by vivid fictional drama can be distressing, even tragic. The incidence of coronaries while cinema audiences watch action films may be only marginally higher than when they walk their dogs. But we might see the pessimists' point with seemingly clear-cut cases like a girl's rapid slide into post-traumatic stress disorder after the BBC1 hospital drama *Casualty* showed a heart-attack in progress (*Radio Times*, 22 October 1994).[1]

Evidently the controversy about media 'causing effects' upon audiences cannot really be about *whether* messages do trigger changes in us (including involuntary ones). Rather, it must concern *which kinds* of effect occur, as well as *how* they are brought about – and whether the outcomes are to be properly judged as harmful. These distinctions should immediately alert us to the moral and political dimensions of the 'harmful effects' debate. Broadly speaking, the spectre of film and television as a dangerous social force becomes emotive when we seem obliged to accept that strong images of anti-social conduct are bound to affect audiences likewise by manipulative or coercive means. And from a mechanistic perspective this view has superficial credibility. A 'cause' of something, in the strongest of its dictionary senses, is said to be an antecedent event (C) which is invariably or *unconditionally* followed by the specified consequent 'effect' event (E). Yet this reading remains both imprecise and unconvincing, although philosophically more formalised conceptions are equally contentious. An account adequate for present purposes can be adapted from Ted Honderich's (1993) notion of a *sufficient causal circumstance* (or SCC). In essence this recognises that a whole cluster of antecedent conditions must be jointly met before the consequence we are interested in can occur, while any one of several alternative causal clusters might suffice to yield the same effect.

Concretely, if the type of E that interests us is the general category of violent acts, there may be many differing kinds of instigating SCC, any of which can be enough to produce some form of violence. Examples might include: imitating a violent role model; following orders in a battle situation; being attacked oneself in a school playground; feeling insulted by someone when drunk; following a plan for a robbery; or suffering the effects of a particular kind of brain tumour. In fact my listing just committed precisely the misleading tactical over-simplification that the SCC concept aims to rule out. But another problem is more immediate. When seeking to explain a broad E like this we risk considering only a few of many possible SCCs and forgetting the rarer ones. Moreover, having found superficial evidence that one set of SCC conditions are present, we may stop looking for signs of a second and stronger SCC which could also happen to be present. (This is one reason why brain tumours are often not diagnosed for long periods.) Such tendencies reflect how so many of our everyday inferences rely appreciably upon *heuristic strategies*, or unconsciously selected short-cuts which restrict what information we consider relevant enough to bring into our more conscious deductive, inductive and probabilistic inferences. In such computations humans thus make errors that computers do not. Our heuristics may help to make us 'profoundly intelligent in a sense that is proving extremely difficult to emulate' (Evans, 1990, p. 111), yet they can sometimes produce nonsense when we diagnose causation too hastily.

In listing some SCCs for behaviours involving violence, it was convenient to identify them just by citing one causal feature in each case. (It would have been tediously long-winded to give an extensive list in any other way.) Yet the point of aiming to delineate causes in SCC terms is precisely that no type of causation really involves just a *single* dynamic event or process. In a world where everything both diachronically and synchronically affects and is dependent upon so many other things, the empirically sufficient conditions to generate any concrete effect must be far more complex. None of the factors listed above can cause a violent act unless many other supporting features are all present as well. Quite characteristically, any formulation of a putative causal law, or of a statistical or more approximate causal generalization, will take many unstated contributory factors for granted (its *ceteris paribus* conditions). Strictly speaking, we should only ever refer to the *total causal nexus* in question (i.e., all the events comprising some specific SCC) as the source of any effect which concerns us. Citing one factor all too readily leads our reasoning astray, if we then ignore equally necessary parts of that given nexus.

The notion of one discrete E-event being the outcome of an SCC proves to be equally idealised in several ways. For one thing, 'violence' is an exceptionally broad functional category of acts with diverse behavioural manifestations. But even a simple reflexive movement like withdrawing a scalded hand from steam involves many dynamic neurophysiological processes – as well as a cluster of lesser movements of other body parts, each with their own internal processes, too. In the realm of planned purposive actions which extend over appreciable time-spans, we are necessarily dealing with long chains of event sequences and feedback loops. It is only by identifying the behaviour functionally – and typically as some goal-directed *intentional action* – that the movements can ever be classified as a single response-event, or effect. But in that case we are constrained in the kinds of causal SCC we can invoke to explain conduct. For human actions the only logically coherent candidates are ones where the causal nexus must include numerous events at a *mental* level. Indeed, multi-way inter-connections between our goal-states, memories, anticipations, internal sensations, external perceptions and gross physical movements are such that the cause/effect distinction almost threatens to break down altogether. It certainly becomes absurd to take some *external physical stimulus*, like a television image, as necessarily being the most significant factor in the SCC for some consequent intentional act.

One fundamental conclusion can now be stated. Concepts of cause and effect are essential in everyday experience, as well as in science, in spite of their ambiguous connotations. Yet in reality what we single out as if it was *the* cause or *the* effect in any dynamic situation is a matter of preference, largely determined by the nature of our selective interest in its processes. In that respect, all causal claims regarding human conduct are partisan. If we look for effects of alterations in just one salient causal variable within a particular nexus, we risk erroneously seeing its influence as uniquely necessary, sufficient or both. That is how media pessimists can so readily mislead us.

## CHOOSING GOOD CAUSES

In the natural sciences, any variable factor's own causal potency can often be confirmed by experiments which rigidly control and keep constant other major parts of the relevant nexus being investigated, as well as excluding other major SCCs for the effect in question. In the biological and human sciences, the vastly greater complexity of phenomena makes such confidence rarely justified. But in the psychological sphere of deliberate actions, identifying which aspects of a given cause/effect nexus to focus upon becomes a quite crucial choice. Differing explanatory paradigms have different priorities. The 'information-processing' models of mind which rely upon computer metaphors occupy a dubious intermediate status; but our main options are ultimately variants of the Behaviourist and Cognitivist approaches. So the most fundamental difference between these paradigms deserves to be brought sharply into view.

Behaviourism aspired to adopt a detached observer's external, and 'objectively' *impersonal* perspective. Thus, in the field of 'media effects', a crude *descriptive causal generalisation* might be operationalised as follows: 'The more explicit pornography anyone watches, the more their misogynistic attitude score on so-and-so's questionnaire scale subsequently increases.' While the older tradition of John B. Watson would invoke physiological processes to explain such a linkage, 'radical' Behaviourists like B. F. Skinner claimed to eschew properly theoretical causal *explanations* entirely. But where all Behaviourists agree is in their focus upon public, objectively measurable stimulus events as the main 'independent variables' in their causal stories.

By contrast, classical Cognitivism – which in its broadest sense does embrace both affective feeling and volition – occupies the stage of mental experience. It aims to understand overt behaviours empathically, as intentional actions chosen by persons themselves. In essence it considers conduct from the 'subjective' *personal* viewpoint of the agent striving to attain anticipated goal-states. Thus more-or-less consciously accessible perceptions, beliefs and desires are assumed to provide fairly coherent and socially intelligible *reasons* for action. In its purer guises it invokes hermeneutic meaning-making, or *interpretive processes*, as essential elements within the SCCs that generate planned behaviours. Only rarely do we just react rigidly to the merely physical properties of stimuli. Rather, our stored knowledge guides perceptual attention in selective ways from the outset. So different people may literally see and hear different things, according to their expectations of how available information has relevance for effectively pursuing personal and multi-layered goals. Such goals include adherence to moral and other subjective standards of conduct for which we feel responsible, and upon which our social reputations and identities depend.

This second psychological paradigm thus has a distinctive explanatory logic. Its various theoretical manifestations aim to formalise and elaborate upon just those structures of meaning presupposed by a person's own experiential, 'inside' view of human agency – our commonsensical or so-called 'folk psychological' understanding of mind. This is what gives Cognitivism intuitive appeal. And many variants of cognitive theorising tacitly acknowledge that in some restricted sense we do experience 'freedom of the will', in *deciding* how to act or to restrain ourselves. Mental reasons for our choices are special kinds of causative elements – quite essential to any causal nexus invoked to explain some deliberate action. Should we ignore reasons, we can at best only explain any act mechanically, as some purely physical sequence of movements for which the notion of *personal responsibility* makes no sense at all.

We can now begin to see why research that fails to take proper account of how people individually ascribe meaning to what they see and hear on-screen must lead to seriously impoverished accounts of how we are influenced by messages. In so far as what we want to explain are intentional reactions of audiences functioning as active and responsible agents, an impersonal Behaviourist approach to 'media effects' simply cannot explain responses in the right way. It is therefore doubtful whether probabilistic statistical predictions of viewers' behaviour from those theories which have not taken agency seriously can ever be empirically robust – at least beyond the artifical constraints of laboratory environments. And, crucially, to dispense with the personal and hermeneutic dimension of human functioning is to do research which loses all contact with *what it is like* to be someone who first makes sense of messages, and then acts according to reflective understandings of their personal relevance.

## CONFLATING CAUSATION AND CONFUSING PERSUASION

Fervent opposition to violent and other morally transgressive screen imagery may derive simply from finding it offensive to one's personal values. But in a nominally pluralist and liberal society a credible case for censorship has to rest upon firm evidence that imagery is a potent cause of social harms. Certainly a mass of empirical data has regularly been given such a confident interpretation. Yet I shall contend that its superficial credibility hinges upon how Behaviourist researchers misrepresent the kinds of causal inference which their results can properly support. Principally, such tendentious impressions stem from investigators assuming rather than measuring how audiences actually interpret message meanings. These problems can be made apparent by exposing how their narrow conceptions of scientific methodology are manifested in both experimental and correlational types of study.

The safest strategies for the fraught task of identifying reliable empirical regularities and genuinely causal relationships concerning screen violence involve laboratory experiments. At its simplest, a one-off presentation of audio-visual stimulus material to volunteer viewers will be followed by behavioural tasks from which some measures of 'aggressive' responding can be obtained (the 'dependent variables'). These subjects will be predicted to score higher on average than similar others exposed to non-violent imagery (the 'experimental' versus 'control group' comparison). If this is confirmed, the acknowledged danger is that such a difference might easily have arisen due to 'sampling errors' – like the experimental group happening by chance to contain more aggressive members in the first place. So statistical tests must be applied to the pattern of scores, to show whether the observed average difference is likely to be an artefact of such accidental variations. If the data emerge unscathed, the experimenter will normally infer that the violent imagery itself caused the stronger aggressive responding by those exposed to it.

Few modern experiments are this simple. Ideally, the 'violent' and 'non-violent' programmes will first have been pre-tested on other audiences, to confirm that the material is perceived as differing in this respect, but not in terms of unwanted 'confounding' variables like the pace of the action or the interest of the narrative. Sometimes physiological measures are taken during the experimental procedure, because the investigator predicts that some arousal process mediates aggressive actions. Commonly, whole batteries of questionnaires are administered to subjects before exposure – sometimes to permit their allocation to the experimental versus control-group samples to be matched for prior aggressiveness, and for other relevant background factors like social class or child-rearing variables. Alternatively, an individual's scores on such measures can be compared with the direct responses to the stimuli, so that appropriate statistical checks can subsequently reveal any part these variables play in the causal nexus.

Harmful violence towards innocent people cannot ethically be encouraged by experimenters, so resorting to tenuous indicators of aggressive inclinations is the norm. In his classic 1960s demonstrations of children's readiness to imitate violence modelled by an adult (either live or on a TV screen), Albert Bandura was able to study distinctive attacking movements towards a large 'Bobo' doll, designed to rock on its base when hit or punched.[2] But with adults the options are largely confined to weak analogues of actual violence like making intensity ratings of felt anger, adopting ruthlessly competitive strategies in social games, or performing social tasks harshly. One variant of the last involves selecting levels of electric shock or noise, supposedly delivered to another subject as punishments for errors during learning of some skilled activity. Dolf Zillmann and others have extended this approach by enlisting subjects' help in attaching physiological apparatus to other alleged subjects (actually stooges in league with the experimenter), following their own exposure to screen imagery. Measures of painful over-inflation of a blood-pressure cuff are then counted as indices of aggression (Zillmann et al., 1981).

Two awkward features of such ingenious experiments on adults have been exposed. First, apparently harmful behaviours cannot be readily and reliably elicited by screen violence unless subjects have already been provoked into anger by being harmed or insulted by the stooge. In short, it is mainly *retaliatory aggression* which may be amplified by viewing the stimulus material during laboratory studies. This must seriously limit the validity of inferring anything about the power of screen violence to motivate other kinds of aggressive action. More significantly still, appreciable degrees of deception are required if subjects are not to detect the fraudulent nature of the situation or guess the predictions being tested. The second outcome must be avoided as rigorously as the first, because 'expectancy' phenomena can turn experimental hypotheses into self-fulfilling prophesies (Orne, 1962; Rosenthal, 1966). It has been established that experimenters convinced of the truth of their predictions can bias results, in ways which include unintentionally conveying to subjects which responses are anticipated. In laboratory situations there are strong incentives to co-operate with the experimenter, often sufficing to make subjects strive to fulfil whatever they perceive to be expected of them. Best-practice 'double-blind' conditions prevent the person testing subjects from knowing and unconsciously communicating the precise hypothesis under examination. Nevertheless, the structure of the experimental situation may itself convey various *demand characteristics* to perceptive participants. Disguising one's predictions is a major reason for deceiving people about the nature of an experiment; yet checks on whether subjects saw through them or were suspicious have often been absent or far from thorough. Worse still, even strongly Cognitivist researchers are reluctant to ask subjects how they subjectively interpret violent and other imagery and judge its relevance to their own behavioural decisions – for fear of tacitly suggesting additional demands.

Tightly controlled experiments are in principle uniquely suited to testing causal theories. Unfortunately this strength is usually bought at the price of 'ecological' validity – the representativeness of the findings for how people function in everyday situations. Naturalistic research in real-world settings can overcome the artificiality of laboratories, and has sometimes achieved quasi-experimental status – notably when levels of anti-social conduct have been measured before and after remote communities gained access to television. Less directly, David Phillips (1986) has compared short-term fluctuations in recorded rates for categories of violent crime, either side of dates on which there was large-scale media coverage of comparable incidents (from nineteenth-century executions in London to boxing title fights in America). He claims to have demonstrated both deterrent and imitative effects upon the incidence of offences; but, because his time-series statistical techniques are fraught with potential artefacts, some scepticism is justified until such associations are shown to be more robust.

The predominant category of naturalistic research studies involves correlating peoples' longer-term consumption of screen violence with their levels of aggressive conduct. This is almost the only way to study later developmental consequences of cumulative exposure to programmes of any content genre. But such correlational studies cannot control other concurrent influences which may be of far greater causal importance, even if the stimulus and response measures are themselves sound (which is all too rare). Suitable measurements and statistical manipulations should be able to take account of complications like prior aggressiveness leading to a greater preference for violent programmes. However, uncertainties regarding proper matching of high- and low-exposure groups on relevant background variables usually mean that causal inferences cannot be made with any rigour. Even in experiments where some nexus of events X definitely does precede event Y, there is always some risk that a still earlier and neglected nexus C has independently caused both X and Y. Uncontrolled correlational studies are still more vulnerable to inferring causal associations spuriously, or just mistaking the direction of causes and effects.

Whichever Behaviorist methods are used in quantitative studies of media impact, the central problem remains. If subjects' own perceptions of programmes are not directly measured, their influence on actions must be ignored or just assumed. Yet the main thrust of the hermeneutic perspective on responsible agency is that interpretation processes themselves have profoundly complex causal determinants, reflecting idiosyncratic as well as socially shared experiences, desires, and beliefs. Consequent behaviour can neither be predicted nor understood without reference to these. The fundamental semiotic concept of *polysemy* refers both to multiple levels of meaning being encoded within a transmitted message, and to the multiple possibilities for its decoding by different individuals. When researchers simply assume how an audience interprets programmes, they necessarily cannot take adequate account of how alternative textual readings by specific members determine their varying reactions. Thus the crucial question of why any programme encourages a particular minority of viewers into anti-social conduct cannot be resolved.

Behaviourist research which is so cavalier about hermeneutic issues readily undermines itself by methodological oversights. Recording children's 'aggressive' responses without distinguishing whether superficially violent acts form part of play-fighting charades is as common as counting a *Tom and Jerry* cartoon as showing more violence than a typical news bulletin. Yet interviews with young viewers readily reveal their early grasp of what semioticians like Hodge and Tripp (1986) call the 'modal fit' between symbolic images and the realities represented. Children as young as 6 perceived and evaluated appropriately the weakness of *modality* (i.e. the low verisimilitude) evident in on-screen violent fantasies, by reference to their prior understandings of real life.[3]

Projecting assumed meanings on to audiences favours over-generalised stereotyping of what is likely to be the most critical determinant in any nexus for media effects. A purported causal analysis might well be true for those viewers who do adopt the investigator's favoured reading of the imagery, yet be quite invalid for sub-audiences who make alternative interpretations. 'Effects' researchers frequently do discuss how imitative and other dangerous consequences of viewing transgressive imagery may be confined to atypically vulnerable viewers, like those too young or naïve to grasp why what they see cannot provide appropriate scripts for real-life problem-solving. But typically these are speculations ungrounded in actual measurements. They are introduced *post hoc*, to explain away why overall predictive associations between viewing and performing anti-social acts are normally quite weak for randomly selected audience samples.

What is most neglected by the pessimists is that, even for those individuals who *do* reflect screen violence in their authentic (rather than playful) conduct, quite different SCCs may generate similar responses. Behaviourist traditions and rhetorics encourage the belief that message stimuli work unconsciously, insidiously and inexorably to change a viewer's dispositions, effectively bypassing rational and moral self-control processes. This postulate conveniently steers academic and public debate away from the most unthinkable possibility of all – that for some young people it could actually make sound functional sense to adopt or adapt coercive or criminal strategies they see enacted on the screen. Once we have dared to contemplate this kind of effect process, it becomes imperative to take closer account of how the Cognitivist paradigm can throw light on media persuasion.

Consider two people who watch a TV commercial promoting a new beverage, then go to buy the product in question. On some cognitive accounts, a dozen or more distinct stages will have to follow initial 'tuning in' of attention to an advert, before we can properly conclude that the viewers really were persuaded by the message into making their purchase. And, even then, the causal routes could be very different for each person. One may have been attending only casually to the screen, but was impressed by features of the advert's form: verbal endorsement of the drink by a football hero; his confident tone of voice; the exciting quality of the music; the bright and memorable decoration of the can; the almost mystical repetition of the word 'isotonic'; and that final scene's crescendo of applause as our hero scores his winning goal. The next time our viewer is rushing through the weekend's shopping, and almost trips over a promotional display of 'Drink-UP!', cheers start to echo in his ears, and a pack pops into his basket. Our other viewer has been wondering for ages whether this new craze for 'healthy' drinks has anything in it beyond the hype. As a student of marketing she knows all the tricks of the advertising trade, and systematically identifies then disregards every ploy that attracted the first viewer. Yet something in the message's content attracts her interest. What's said to be distinctive about 'Drink-UP!' is its low content of sweeteners, coupled with that slightly tart taste of real cherries. On reflection she decides it could be a truly refreshing change from all those sickly fizzes on the shelves. She puts it on her shopping list.

This fictitious example contrasts two modes of persuasion, identified by Richard Petty as 'peripheral' versus 'central' routes (Petty and Priester, 1994). The latter kind of processing can legitimately be called *rational*, since any change of mind arises from deliberating upon how new information shifts the balance of realistic incentives to behave one way rather than another. When peripheral processing is dominant, careful reflection is largely replaced by heuristic short-cuts whose form is inferentially defective (such as: 'If it's good enough for my role model, it must be good for me'). And of course we would prefer to think that if a diet of crime and war movies induces a youngster to join a street gang this must involve such irrational persuasion. Yet for poor young Blacks struggling for sheer survival in the violent culture of some American inner-city ghetto there are strong pragmatic incentives for joining gangs or acquiring weapons. Indeed, if such forms of activity are preceded by donning an army uniform, even outsiders may concede that the influence process was rational. We must beware of invoking mechanistic causal accounts of media 'effects' simply because we morally deplore the outcomes of persuasion processes.

## THE GREAT RESEARCH FIASCO

People are necessarily concerned about those phenomena which appear to pose the strongest challenges to their personal physical safety and mental security. Rightly or wrongly, it is widely believed that the incidence of anti-social offences, and especially violent crimes, has long been rising steadily throughout Western countries.[4] Such perceptions make it more than understandable that the general public casts around for simple explanations and scapegoats, and for corresponding forms of social engineering which can promise easy solutions.

In this regard, sociological research by George Gerbner and colleagues under the rubric of *cultivation processes* blames the long-term impact of screen media for amplifying people's fears (Gerbner *et al.*, 1994). Although his methods are undoubtedly flawed, the central claim probably holds some validity for audiences in the USA. This is that perceptions of risk are somewhat elevated for the heaviest viewers of American TV drama – whose characters are on average far more frequently involved in violent incidents than ordinary citizens would be. Such unrepresentativeness should partly explain the prominence of violent crime in the perceptions of social reality held by many Americans. However, research has also confirmed how far topics of public concern are subject to *agenda-setting* via the selectivity of news coverage accorded to events (McCombs, 1994). Our susceptibility to media-induced panics is evident when there is nominally factual saturation reporting of violence (including coverage of alleged copy-cat effects of screen violence). Thus news and documentaries seem likely to create more impact on exaggerated beliefs about risk than fictional scenarios can exert. Sadly, it is the very rarity of the most extreme incidents – like murders of and especially by children – which gives them sufficient news value to justify many pages of graphic coverage, and thereby to amplify public fears about people's vulnerability.

Before turning to a brief examination of what 'effects' research actually reveals about the dangerousness of transgressive imagery, it is appropriate to highlight how limited its causal impact on audiences could possibly be. National differences in the proportions of a population claiming to have suffered as victims of crime can be large. One comparison of assaults during 1988 gave 3% for the USA, 2% for Holland as the worst European nation, yet only 0.6% for the UK.[5] There are quantum differences between American and other rates for the most serious offences; but most conspicuously there are huge geographic variations within the USA itself. In 1993, New York no longer made the 'top ten' list of deadly cities, while Los Angeles just qualified with a rate of 31 murders per 100,000 persons – a sum of 1,035, well exceeding Britain's national total for all homicides. Top rates were found in the smaller urban districts of East Palo Alto, California, and East St Louis, Illinois, with 175 and 143 per 100,000 respectively.[6] Alienation associated with economic depression (and thus ethnicity), the accessibility of guns, plus the presence of rival gangs of dealers in 'hard' drugs are amongst the strongest correlates of such massive variations. The absurdity of considering that variations in levels of TV viewing might explain such differences as these is patent.

Given that serious violent crime is relatively so common in the USA, associated public pressures explain why social scientists have been so obsessed with finding its causes. The modern Hollywood cinema's graphic focus upon extremes of violence has made screen imagery an obvious candidate for investigation. This attention is to be expected in the light of the heuristic processing which readily distorts our rational judgements. Particularly when emotional stress clouds our capacity for detached, systematic, reflective reasoning, we are apt to attribute causal responsibility for an event prematurely, to the most *perceptually salient* amongst plausible candidates. In turn, *resemblance* between an event to be explained and one of several prior events can make the similar one more salient, and thus more likely to be singled out as the cause (Nisbett and Ross, 1980). (This is of course a key principle in imitative or 'sympathetic' magical practices.)

Nor is such readiness to scapegoat screen representations of anti-social conduct as causes for the real thing anything new. Soon after the cinema arrived in the small Yorkshire town of Bingley in 1913, films were blamed in the Children's Court for the 'gangsterism of a boy of nine'.[7] The recent trend for educated American liberals to reject their long-standing belief that screen events *reflect* rather than cause social reality is nominally based upon accumulating evidence for harmful 'effects'. But one might suppose that where violent crime is rising close to home, and screen explicitness has reached new peaks, the search for simple answers has merely become more desperate.

Public fears now refer to how video recorders and multi-media computers have brought the most explicit celebrations of violence and grotesque spectacles of horror from the cinema into the home, where material meant only for adult eyes may be watched by quite young children. It is very hard to get meaningful estimates of how often this happens (Barker, 1984). Hagell and Newburn's (1994) recent survey of teenage samples indicated that many had seen films or videos which would have been classified for older ages, and that violent 'mainstream' material (like the *Terminator* movies) was popular. Television viewing was substantial, with about half watching for four to six hours daily, even on weekdays, and often after the 9 p.m. 'watershed'. What was most interesting was the absence of substantial differences in viewing or content preferences between juvenile non-offenders and offenders, even ones convicted for violence.[8] However, a distinctly moralistic and minimally violent police series, ITV's *The Bill*, was appreciably more popular for the latter group, presumably because of its relevance to their own experiences.

It must be noted that, when all categories of violent act are lumped together, British television shows far less violence than do most American channels – and the rate has decreased. Barrie Gunter's recent content-analysis comparison suggested that since 1986 the quantity has halved, and occupies just half a per cent of programme time on terrestrial TV (except for ITV at 1.1%). Yet quite unhelpfully the story's headlines in *The Times* (22 August 1995) emphasised: 'Children's shows blamed for fifth of all television violence – *Power Rangers* and puppets are most frequent offenders.' This glosses over the fact that youngsters do not normally equate cartoon violence with real-life harmful acts. But the more general problem is that, even if discrete acts are sub-divided by type and rated for the intensity of violent action, no account is normally taken of the narrative context which can fundamentally affect the nature of the meanings likely to be attributed to particular violent episodes.

Turning now to the systematic evidence from hundreds of published studies of the relationship between viewing violence and subsequent problematic behaviours, the most certain conclusion is that there is no genuine consensus of findings. The more sceptical reviewers remind us that for every research design which has delivered at least a statistically significant positive correlation there will be apparently comparable investigations which fail to confirm the result. Another conclusion is that rigorous research has almost neglected to look for *personal harms* associated with fear reactions to specific categories of violent content. That younger children sometimes suffer such harms is probably not in doubt, so long as we acknowledge that these are in most cases confined to nightmares and similar short-term consequences (Cantor, 1994). The limited evidence here suggests that what will seriously upset particular children varies idiosyncratically; but one survey of parents revealed that almost half said news coverage of the 1991 Persian Gulf war caused distress.

Research on *social harms* has primarily dealt with reactions deemed to be aggressive or callous. In the absence of consensus between individual studies, we may first survey the literature reviews which have sought to sift through the mountain of reported data (from around the world, although predominantly American). American reviewers like Russell Geen (1990, 1994), Harris (1994), Liebert and Sprafkin (1988), and Judith Van Evra (1990), amongst others, accept that laboratory studies have predominantly shown substantial short-term attitudinal and behavioural consequences of viewing violent programme material. They also agree with Turner *et al.* (1986) that descriptive correlations between long-term heavy viewing patterns and anti-social inclinations, from naturalistic studies, are fairly reliable reflections of causal relationships. However, there is little enthusiasm for crude, mono-causal forms of 'effects' theory within this section of the media pessimists' camp – just a failure to grasp how seriously the dominant methodologies trap researchers into 'effects' assumptions. Stimulus variables like realism or the context of the violent imagery are nominally accepted as important, while background variables like age, gender, and socialisation history are acknowledged as affecting stimulus impact on behaviour.

Several reviewers from the USA and Canada have reached more fundamentally sceptical conclusions, notably William McGuire (1986) and Jonathan Freedman (1984) respectively. They have questioned whether the artificiality of the laboratory experiments gives these any validity for the real world, and whether the small and unreliable correlations found in naturalistic research can reveal anything about causation, once factors like socio-economic background and viewers' prior levels of aggressiveness are discounted. And, when we turn to reviews by British media researchers, opinion generally varies from those showing moderate scepticism over 'effects' data, like Gunter (1994), to stringent critics like Cumberbatch and Howitt (1989) and David Gauntlett (1995). The same tendency towards transatlantic polarisation occurs amongst reviewers of the many studies on whether the presence of violence in erotic/pornographic imagery viewed by men induces aggressive conduct or other anti-social reactions towards women.

In deference to the critics' doubts about the empirical data, 'effects' researchers now rarely claim that there are very strong relationships between exposure to violence and aggressive behaviours. Exceptions include Brandon Centerwall (1989), whose study using aggregate statistics compared the rise from around zero to saturation ownership of television sets, in North America between the early 1950s and 1975, with a corresponding leap in certain violent offences (committed by Whites). His remarkable conclusion was that: 'exposure to television is etiologically related to approximately one half of the homicides committed in the United States, or approximately 10,000 homicides annually' (p. 651). Of course, the credibility of such a causal influence hinges entirely on how adequately the analyses discounted demographic changes in age distributions, sources of socio-economic stress and so on. More typically, even the more pessimistic reviewers now infer that television's measurable 'effects' in the real world are far more modest. A figure of 3–10% is often canvassed as an estimate of the amount of variability in people's violent conduct attributable to variations in viewing violent programmes (e.g. Harris, 1994).

In recent years, statistical innovations have permitted attempts to overcome the erratic patterning of data from different studies, using 'meta-analysis' techniques to produce a kind of averaging of 'effect-size' measures. Susan Hearold (1986) integrated results from some 230 empirical studies of all kinds of screen stimuli and responses, published before 1978. Her analyses confirmed that in laboratory studies facilitation of anti-social behaviour was weakest for unjustified violence by cartoon characters, in which serious harm to victims was not shown. In contrast, strong modality images – like news footage of American soldiers – had the greatest harmful impact. Effect-sizes for pro-social programmes, which are typically *designed* to produce their observed improvements in conduct, were stronger than those where violent imagery was shown. Marked sex differences, showing greater male aggressiveness, emerged rapidly during the adolescent years.

Paik and Comstock (1994) took 217 mainly newer studies using only violent stimulus materials. Findings were generally similar; but the analyses were able to show that effect-sizes for laboratory experiments were well over twice as strong as for naturalistic correlational surveys, and that pre-school children were far more susceptible than adults. In experiments the type of programme is specified fairly precisely, so genre differences could be compared. Strong 'effects' of cartoon and fantasy material almost certainly reflect the young age of the subjects exposed to it; while potent influences from violent pornography may be attributable to the typically strong demand characteristics found in these studies, too. The weak impact of news and documentary material in this analysis versus Hearold's remains unexplained, but weaker sex differences could reflect the new presence of more aggressive female characters on screens.

Such meta-analytic investigations do confirm that, even in tightly controlled experiments, contrasts between the screen stimuli pre-schoolers are exposed to rarely explain more than a quarter of the statistical variance of their response behaviours. For adults the strength of the 'causal' relationship is roughly halved. In survey studies covering mainly later childhood and adolescence the figure is often well below 10%. Even taking the 'causal' impact of violent imagery at face value, it has real but modest impact on general audiences. Yet we are still left with the issue of validity. Efforts have been made to code some 'quality' features of the studies collated for meta-analytic treatment, although the primary criteria for inclusion are technical ones. Hearold reported the uncomfortable finding that 'the effect-size is smaller for the more ecologically valid studies' (1986, p. 95) – those with measures and situations most representative of the real world. Most seriously, she found that those most likely to be influenced by experimenter-bias factors obtained far stronger effect sizes. Those researchers who confidently predicted harmful effects found them far more often than did neutral experimenters.

Without going into further details of particular 'effects' studies, including the plausibility of their assumptions about how subjects ascribed meanings to stimulus materials and response situations, the myth of potent corrupting 'effects' already looks fragile. We are left with a predominantly transatlantic divergence regarding whether media violence has convincingly been shown to have any behaviourally significant causal impact at all. Part of the reason concerns differences in the cultural facts, and the parochial tendency to give more weight to data nearer home. Mallory Wober (1989), who is unusual amongst British media researchers in locating himself towards the 'proven harms' pole, notes that there is less evidence of British adolescents being influenced by violence in programmes, less of such content on TV, and good reason to believe that our youth are habitually less aggressive anyway. To that extent, the scope for real 'effects' may simply be weaker here. It should also be said that the understandably greater concern of Americans to find scapegoats for violence in society, and its greater salience on their screens, is likely to bias reviewers towards being less critical of findings of strong 'effects'. But, conversely, British reviewers may be less critical of research showing lesser impact of screen violence. It would be invidious to cite examples, yet both media pessimists *and* sceptics reveal imperfect scientific impartiality in which studies they single out to approve or demolish.

Yet the primary divide must involve methodological and theoretical allegiances. The USA was the home of Behaviourism and its 'effects' theory spin-offs in media research and other fields, whereas Cognitivism has always been more deep-rooted amongst British academics, who are close enough to Europe to be more influenced by its hermeneutic traditions. One might thus invoke an 'ideological' bias, which makes Americans more likely to practise and respect hard-headed experimentalism and the externalist methodology of the natural sciences. Their precise stories of how screen imagery influences us have become steadily more cognitive. Newer theories may invoke mental 'scripts' and viewers' judgements of the relevance of media scenarios for personal conduct, or 'priming' of associative mental networks by what we see, so that any threatening environmental stimulus is more likely to trigger aggression (Geen, 1994). What has not yet changed is the reluctance to talk to viewers about their thoughts and feelings. If any experiential reports are elicited, answers are likely to be counted simply as response variables – not as crucial determinants of how stimuli are assigned meaning in the first place.

## CONCLUSION: HOPES AND FEARS

The inadequacy of simple mechanistic 'effects' models for explaining how the media do normally influence us is beyond question. But that is not to deny that we can often allow ourselves to be influenced by media messages in ways which are not fully conscious, or which bypass our rational powers of critical thinking and evaluation. Indeed, the theoretical differences between academic representatives of media pessimism and media scepticism or optimism are becoming smaller. What we are left with is a confused and conflicting assemblage of empirical data. As to whether exposure to an excessive diet of screen violence can have some causal impact upon viewers, if the overall pattern of results is taken at face value, then the answer is modestly affirmative. Yet the extreme sceptics' case against this evidence cannot be ruled out entirely, since in principle the positive findings could result from methodological artefacts.

It is tempting just to conclude that one must suspend judgement until more suitable kinds of data are gathered, since neither side has yet established its case beyond reasonable doubt. However, it will be more productive to end by offering pointers for the future, initially through spelling out what sense can usefully be made of the notion of 'some causal impact'. Anyone tuning into a known TV programme wants and expects to be influenced in some sense, whether what is sought is diversion, excitement, information, education, company or whatever. Such varying and usually interwoven motives for active media consumption have long been explored under the rubric of 'uses and gratifications' research (Rubin, 1994). In so far as a programme's messages offer us the kinds of thought and feeling that we broadly anticipate and want – but with enough surprises to sustain our interest – we will find it satisfying. These are effects, of course; but the point is that their causal influence upon us only operates like that because the external stimulus input meshes with a host of equally essential mental motives and acts of appropriate kinds. Without such parts of the SCC all being provided within ourselves, the effects would be different, too.

What is so objectionable in simplistic 'media effects' hypotheses in general is not that messages influence us – but that a single and overt, albeit essential causal factor is highlighted to the apparent exclusion of so many more, equally necessary, internal causal elements. Typical empirical studies reveal so little of the complex multi-way lines of influence within SCCs for observed behaviour because they make no effort to expose processes of making meanings. In a conceptual reanalysis of a typical experiment on media-induced aggression by Zillmann, I was readily able to show how the behavioural responses obtained presupposed several dozens of mental-process events, of which he actually measured just two (Vine, 1994). The objectivist and externalist prejudices of Behaviourist methodologies leave us, after decades of empirical studies, having scarcely scratched the surface of bringing the causal dynamics of reacting to media messages into the realm of rigorous investigations.

We have reasons to worry about only *some* effects of media messages upon us. Primarily these are ones resulting in personal harms which audience members cannot be expected to foresee and control, or corresponding social harms they subsequently inflict upon others. Only then does it really make sense to blame anti-social conduct upon media stimuli, rather than on features of the offenders' own states of mind and moral choices. We may assume that next to no one would knowingly *choose* to have their rational and moral powers corrupted from without. Therefore, frightening, anger-inducing, and otherwise disruptive screen images can only be properly regarded as inherently dangerous to the extent that they *do* affect people against their will, or in unavoidably insidious ways. The pessimists are only right to talk of 'effects' in their strong sense, and to scapegoat transgressive media messages as such, if genuinely involuntary psychological changes can be demonstrated within normal audiences.

Even where younger children view adult material, the dangers have very probably been overstated. Besides, the primary solution has to lie in educating young people as critical viewers, who can weigh up a given screen message against many other sources of information and moral example. Unfortunately, mainstream screen-violence research of the kinds predominating to date has not addressed hermeneutic questions sufficiently for us to ascertain how far any of the many forms of 'violent' imagery are likely to operate in dangerous ways upon typical viewers. Nor can we say with any precision who are the most vulnerable minorities. We know from other research areas that irrational, peripheral-route persuasion can often occur – essentially because people can become content with lazy habits of processing information. But what role this plays in explaining such correlations as do arise between exposure to violent imagery and anti-social conduct is still largely a matter of guesswork.

In particular, future studies need to address whether becoming more callously desensitized towards others' suffering, or disposed towards social aggression in any of the various ways theorists have proposed, is a matter of real *inability* to resist some potent forms of peripheral persuasion. If instead it reflects poor media literacy skills or failures of moral learning within certain groups of viewers, the fault lies in our living rooms and classrooms, rather than on our television screens.

Even for vulnerable audience categories, a central theoretical point must be emphasized again. The primary factors in the causal nexus leading to harmful reactions lie within the vulnerable individual's own interpretive powers and various dispositions – such that the imagery itself is no more than an external triggering cause of any consequences. If there are occasional dramatic cases of authentic 'copy-cat' crimes which closely follow screen narratives, it is meaningless simply to equate them with ordinary imitative learning – which even young children soon start to bring under voluntary and eventually moral self-control. In all probability a host of internal predisposing causes must already be firmly in place and in favour of some category of starkly anti-social and compulsive outbursts of activity. Mostly, we can readily envisage how some alternative trigger would soon have set off some functionally similar response. Scapegoating media imagery is an easy and perhaps comforting, but ultimately futile and self-defeating, way of avoiding uncomfortable realities in our real and conflict-ridden social worlds.

The 'harmful effects' approach to the media is moribund and reactionary. If the proper development of hermeneutic and Cognitivist research and praxis on critically interpreting screen messages also makes young people more critical of the social systems which generate these, that may be more of a cause for relief than for moral panic.

## NOTES

1 But I have omitted a rather crucial piece of information. Imagery concerning a heart attack had very special significance for the girl, since her mother had suffered severe chest pains just a fortnight previously. In all probability a whole cluster of relevant thoughts and fears were still prominent in her memory, and the strong personal relevance of the scenario induced intense attention and emotional responsiveness. Nothing short of knowing the precise fragment of

relevant biography about the girl could have led to classifying her as at risk for an involuntary harmful reaction to screen 'violence'. Unless she was totally innocent of the nature of the series, or encountered the episode quite accidentally, there is little reason to suppose that other equally dramatic or graphic and gruesome scenes that can be expected within the same genre would have had any untoward consequences.

2 Bandura (1994) currently espouses a complex Cognitivist theory of media influence, in which factors like moral evaluations determine whether a model's conduct is imitated or not.

3 This is not, however, to deny that screen literacy remains imperfect amongst much older children, and that subtler aspects of the realism of what is seen on-screen may still elude some adult viewers. See also Clifford et al. (1995) and Greenfield (1984) for research on perceptual/cognitive aspects of how children interpret what they see.

4 There are many reasons for doubting just how true such claims are. Serious ambiguities and inconsistencies attach to the official crime statistics upon which the inferences are based (Bottomley and Pease, 1993). These permit politicians whose priority is to promote their own electoral agendas, or journalists in search of dramatic stories, to create highly misleading impressions according to just which data they choose to emphasise. Because the public reporting, official recording and eventual prosecution of crimes typically falls far short of their real frequency, police and court statistics are subject to many extraneous social influences which can themselves vary substantially over time. Modern increases in the recorded incidence of certain violent assaults, like rape, are undoubtedly due mostly to victims becoming more prepared to face the additional traumas of making their experiences public. Statistics for serious offences least susceptible to such sources of distortion, notably homicides, do not usually show dramatic rises. According to Jib Fowles (1992), unlawful killings in the USA were probably falling until around 1960; and subsequent increases were mainly attributable to demographic population changes. Since most crime and most violence are committed by younger males, the transition of the post-war 'baby boom' generation into adolescence may well explain that turning point.

5 Data collated by Jones et al. (1994), as cited by Hogg and Vaughan (1995, p. 362).

6 The figures were reproduced by Eugene Robinson in 'Home of the killing spree', in the magazine Hustler (UK edn, 1:2, 1994).

7 Quoted from Dodd (1958, p. 186). I am grateful to Mrs Amanda Huggon for providing me with this rather quaint example.

8 Other studies have made opposing claims, like one cited in Elizabeth Newson's (1994) report. Susan Bailey (1993) inferred from assessments of 40 adolescent murderers and over 200 sex offenders that 'repeated viewing of violent and pornographic videos' was amongst the most substantial causal factors (p. 6). My request for further clarification of her ill-specified methodology met with no response. There is no reference to comparison of viewing habits with control groups of non-offenders or non-violent offenders with comparable backgrounds.

## REFERENCES

Anon. (1994), 'Televised violence and kids: a public health problem?', ISR Newsletter, 18:1, February, pp. 5–7.

Bailey, S. M. (1993), 'Fast forward to violence', Criminal Justice Matters, 11, Spring, pp. 6–7.

Bandura, A. (1994), 'Social cognitive theory of mass communication', in J. Bryant and D. Zillmann (eds), *Media Effects: Advances in Theory and Research*, Hillsdale, NJ: Lawrence Erlbaum Associates, pp. 61–90.

Barker, M. (ed.) (1984), *The Video Nasties: Freedom and Censorship in the Media*, London: Pluto Press.

Bottomley, K. and Pease, K. (1993), *Crime and Punishment: Interpreting the Data*, Milton Keynes.: Open University Press (originally published in 1986).

Cantor, J. (1994), 'Confronting children's fright responses to mass media', in D. Zillmann, J. Bryant and A. C. Huston (eds), *Media, Children, and the Family: Social Scientific, Psychodynamic, and Clinical Perspectives*, Hillsdale, NJ: Lawrence Erlbaum Associates, pp. 139–50.

Centerwall, B. S. (1989), 'Exposure to television as a risk factor for violence', *American Journal of Epidemiology*, 129, pp. 643–52.

Clifford, B. R., Gunter, B. and McAleer, J. (1995), *Television and Children: Program Evaluation, Comprehension, and Impact*, Hove, Lawrence Erlbaum Associates.

Cumberbatch, G. and Howitt, D. (1989), *A Measure of Uncertainty: The Effects of the Mass Media*, London: John Libbey.

Dodd, E. E. (1958), *Bingley: A Yorkshire Town through Nine Centuries*: Bingley: Harrison.

Evans, J. St B. T. (1990), *Bias in Human Reasoning: Causes and Consequences*, Hove: Lawrence Erlbaum Associates.

Fowles, J. (1992), *Why Viewers Watch: A Reappraisal of Television's Effects*, rev. edn, Newbury Park, Calif.: Sage Publications.

Freedman, J. L. (1984), 'Effect of television violence on aggressiveness', *Psychological Bulletin*, 96, pp. 227–46.

Gauntlett, D. (1995), *Moving Experiences: Understanding Television's Influences and Effects*, London: John Libbey.

Geen, R. G. (1990), *Human Aggression*, Milton Keynes.: Open University Press.

Geen, R. G. (1994), 'Television and aggression: recent developments in research and theory', in D. Zillmann, J. Bryant and A. C. Huston (eds), *Media, Children, and the Family: Social Scientific, Psychodynamic, and Clinical Perspectives*, Hillsdale, NJ: Lawrence Erlbaum Associates, pp. 151–62.

Gerbner, G., Gross, L., Morgan, M. and Signorelli, N. (1994), 'Growing up with television: the cultivation perspective', in J. Bryant and D. Zillmann (eds), *Media Effects: Advances in Theory and Research*, Hillsdale, NJ: Lawrence Erlbaum Associates, pp. 17–41.

Greenfield, P. M. (1984), *Mind and Media: The Effects of Television, Video Games and Computers*, Glasgow: Fontana Paperbacks.

Gunter, B. (1994), 'The question of media violence', in J. Bryant and D. Zillmann (eds), *Media Effects: Advances in Theory and Research*, Hillsdale, NJ: Lawrence Erlbaum Associates, pp. 163–211.

Hagell, A. and Newburn, T. (1994), *Young Offenders and the Media: Viewing Habits and Preferences*, London: Policy Studies Institute.

Harris, R. J. (1994), *A Cognitive Psychology of Mass Communication*, 2nd edn, Hillsdale, NJ: Lawrence Erlbaum Associates.

Hearold, S. (1986), 'A synthesis of 1043 effects of television on social behavior', in G. Comstock (ed.), *Public Communication and Behavior*, vol. 1, Orlando, Fla: Academic Press, pp. 65–133.

Hodge, B. and Tripp, D. (1986), *Children and Television, A Semiotic Approach*, Cambridge: Polity Press.

Hogg, M. A. and Vaughan, G. M. (1995), *Social Psychology: An Introduction*, London: Prentice Hall/Harvester Wheatsheaf.

Honderich, T. (1993), *How Free Are You? The Determinism Problem*, Oxford: Oxford University Press.

Jones, B., Gray, A., Kavanagh, D., Moran, M., Norton, P. and Seldon, A. (1994), *Politics, UK*, 2nd edn, Hemel Hempstead: Harvester Wheatsheaf.

Liebert, R. M. and Sprafkin, J. (1988), *The Early Window: Effects of Television on Children and Youth*, 3rd edn, Elmsford, NY: Pergamon Press.

McCombs, M. (1994), 'News influence on our pictures of the world', in J. Bryant and D. Zillmann (eds), *Media Effects: Advances in Theory and Research*, Hillsdale, NJ: Lawrence Erlbaum Associates, pp. 1–16.

McGuire, W. J. (1986), 'The myth of massive media impact: savagings and salvagings', in G. Comstock (ed.), *Public Communication and Behavior*, vol. 1, Orlando, Fla: Academic Press, pp. 173–257.

Newson, E. (and 25 co-signatories) (1994), 'Video violence and the protection of children', University of Nottingham, March (reprinted as Memorandum 13 in House of Commons Home Affairs Committee, *Video Violence and Young Offenders*, Session 1993–4, Fourth Report, London: HMSO, pp. 45–59).

Nisbett, R. E. and Ross, L. (1980), *Human Inference: Strategies and Shortcomings of Social Judgment*, Englewood Cliffs, NJ: Prentice-Hall.

Orne, M. T. (1962), 'On the social psychology of the psychological experiment: with particular reference to "demand" characteristics and their implications', *American Psychologist*, 17, pp. 776–83.

Paik, H. and Comstock, G. (1994), 'The effects of television violence on antisocial behavior: a meta-analysis', *Communication Research*, 21, pp. 515–46.

Petty, R. E. and Priester, J. R. (1994), 'Mass media attitude change: implications of the elaboration likelihood model of persuasion', in J. Bryant and D. Zillmann (eds), *Media Effects: Advances in Theory and Research*, Hillsdale, NJ: Lawrence Erlbaum Associates, pp. 91–122.

Phillips, D. P. (1986), 'The found experiment: a new technique for assessing the impact of mass media violence on real-world aggressive behavior', in G. Comstock (ed.), *Public Communication and Behavior*, vol. 1, Orlando, Fla.: Academic Press, pp. 259–307.

Rosenthal, R. (1966), *Experimenter Effects in Behavioral Research*, New York: Appleton-Century-Crofts.

Rubin, A. M. (1994), 'Media uses and effects: a uses-and-gratifications perspective', in J. Bryant and D. Zillmann (eds), *Media Effects: Advances in Theory and Research*, Hillsdale, NJ: Lawrence Erlbaum Associates, pp. 417–36.

Turner, C. W., Hesse, B. W. and Peterson-Lewis, S. (1986), 'Naturalistic studies of the long-term effects of television violence', *Journal of Social Issues*, 42:3, 1986, pp. 51–73.

Van Evra, J. (1990), *Television and Child Development*, Hillsdale, NJ: Lawrence Erlbaum Associates.

Vine, I. (1994), 'Illusory causes and "harmful" effects: or why the media effects research tradition has failed us', paper to conference on 'The "Effects" Tradition – Its Problems, Politics and Supersession', West Drayton, Middlesex, 26–7 November.

Wober, J. M. (1989), 'Screen violence: a psychologist's view', *The Psychologist*, 4, pp. 162–5.

Zillmann, D., Bryant, J. and Carveth, R. A. (1981), 'The effects of erotica featuring sadomasochism and bestiality on motivated intermale aggression', *Personality and Social Psychology Bulletin*, 7, pp. 153–9.

# Chapter 9

# On going public

One of the most common complaints of serious media researchers concerns what happens when we 'go public'. What happens when we try to inform the public what our research is finding? What happens, importantly, when research on the media and its audiences contradicts 'common sense'? And what happens, most crucially of all, when the publication of research coincides with a current moral campaign? There is hardly a happy tale to be told, anywhere. The short reports which follow summarise what happened in three cases, and make some simple recommendations to those who may – no, must – come after.

## GOING PUBLIC WITH *YOUNG OFFENDERS AND THE MEDIA*

*Ann Hagell and Tim Newburn*

In April 1994, we published a short paperback report presenting the results of a comparison of the viewing and reading habits of a group of 78 offenders aged 10–16 and a representative sample of over 500 schoolchildren of the same age. The primary purpose of the research was to provide basic factual information on which a more reasoned discussion of the role of the media in young people's lives might take place. We have always emphasised that this limited piece of work did not consider possible links between viewing habits and criminal behaviour. Rather, its main aims were: first, to examine whether there were differences in the viewing habits of young offenders and their peers; second, to look at differences in viewing preferences; and, finally, to look at how television and viewing fitted into these children's lives.

One of the main strengths of the study was the offending sample, who had all been arrested several times within one year. They had, on average, nearly eleven offences attributed to them within that year, most commonly non-residential burglary, road traffic violations, criminal damage and theft from shops. They were all personally interviewed, providing background information as well as details about viewing habits. As far as we knew, the size of the sample and the frequency of the juveniles' offending made the study unique.

The research revealed few differences in the viewing habits of young offenders and schoolchildren. Soap operas and similar dramas dominated the television choices of both sets of children. The boys in both samples nominated the same favourite film: *Terminator II*. Offenders did not watch more television or select more violent programmes or films than schoolchildren generally. Importantly, but hardly surprisingly, it was found that offenders were more likely than schoolchildren to have disrupted living circumstances and to come from poorer backgrounds. Lack of money and household disruption led to fewer television sets within their households, and they had less access to videos and other such equipment than other children. This may have accounted for the fact that the young offenders seemed less interested in both written and visual media than the comparison group.

Our main point in presenting the study to the media was that television, video and film viewing had to be understood in the context of the sorts of life young offenders lead. Our results did not suggest that violent videos were watched more by young offenders, and neither group viewed so-called 'video nasties'. Therefore to maintain that violent videos were to blame for a perceived rise (which may not be actual) in juvenile crime was far too simplistic.

In retrospect, there were two striking features of the story of 'going public' with our report. The first was the relationship of the project to the sponsors. It was funded, as most projects are, with specific agendas in mind, and the management of its publicity inevitably reflected this. The second was timing, in terms of the broader context of the media's preoccupations at the time. We were initially funded by the British Board of Film Classification (BBFC), who were aware that we were involved in research on young offenders. They were under some pressure as a result of a brief furore over, amongst other films, *Silence of the Lambs* and wanted to commission research that would shed some light on what 'young criminals' liked to watch. The BBFC were eventually joined by the BBC, BSC (Broadcasting Standards Council) and ITC (Independent Television Commission) as co-sponsors of the research. Essentially, they, too, wanted to know what young offenders liked to view. The fact that they, and the media, were actually primarily interested in violent offenders was a problem, as our sample was typical of young offenders and as such did not include many individuals with records of violence. The confusion between young offenders and violent teenagers was one that recurred again and again in the process of 'going public', and still remains.

The media furore over the murder of James Bulger, and the impending trial of Robert Thompson and Jon Venables, gave renewed impetus to public concern over the role of the media in juvenile crime. At least one of our sponsors saw the funding of this research project as a way of indicating publicly that it was taking the whole issue seriously. At the outset of the project, a press release from one of the funders announced its commencement and the expected date of publication later in the year. This set the media up to expect something from us, and the project was referred to in the press and in the House of Commons several times in the year before publication. At the time of publication, the BBFC hosted and chaired the press conference that launched the report and issued their own press release.

We, at the Policy Studies Institute (PSI), separately press-released the report with a somewhat different slant from the BBFC. Attempting to keep some control over the way in which the research was presented to the public was therefore a central concern for us.

By chance our release coincided with Elizabeth Newson's publication of her 'report' on 1 April. We had already decided on a publication in April at this point, and had no idea that Professor Newson was going to enter the debate at around the same time. Media interest was fuelled by the apparent but totally unintended confrontation between the two reports. Then Liberal Democrat MP David Alton announced an attempt to amend the law relating to the home rental of videos, and a Commons debate on the Criminal Justice Bill was thus timetabled – for several days before our planned publication. Given that one of PSI's stated aims is to contribute to policy debates, to publish several days *after* such a debate would have been a failure, and might have made us look slightly foolish. Publication was therefore brought forward to the day before the debate.

Given the timing of the report, the response by the media was overwhelming. Anticipating this, we had employed the services of a public relations company, as it seemed likely that our press office's resources would be stretched. After the BBFC's press conference, dominated by the media-friendly presence of James Ferman, we spent the day in front of television cameras, in radio stations and, in between times, in the PR company's office, eating promotional tubs of Ben and Jerry's ice cream and waiting for the next call.

All the major stations and papers carried the story on the day of publication. Comment fell into two broad categories. Either our research provided a balanced response to Newson's more emotive position and highlighted the scapegoating by the media of a problem really caused by more complex social factors; or our research did not and could not answer the question about whether watching violent videos caused criminal behaviour, and was therefore irrelevant. The primary problem with both these positions was that they talked of 'causes'. We endlessly reiterated that our research was not about causes. Our starting point was that the majority of debate was based on the untested and unsupported assumption that violent offenders watched and liked more violent material than other children. Our research, though small-scale, was important for the simple reason that it provided some rigorous information about what young people actually watch and like. Equally important was the fact that the research highlighted what was really different about the lives of young offenders. Used properly, therefore, it provided the opportunity to inject a note of sanity into an increasingly hysterical debate. Needless to say, our voices of caution, casting doubt on the likely efficacy of further increasing levels of censorship, were often drowned out by others screaming in populist outrage.

David Alton and the Home Secretary, Michael Howard (who was against further censorship, but also did not want to be defeated in the Commons), reached an eleventh-hour compromise. Howard promised to bring forward various changes relating to videos, and Alton withdrew his amendment to the Criminal Justice Bill. James Ferman, the most vocal of our sponsors, suddenly went silent (well, quiet), whilst the details of a 'workable compromise' were hammered out. The eventual changes included tougher penalties for retailers or distributors who sold or hired unclassified videos, and new obligations for the BBFC when considering classifications for films. All without reference to any research evidence. 'No way to run a video shop, let alone a sentient legislature,' commented the *Guardian* (10 April 1994).

There were several lessons that we would draw from this episode. First, we were and will continue to be selective in our choice of journalists to whom we respond. Some sorts of publicity are important to PSI. We are entirely grant-funded, so publicising the nature of our research is vital in maintaining the sort of public profile we need if we are to sustain ourselves. Not all publicity is good publicity however. Given that in this particular case our research was going to be publicly discussed even if we did not talk to a single journalist, it was important that we dived in and tried to manage the publicity rather than responding in a passive manner. We generally refused to do chat shows or other programmes that we felt would not help further the debate (such as the Granada television 'trial' of media research). However, we did take part in a *Newsnight* debate where the quality of discussion was likely to be high, and also a short debate on Sky television with Sir Ivan Lawrence, MP, chair of the Home Affairs Select Committee. We refused, fairly early in the proceedings, before publication, to be involved with a BBC television programme about crime and the media because of concerns we had about editorial control. Media training alerted us to the importance of understanding what the journalist's aims are in producing the article or programme.

Second, any very public discussion of your work is likely to get personal, and it might help to be prepared for this. Obviously this was the case with Elizabeth Newson ('The 64-year-old professor of child psychology . . . wears a smile that has won the trust of generations of young mothers and their offspring. . . . Much of her own leisure time is spent with her grandchildren . . .', as one sympathetic journalist wrote in the *Daily Telegraph*, 2 April 1994). It was a surprise for one of us to be similarly profiled ('She [Hagell] was not the only cinema-goer in the country to leave halfway through *The Cook, the Thief, His Wife and Her Lover*, although her squeamish early exit during a screening of *Gremlins* reveals a rather more delicate constitution', *Guardian*, 13 April 1994). The press are far more interested than the academic community in the juxtaposition of you with the work you do. Women doing research on violence are more interesting than men doing similar work, and we received many requests for a female to balance studio discussions and satisfy producers' half-hearted political correctness about the male/female ratios on the screen.

Third, we learned to be clear and positive about what the research showed, and to speak in media-talk. It is important to swallow your academic wordiness and produce a couple of punchy lines to repeat. One of the statements we used – 'The results of this research reinforce my view that those who blame the media for crime are on a doomed mission in search of a simple solution to a complex problem' – was repeated in almost every article that mentioned the research. Similarly, the comment that 'I was overwhelmed by the sadness of their lives rather than the badness of them' was much repeated. We prepared responses to most of the questions we thought we were likely to be asked, and practised these on tape and on video with professional help. We had two or three sentences summing up what we found and how this fitted into the debate, and this is usually all you will have time for.

Fourth, some advice for those that actually want publicity: find a hook for your work and present it to the media as a *fait accompli*. In our case, the hook was provided by Professor Newson and the Alton amendment. Juvenile offending is usually newsworthy. However, even with pieces of research that are less obviously exciting to journalists, timing and context are going to be all-important.

Finally, grit your academic teeth and get the help of professionals. At PSI, we find media training very helpful and it is part of our ongoing staff development. The services of a PR company probably also increased our control over how the research was presented, as the company were prepared to fight battles on our behalf about misrepresentation of our work, and they already had personal contacts with journalists, as well as talking the same language.

## GOING PUBLIC WITH *CHILDREN AND VIOLENCE*

*Julian Petley*

In 1993, in the wake of the murder of James Bulger and the national soulsearching which followed it, the Gulbenkian Foundation conceived the idea of a commission which would look into the whole question of children and violence. Its seventeen members included representatives of the National Society for the Prevention of Cruelty to Children, Save the Children, the National Children's Bureau, Young Minds, the Council for Disabled Children, and the writers Penelope Leach and Claire Rayner.

The aims of the commission were to 'provide as accurate a picture as possible of the level of all kinds of violence to and by children and young people' and to 'propose ways of challenging social and legal endorsement of any form of inter-personal violence and policies and practices which tend to increase violence involving children and young people' (Gulbenkian Foundation, 1995, p. 4).

The commission's report, *Children and Violence*, was published in November 1995. It made a series of recommendations under five main headings. The first, 'Making a commitment to non-violence', argued that we need to 'work towards a society in which individuals, communities and government share non-violent values and resolve conflict by non-violent means' (ibid., p. 13). This would involve

> understanding the factors which interact to increase the potential for violence involving children, and those which prevent children from becoming violent; action to prevent violence in all services which work with families and children; and consistent disavowal of all forms of inter-personal violence – in particular by opinion-leaders.
>
> (ibid., pp. 13–14)

Furthermore, all relationships involving the care and education of children should be based on non-violent principles, such as: 'all discipline should be positive, and children should be taught pro-social values and behaviour, including in particular non-violent conflict resolution', and 'non-violence should be clearly and consistently preferred and promoted' (ibid., p. 14).

Under the second heading, 'Legal reforms', the commission made a number of recommendations designed to 'remove legal tolerance for any level of violence to children, and to ensure that responses to violent behaviour contribute to violence prevention, rather than to the problem of violence' (ibid., p. 21).

Among other things this would: remove the common-law defence of 'reasonable chastisement' in so far as it justifies physical punishment or other humiliating treatment; introduce laws which would provide a definition of parental responsibility, and of parental rights necessary to exercise that responsibility, based on the principles of the UN Convention on the Rights of the Child; ensure that the criminal justice system for under-18-year-olds complied with the UN Convention and relevant UN instruments; raise the age of criminal responsibility to at least 14 throughout the UK; require institutions that dealt with children to implement anti-bullying policies; and strongly discourage children's involvement in boxing.

The third set of recommendations was grouped under the heading 'Support and services for children and families'. This noted that 'inequality, discrimination and lack of appropriate support and services for children and families all increase the potential for violence', and recommended 'urgent and concerted government action to challenge the extent and growth of child poverty in the UK' (ibid., p. 23), proper financial support for working parents, provision of good-quality day-care for all who seek it, the rapid expansion of pre-school education, the recognition of non-violence as a priority within the curriculum, the provision of adequate play and leisure opportunities for children, the establishment by the Department of Health of a programme of violence-prevention based on research and sufficient resources to ensure that child victims of violence were properly compensated and rehabilitated.

The fourth group of recommendations concerned 'Other issues'. These included raising the tax on alcohol to make it less attractive to children, setting up a UK-wide review of law, policy and practice relating to child deaths and trying to reduce suicides and attempted suicides by young people. This section also included recommendations on the media. Here the media were urged to promote pro-social behaviour and non-violent conflict resolution and to discourage inter-personal violence; the BBFC was urged to monitor the effectiveness of its classification schemes; broadcasters were encouraged to observe rigorously the evening watershed, and to provide viewers with warnings about violent scenes, especially in non-fiction programmes; and finally: 'all teachers and schools should seek increased critical understanding by pupils of the new communications technologies: the importance of this should be reflected in arrangements for the curriculum throughout the UK' (ibid., p. 26).

Under the fifth heading, 'Information and research on violence involving children', the commission recommended all relevant government departments to commission a review of available information on levels of violence to and by children in the UK, and recommended the appropriate research bodies to undertake a review of the antecedents of violence in children.

Quite clearly, then, this was an extremely wide-ranging piece of work, undertaken by members of diverse, reputable and highly authoritative organisations. This is not the impression given by press coverage of the report. Things started off unpromisingly when the *Telegraph* broke the Gulbenkian's embargo, and this may have made it more difficult for the organisation to manage the report's official release. On the other hand, the report's measured and liberal tones may simply have offended Fleet Street's finest, who decided to rubbish it. Whatever the case, the report is barely recognisable from many papers' accounts of it. Almost without exception the national daily press focused on the smacking issue which, though important in the context of the report's discussion of forms of domestic violence, is given nothing remotely like the prominence which the press afforded it, and takes up only nine of the report's 300 pages. Admittedly certain newspapers focused on the smacking issue in a reasonably balanced way, giving space to arguments both for and against, but this does not obviate the fact that their coverage of the subject was out of all proportion to the place which it occupies in the report itself.

It is extremely hard to avoid the conclusion that, for certain newspapers, *Children and Violence* was simply a pretext for a tirade against the hated 'liberal values'. For example, the *Daily Express* on 10 November devoted a front-page article to it under the heading 'Fury at call to ban smacking', and although, in an inside double-page spread, the paper does give space to both proponents and opponents of smacking and covers other aspects of the report more fully than most other papers, there can be little doubt where its real interests, and sympathies, lie. These become especially clear in its editorial, entitled 'A soft road to violent crime', which calls the report a 'jargon-laden hymn to social engineering and political correctness' in which 'every fashionable liberal hobby-horse is ridden into the ground'. Similarly the same day's *Telegraph* covered a number of the report's recommendations, but critics of the report were more numerous that supporters, and the headline over the main story, 'Report attacked over call to stop hitting children', reflected more accurately the main thrust of that story than that of the report itself. And, later in the week, the paper gave Ann Davis, the child-minder who won a legal battle against Sutton council over the right to smack, a whole article to herself in which to attack the report (she also featured prominently in the earlier *Telegraph* piece).

The *Telegraph* and *Express*, however, were far more balanced in their coverage than *The Times*, the *Sun* and the *Mail*, in which opinion almost entirely replaced reportage. The *Sun* devoted an editorial to the subject which stated that

> the busybodies are at it again. And they are so, so wrong. . . . They cannot see that the yob society has been caused by the trendy claptrap that has been preached since the Sixties. . . . Society has gone soft and we are paying the price.
>
> (10 November 1995)

Similarly *The Times* ignored the report in its news columns but devoted no less than two opinion pieces to it – one by Libby Purves on 11

November and another by Janet Daley on 26 October, both predictably hostile. Even this, however, was preferable to the *Mail* of 10 November, which ran what can only be described as a long editorial in the guise of a news story under the headline 'Report that's a smack in the face for common sense'. What is most extraordinary, however, about this biased, jaundiced piece is that it has the gall to attack the BBC Radio 4 programme *Today* for covering the report in a detailed and balanced fashion! Thus we find gripes about 'the same liberal agenda, the same reverence from the BBC' and the complaint that 'predictably the "progressive" agenda mapped out by the team of social workers, academics and childcare professionals captured the headlines on BBC Radio 4's *Today* programme'. The *Mail* also ran a full-page article by the former Chief Rabbi Lord Jakobovits under the curious headline 'I smacked my children because I love them' (although not as curious as 'I hit my children because I love them' which is how the article is trailed elsewhere in the paper). Here the report is attacked as 'deeply flawed' and as having a 'biased agenda' – unlike the *Mail* itself, of course. Jakobovits confesses himself 'taken aback by the weak and fashionably permissive tone it adopts', though he is unsurprised by its 'limp conclusions' given the 'politically correct composition' of the commission.

It's 'reporting' such as this which makes one doubt that certain newspapers would have covered *Children and Violence* accurately, however carefully the Gulbenkian Foundation had handled its release. It's also extremely significant that virtually no coverage at all was given to the report's comments on the media, and it's very hard to avoid the conclusion that these were not what the press wanted to hear – unlike, of course, those of Professor Newson. Indeed, the report even has the temerity to suggest that the Newson document 'made insufficient reference to criticisms of the methodology of the research' which it cited, and actually dares to quote approvingly Martin Barker's and others' reply to Newson, which was totally ignored by the national press, with the exception of Richard Boston in the *Guardian*. Nor was a sensation- and scapegoat-hungry press likely to be attracted by sentiments such as the following:

the Commission does not subscribe to the view that media violence is a major factor in the development of violent attitudes and actions. A particular focus on violent videos such as we have seen recently in the UK can distract attention from other more potent factors, including in particular children's direct experiences of violence in the home. A useful debate about causes and prevention of violence involving children is hindered by the sort of misinformation about the role of particular videos which followed the Bulger trial and two other brutal murders in 1993.

(ibid., p. 202)

It's a sad comment on the British press that it so comprehensively failed to cover the Gulbenkian report accurately, adequately or fairly. The overwhelming concentration on one aspect of the report at the expense of all others illustrates all too clearly the rat-pack nature of British journalism, with its pre-set agendas and ideological blinkers. In this context at least, the possibilities for serious debate about the role of the media in modern life, or about anything else for that matter, remain strictly limited.

## References

Gulbenkian Foundation (1995), *Children and Violence*, London: Gulbenkian Foundation.

## TAKING ON THE MEDIA

*Bill Thompson*

In 1989 I had just secured my first permanent job, had a PhD to publish, and had brought the house down in my first international academic conference. Then I met the media. I was not completely naïve, having already been rolled a couple of times by those who prefer a good 'story' to the truth; but I was to learn so much more.

The year before, Gregg Barak, in a *Justice Quarterly* article, had encouraged criminologists to become media pro-active (Barak, 1988). He believed that proffering expertise rather than avoiding interviews could help create a more realistic assessment of society than that offered by the sensationalist media. Although sceptical of Barak's aspirations that interventions could alter public attitudes, and thereby establish a credible voice in policy formation, I have always believed that all social scientists, being 'privileged observers', have a responsibility to offer a rational alternative to the various vested interests which exploit the media for their own ends.

If we discount fear and lack of access, which can be easily overcome, the major reason social scientists have ignored or shied away from the media is the obvious difficulty in presenting complex concepts, research and theories within the typical media frames. As Weiss and Singer have noted, reporters can strip social science of its meaning and recast it, creating a completely different product (Weiss and Singer, 1988, p. 2). Amongst the most annoying results are the over-interpretation of statistics and correlations, and the simplistic presentation of concepts like 'aggression', 'arousal' and 'habituation'; though there are many more (see Baker, 1987; Barrile, 1984; Benderly, 1989; Ericson, 1991; Fishman, 1980; Wong and Alexander, 1991).

Perhaps the first and most important lesson to learn is that our media contribution amounts to a political act whether we realise it or not. Consequently, while I would encourage every social scientist to follow the advice in the Economic and Social Research Council's *Pressing Home Your Findings*, a comparison of the approaches adopted by myself, and a friend and colleague, Dr Cecil Greek of South Florida University, might provide even more valuable lessons.

Impressed by Barak's advice, Greek's media 'career' began with him signing up on his university's and the American Sociological Association's media contact lists. In order to overcome the major problem of access, he also joined the local boards of the American Civil Liberties Union (ACLU) and Friends of the First Amendment, invited local crime reporters to address his classes, and then issued press releases related to his research, employing 'teasers' for the local news media. These initial efforts paid off. Apart from interviews by newspaper and TV journalists, appearances on radio and TV talk-shows, and having his views at public forums reported, Greek developed numerous contacts. His appearance rate soared from one or two per year to between ten and twenty. But everyone appeared to be interested in only two topics: community corrections and pornography policy.

The corrections issue, centring around the usual probation/paroled recidivist shock-horror stories, presented several difficulties, but Greek utilised his opportunities to place such cases in the wider perspective and promote rational discussion about cost-effective community-based alternatives to prisons. In this way, he was able to make an impact and widen the otherwise narrow debate. His excursion into the second issue was not as successful. Not only was he battling with the ever-popular sex-crime stories (Zoglin, 1992), but living in Florida ensured that Greek had his hands full. At the turn of the decade, a moral crusade was led by the American Family Association and local Republican politicians seeking re-election, which targeted the 2 Live Crew stage-show, workplace centre-folds, adult entertainment, T-back bathing suits worn on the beach or by hot-dog vendors on the highways, Pee Wee Herman and Madonna's *Sex*.

Greek again sought to encourage rational discussion by countering the usual myths and horror stories about the content, nature and effects of the 'adult entertainment' industry. Greek's interviews, however, did not go as he anticipated; not only did he make mistakes, he also walked into several 'ambushes'. The first difficulty followed from agreeing to do as many interviews as possible. His aim was rational enough: to learn from experience, by noting which standard mistakes go with which media format. While one can get away with brightly coloured socks and hiking shoes on radio, they detract from contributions when sitting on a couch in front of TV cameras. Though he could quickly remedy this, 'ambushes' set by opponents are more difficult to eradicate. One of Greek's worst occurred during the taping of the half-hour-long programme *Pro and*

*Con*, on which Greek was the only guest. Having agreed to discuss Federal sponsorship of controversial art shows, like the Cincinnati Robert Mapplethorpe show, Greek was fazed when, half-way through, the host suddenly began to bait him by accusing the ACLU of removing prayer and Bible reading from public schools, and of defending gays in the military. These questions were not within Greek's expertise, so he remained cool and simply but politely remained adamant about returning to the original topics. The next, very common, problem Greek faced was over-estimating the honesty of fellow participants. On one show, covering the volatile issue of adult video stores, the producers held a pre-broadcast meeting in the hope that establishing ground rules would ensure a rational discussion. This went well, with a local member of the American Family Association having several erroneous beliefs (e.g., that a proposed Ordinance was already law) corrected, and everyone present agreeing to avoid the red herring of child pornography. Yet once the programme started the AFA member not only repeated his erroneous assertions, he kept talking over Greek's comments by shouting: 'The ACLU supports child pornography!'

Otherwise, Greek faced the common trials and tribulations such as having segments from public speeches quoted out of context by newspaper columnists wishing to present his rational views in a poor light, and finding his 'teasers' printed without a follow-up interview. Perhaps his most unexpected experience was finding his contribution on civil liberties issues being used as 'voice-over' on filler clips featuring nude dancers!

**Personal experience**

In contrast to Greek, my media involvement began by accident. Being at media-aware Reading University, where the Sociology Department fills a considerable number of column inches and broadcasting minutes each year, I have the help of a good PR department which monitors coverage, and an administration which accepts controversy as long as the contribution is supported by genuine research.

Following my attendance at the Liberty AGM in 1989, I organised a small project team at Reading in order to test two assertions made by political activists seeking to justify a motion supporting stringent controls on sexually oriented material: the first was that British pin-up magazines contained increasingly violent imagery; the second was that social scientific research had demonstrated a clear link between consumption of this material and the commission of sex crimes. Having just spent ten years following moral crusades against sex shops and video nasties, ploughing through research data on media effects, completing a content analysis of European hard-core material, and clerking for a barrister specialising in obscenity trials, I held a contrary impression; but with the help of half a dozen students set out to quantify British content over the last thirty years, and to review thoroughly the effects literature.

The subsequent Reading study, and four reports which followed, clearly demonstrated that British material was completely non-violent, that European content had become less violent and that the research literature gave soft-core material a clean bill of health. This attracted considerable media attention. I quickly discovered that one is not allowed to maintain a 'disinterested position', to dare to be 'objective', or to let the results speak for themselves when your research can feed into an emotive debate. At best, the media wanted me to take sides in 'the pornography debate'; at worst they insinuated that I already had. At various times I was accused of being in the pay of porn barons, and our hard data was frequently ignored in order to justify the media's sensational 'panic approach' to the subject. This gross misrepresentation of the study culminated in me being 'door-stepped' by someone claiming to represent a tabloid, following an appearance on TV, threatening to expose me as 'Dr Dirt', complete with a collection of snuff movies, a diary full of orgies and doubtlessly sexually harassing my female students, if not selling them into White Slavery. Their claim that they had pictures to prove this was obviously bogus; but, given their knowledge of my movements, someone had been tracking me for some time. Such allegations are now water off a duck's back as the threat of such 'exposures' is ever-present – my work on the Spanner judgement led to rumours that I was really a gay sadomasochist, and my activities debunking the Satanic panic led to charges of being a baby-eating Satanist; but, in some quarters, mud sticks.

This attempt at character assassination occurred despite the fact that, in contrast to Greek, my media involvement has been completely passive. I have never issued a press release or initiated contact with a journalist, though I am registered on my university's and the CIBA Foundation contact list. It occurred because the Reading study – born of a rigorous methodology, open to peer review and supplied to anyone who asked – embarrassed those whose case against publications featuring nudity rested upon erroneous assertions. It was these people rather than the media who attempted to undermine my credibility.

During the same period, however, I saw some fellow academics engage in gross misrepresentation, exaggeration and obfuscation in order to promote their political agendas; align themselves with vested interests and agencies of social control; and attempt to manipulate public discussion by trying to lay down the rules of debate to programmers by refusing to appear if a knowledgeable person 'from the other side' did. As a result, the 'public' debate about an important issue was a disgrace.

It finally came to the point where I had to threaten legal action against one programme promoting one 'academic' view who had revealed their intentions in a phone call which I had fortunately recorded. Ultimately, such attacks and consequences – which included losing several publishing deals – became so dire I was finally forced to go on the counter-attack in a book *Soft-core* (1994) which, while actually targeting the low academic standards and poor practice of my detractors, will inevitably be read as 'taking sides'.

It was time to move on. I had been tracking the rise of Satanic abuse allegations since 1984, owing to my interest in the social and political use of social group urban legends. Academic conference papers led to invitations on talk-shows, and interviews for news reports from March 1991. My reviews of the interview tapes and other material in Britain's largest cases confirmed what I had deduced from the American experience: the children were neither lying nor telling the truth; they were being coerced into making allegations. Once again, media appearances led to hate mail and character assassination at the hands of evangelical Christians, social workers, ideologically motivated journalists and therapists with a vested interest.

In both cases, I had striven to inform the public debate by drawing attention to major issues that should be considered before deciding policy: in the case of the pornography, highlighting the simplistic application of research studies and bogus claims about content; in the case of Satanic abuse allegations, the possibility of interviewers with prior convictions inducing children to confirm them.

During Easter 1991, I spent up to ten hours a day, over a four-week period, fielding questions from numerous media sources on any and every aspect of the 'Satanic abuse controversy'. Contrary to the uninitiated's imagination, this media contact is far from glamorous. In many cases programme researchers will ring to save themselves time, and trying to find 'angles' rather than grasp the complexity of some issues. While I was happy to oblige, being mindful that I was paid by the public purse, I discovered that others, far less knowledgeable, were securing consultancy fees for the same service. Some media are far more responsible. When a national paper envisaged running a series of articles and had their journalists repeatedly checking aspects of the stories with me, I was offered a more than generous fee which helped fund my own investigations; and that is how it should be.

In contrast to Greek's experience of finding segments quoted out of context, I have more often found my contributions 'pulled' from programmes, as I can be quite dogmatic about contextualising my comments, knowing some material will be cut. This makes it difficult to use 'soundbites'; hence they are pulled. If I find myself rambling, or being too simplistic, I simply say 'Cut'; and insist on filming it again. No matter how careful you are, however, you are not the programme-maker: they have the final say. Despite constantly trying, I have never managed to get my suggestion, made in the original Reading study, that top-shelf material may have a 'normalising effect' – when it comes to once-taboo sexual practices – aired on the screen; such a view does not square with the pro-/anti polarisation such programmes like to take. Everyone will be 'pulled' at one time or another, simply because the needs of a programme can change. My best filmed interview ever, for *Newsnight* on the nature of drug panics over the years, was 'pulled' simply because by the time it reached the studio the 'balance' of studio guests had changed. This has to be accepted. What is not acceptable is the political manipulation of contributions. My most irritating experience in this area was having the whole of my contribution pulled from a *This Week* programme entitled *Pornography and Violence*. It was not just the time I lost, nor even that the production team obviously found the results were too awkward for their general approach; what annoyed me was that in my place another 'academic' appeared, with a desk full of top-shelf material, asserting that her recent trawl demonstrated growing violent trends. The makers of this programme clearly misled the public regarding the nature of contemporary research.

Amongst the obvious lessons to be learnt from the Thompson–Greek experience is to keep to subjects you have researched yourself or have an extensive teaching background in. I never agree to discuss, let alone debate, issues that I am not conversant with. I may proffer an overview, but I prefer to suggest a viable alternative 'expert'. While this can easily annoy some young programme researcher or journalist facing a deadline, it also gains some respect in the profession. As a consequence, I have enjoyed regular appearances on programmes such as Radio 5 Live's *Magazines* and BBC Wales' *Week In: Week Out*; and must be one of the few 'straights' trusted by the gay press.

To achieve this, one should be prepared with simple explanations of scientific terms and presentations of figures that do not misrepresent their findings when completing research. I never assume that even a chief correspondent will necessarily know what I do, though I dare not patronise such people, either; they frequently know far more about the ramifications of issues and the other players than an academic would.

As part of your preparation, research your 'programme'. Know its style and format; and remember, different programmes require different responses. Be aware of how the debate is likely to be framed, but do not be bamboozled. If you think an issue is important or vital, say so. Explain why you think the frame they are using is erroneous.

It is not unusual for TV researchers to want much more time, effectively picking your brains rather than doing their own research. This can always pose a dilemma. If you do not offer the time, there may be no counter to erroneous beliefs shaping the programme; but you could find yourself wasting hours. One experience that always made an impression upon me concerned a nationally renowned academic who was obviously pleased a programme researcher had been so interested in his painstaking research on the 'underclass'. What he had failed to secure from the researcher was not only a fee, but an indication of the programme's particular format and footage. This turned out to be constant sweeps and close-ups of a large council-housing estate, where the residents, far from being members of an underclass, were proud of the number of those taking up their 'right to buy' and attempts to curb the problems found on many other estates. The end result of the programme was local uproar, and another boost to the popular image of sociologists knowing everything about nothing.

If you are not quite sure of your ground or data, but know you have a contribution to make, take Greek's advice: make an excuse to call the journalist back, do a little research and prepare some sound-bites, or snappy but comprehensive quotes. Do not leave it too late, because they are working to deadlines. While this can not eliminate misquotes, it can dramatically reduce them in number. Greek also reminds us that newspaper journalists should not be treated with scorn, for they are often better prepared than their electronic media counterparts. They are usually more thorough than TV journalists because they have more time, if not collecting 'hard-news' quotes, and being assigned to the same areas are often better-informed about their stories.

Television interviews and talk-shows are more difficult because of the visual dimension. Greek reminds us that we also need to recognise the way the TV camera has fundamentally changed public speaking in that it reveals you face-to-face with the mass audience. As a result, TV viewers receive clues to a person's attitudes and state of mind that are hidden on radio. You therefore have to pay much more attention to advance preparation and 'on-camera demeanour'. Greek suggests we should be more cautious in accepting requests for TV interviews and, prior to agreeing, ask a reporter the following questions: What is the purpose of the interview? What type of interview will it be, e.g., live or taped? Will the video-tape be edited or broadcast in its entirety? Why have I been selected? Who will be conducting the interview? What is the technical and physical setting of the interview? How long will the interview be? Who will the audience be? (see Blythin and Samovar, 1985, p. 180). Likewise, he is correct to note that it is not inappropriate to ask the interviewer to agree to ground rules.

When it comes to an open debate, your preparation should include finding out who the other interviewees/guests will be and their perspectives, preparing answers to all questions you think you might be asked – interviewers will often discuss this with you, as they need to know your perspective. If you are facing a one-on-one and are not familiar with the interviewer, you must expect any type of questioning, including the following: false facts; reinterpretation of your response; putting words in your mouth; false assumptions or conclusions; hypothetical premises; baiting you into accusations; leading questions; multiple-part questions; forced-choice questions; and loaded questions. On talk-shows other guests may try to use these techniques against you if they disagree with your position.

To overcome the problem of presenting intellectually oriented material to a mass audience, Blythin and Samovar (1988, pp. 188–93) suggest the following techniques for media presentation: start with your main point first; be brief; relate to your audience; be accurate; do not flaunt your expertise; do not be evasive; stay calm, even during difficult moments; make effective use of language; try to establish and maintain your personal credibility.

If the situation turns into a debate or heated discussion, the following suggestions may prove helpful: be quick to identify which questions are being used to bait you and which are legitimate; never allow incorrect statements to stand – respond to them immediately, otherwise the audience will believe they are true; avoid debating, by being the rational and calm one; do not repeat negative questions, and make only positive points; be very cautious in the use of statistics, never using more than two per sentence, preferably in the same 'denomination' and as points of comparison. Be aware that your more experienced 'opponents' will probably engage in 'creative confrontation' – making sure that they go first in a potential debate, being very well prepared and 'grabbing' all the good points for themselves (Schmertz, 1986).

The key differences between live and taped interviews also need to be considered. Taped interviews are problematic because that taped ten-to-thirty minutes interview will be edited down to one or two ten-second sound-bites, leaving you with little control over the context of your remarks. You can ask to have your pre-recorded answers kept intact, but any promise is likely to be broken. Making 'deals' is much easier with newspaper journalists. I always warn them that while I am willing to speak generally for their benefit I would appreciate agreement over the obligatory direct quote. Consequently, the best bet on TV is to offer one or two select sound-bites that typify your position, encouraging them to pick those.

Live interviews are easier, but also a real test of your ability; and there is no doubt that deliberately pacing myself on the three-hour *After Dark* did much to enhance my reputation in the news media, even though my first perfect rebuttal of my 'opponent's' main point was lost during the first commercial break; a fact I did not realise until afterwards, otherwise I would have repeated it.

On the other hand, any mistakes you make cannot be edited out. Consequently, anticipation and flexibility are the best form of preparation.

Consider every type of question and response. Failure to do so could lead to someone else making you look foolish; but doing so can also enable you to turn the tables. On the *Up Front* programme, I had warned the production team that mention of my name would lead to difficulties with the main guest, who had studiously avoided me for three years, but could hardly flee the studio when they finally saw me. Likewise, I had read every word of their book, knowing that it would be hyped on the show. Having played it very cool, presenting the academic consensus on media effects and avoiding any controversy, when the other guest attempted to ridicule a point I was making by insisting that they could not imagine where I could get such ideas from, I quietly retrieved their book from under my seat and quoted the page number. The studio audience erupted in laughter; the fact that the guest did not understand the data in their own book was not lost on them. It had taken me twenty-four hours – it was a large book – but the effect was worth every minute. Social science had triumphed over 'advocacy research'.

If the cause of social science begs that academics not only pay more attention to the media, but also actively engage with them, a sane society requires all social scientists to realise that, while the media present a challenge, one has little to fear if prepared and aware of the pitfalls. Like Barak and Greek, I would encourage all my colleagues to seek access to the media and to become actively involved in public presentation of their work, for there are too many issues which, if not being controlled by us, are being effectively left to those whose credentials are unknown.

## Note

This article and the original presentation on which it is based would not have been possible without the help of Cecil Greek, South Florida University.

## References

Baker, Mary *et al.* (1987), 'The impact of a crime wave: perceptions, fear, and confidence in the police', *Law and Society Review*, 17:2, pp. 319–35.

Barak, Gregg (1988), 'Newsmaking criminology: reflections on the media, intellectuals, and crime', *Justice Quarterly*, 5:4, pp. 565–87.

Barrile, Leo (1984), 'Television and attitudes about crime: do heavy viewers distort criminality and support retributive justice?', in Ray Surette (ed.), *Justice and the Media*, Springfield, Ill.: Charles C. Thomas, pp. 141–59.

Benderly, Beryl (1989), 'Don't believe everything you read . . . a case study of how the politics of sex-difference research turned a small finding into a major media flap', *Psychology Today*, November, pp. 67–9.

Blythin, Evan and Samovar, Larry (1985), *Communicating Effectively on Television*, Belmont, Calif.: Wadsworth.

Cohen, Akiba (1987), *The Television News Interview*, Beverly Hills, Calif.: Sage Publications.

Ericson, Richard *et al.* (1991), *Representing Order: Crime, Law, and Justice in the News Media*, Toronto: University of Toronto Press.

Fishman, Mark (1980), *Manufacturing the News*, Austin, Tex.: University of Texas Press.

Greek, Cecil (1992), 'Becoming a media criminologist: is "newsmaking criminology" possible?' Paper presented to the 'Annual Academy of Criminal Justice Sciences', Pittsburg, Pa.

Schmertz, Herb (with William Novak) (1986), *Good-bye to the Low Profile: The Art of Creative Confrontation*, Boston, Mass.: Little, Brown.

Sherman, Lawrence and Cohn, Ellen (1989), 'The impact of research on legal policy: the Minneapolis domestic violence experiment', *Law and Society Review*, 23:1, pp. 117–44.

Thompson, William (1994), *Soft-core: Moral Crusades against Pornography in Britain and America*, London: Cassell.

Weiss, Carol and Singer, Eleanor (1988), *Reporting of Social Science in the National Media*, New York: Russell Sage Foundation.

Wong, Linda and Alexander, Bruce (1991), ' "Cocaine-related" deaths: media coverage in the war on drugs', *The Journal of Drug Issues*, 21:1, pp. 105–19.

Zoglin, Richard (1992), 'Prime time lively', *Time*, 17 February, p. 8.

# Index

Note: this index does not include references to categories such as 'media effects' and 'violence' as these are central to all the discussions throughout.